Praise for
*Walking in the Land of Many Gods*

"With compassion and love—*emee'ih eh ah'moo'oh nhiyah* in the Acoma Pueblo language—we are within sacred reason when we sincerely and fully participate in the ecology of life, i.e., the organic forces of nature, Wohlpart observes in *Walking in the Land of Many Gods*. And he confirms and affirms this teaching by the questioning yet insightful articulation offered by Linda Hogan, Terry Tempest Williams, and Janisse Ray to help us realize it is possible to attain beneficial communion with *sacred Mother Earth*. And with some help from Martin Heidegger also. Thank you—*Dawaa-eh*—for the knowledge!"

—SIMON J. ORTIZ, Acoma Pueblo author of
*Woven Stone, Out There Somewhere, from Sand Creek*

"A. James Wohlpart has given us a lucid, large-spirited study of environmental literature that contributes directly to a central issue in contemporary ecocriticism: how to understand humanity's fundamental connectedness to the world. Wohlpart embraces this conundrum with eloquence, optimism, and an enthusiastic sense of mystery. His emphasis on spirituality and 'sacred reason' is a particularly valuable addition to the current conversation about ecomaterialism."

—SCOTT SLOVIC, University of Idaho, editor of
*ISLE: Interdisciplinary Studies in Literature and Environment*

"A. James Wohlpart both carries out highly perceptive readings of Janisse Ray, Terry Tempest Williams, and Linda Hogan and makes his own valuable contributions to the broader project that their books serve. Central to his discussion is the importance of 'sacred reason,' which he defines as an ecological model for relationship and healing. Just as this concept reinforces the ceremonial intentions of the authors on whom he focuses, so too does it help him explain how both caring for the land and writing can offer ways to 're/place' ourselves in the intricacy and wholeness of this world."

—JOHN ELDER, *Imagining the Earth*

"An innovative ecocritical study, *Walking in the Land of Many Gods* makes a real contribution to our understanding of contemporary environmental literature and to our current environmental situation. Wohlpart articulates an alternative view of the human place in the world, suggesting ways we can live richer and more ecologically sustainable lives."

—PHILIP CAFARO, *Thoreau's Living Ethics:*
*Walden and the Pursuit of Virtue*

# Walking in the
# Land of Many Gods

E S T. 75 1938
YEARS
THE UNIVERSITY OF GEORGIA PRESS 2013

# Walking in the Land of Many Gods

## REMEMBERING SACRED REASON

## IN CONTEMPORARY

## ENVIRONMENTAL LITERATURE

A. JAMES WOHLPART

THE UNIVERSITY OF GEORGIA PRESS

ATHENS AND LONDON

© 2013 by the University of Georgia Press
Athens, Georgia 30602
www.ugapress.org
All rights reserved
Designed by Kaelin Chappell Broaddus
Set in by 10/13 Dante MT Std.
Manufactured by Thomson-Shore, Inc.
The paper in this book meets the guidelines for
permanence and durability of the Committee on
Production Guidelines for Book Longevity of the
Council on Library Resources.

Printed in the United States of America
13 14 15 16 17 P 5 4 3 2 1

Library of Congress Cataloging-in-Publication Data
Wohlpart, A. James, 1964–
Walking in the land of many gods : remembering sacred reason in
contemporary environmental literature / A. James Wohlpart.
pages cm
Includes bibliographical references.
ISBN 978-0-8203-4523-9 (hardcover : alk. paper) — ISBN 0-8203-4523-7 (hardcover : alk. paper)
ISBN 978-0-8203-4524-6 (pbk. : alk. paper) — ISBN 0-8203-4524-5 (pbk. : alk. paper)
1. American literature—History and criticism. 2. Environmental literature—
History and criticism. 3. Ecocriticism. 4. Nature in literature in literature.
5. Human ecology in literature. 6. Ecology in literature. I. Title.
PS169.E25.W64 2013
810.9′355—dc23
2012043942

British Library Cataloging-in-Publication Data available

This book is dedicated

to my father,

my elder, my friend, and my hiking partner,


who introduced me to all my relations.

# CONTENTS

# PREFACE

The founding premise of *Walking in the Land of Many Gods* is that a creative force animates the universe—a force that became manifest in the Big Bang nearly 14 billion years ago and that led to the formation of Earth 4.5 billion years ago, which in turn fostered a life-sustaining system, call it Gaia or what you will—and that humans, like all animate and less-than-animate beings, have the potential to participate in this creative force.

Our participation as a species might perhaps differ from that of other species in that ours includes a self-consciousness that allows us the opportunity to reflect on our connection to and participation with, or, alternatively, our separation from and reaction against, this creative energy. Central to the human ability to participate in or separate from this flow and exchange of creative energy is the role of language, which originally derived its force from our sensuous participation with the world around us but which now acts as an endless game of tag.

The poststructuralists seem to have it right. Language is now too often an endless play of signification, cut off from the reality of what it purports to signify. We have become, at the beginning of the twenty-first century, trapped in our own mental machinations seemingly without a way out. This entrapment is the logical conclusion of a separation from the natural world that began ten thousand years ago on the floodplains of Egypt and Sumer, heightened with the advance of a historical mind-set and the scientific revolution, and fully closed around us with the rise and domination of the techno-industrial-urban world.

But, I would contend, there is another way. *Walking in the Land of Many Gods* is my attempt to point in this direction. What I hope to show is that we can remember an ancient wisdom of Earth and elders that reconnects us, bodily, sensuously, spiritually to the world that sustains us and nurtures us and that is the very foundation—in an evolutionary and biological sense but also in an emotional, psychological, and spiritual sense—of our being.

The central question becomes, then, about our place in this world. I want to ask, can we re/place ourselves bodily, emotionally, intuitively in the natural world in such a way that we reopen the channels through which the creative energy of the universe flows, so that we become once again participants in the ongoing dialogue between all species, indeed participants in the omnipresent conversation that occurs within the totality of the natural world including the plants and the animals, the mountains and the valleys, the rivers and the streams, the sky, the thunder, and the sun? Can we reanimate our own words, both spoken and written, so that they participate in this creative energy and become, rather than the means of our disconnection from the world, a way of reengaging the flow of energy that invisibly surrounds us? Finally, can we remember an ancient way of thinking and being in the world that heals our bodies and our spirits and that assists us in returning to our rightful place in our communities, human and nonhuman, allowing us to heal the rift between ourselves and nature?

The problem of the twenty-first century is the problem of the human relation to the natural world, a problem too great for any one individual to answer comprehensively or definitively. We light candles along the way, hoping to illuminate our path and see our next step. *Walking in the Land of Many Gods*, I hope, is one candle among many, offering some glimpse of the journey before us.

# ACKNOWLEDGMENTS

In deepest gratitude, I would like to recognize the many students who took my Environmental Literature course over the years and walked the journey of this book with me, including especially the fall 2009 class. My students helped me develop the ideas presented in this book, but more than that, they also helped me remember that the ideas must be lived. Many of them have touched me deeply.

I am also appreciative of the faculty members who have taught the course with me, Peter Blaze Corcoran and Kevin Aho. I have learned much from them. Thank you, Peter Blaze, for originally conceiving of the course with me and for working together to bring many of the authors we taught to our campus. And thank you, Kevin, for sharing with me your deep and rich understanding of Martin Heidegger both in our class and during our long runs in the southwest Florida wilderness; anything profound in this book surely has your influence, just as any errors are my own.

The seed for this book was planted in the fall of 2000 when the Orion Society brought the Forgotten Language Tour to our campus. That seed has fully germinated with the support and assistance of everyone at the University of Georgia Press, including especially Nancy Grayson, John McLeod, and John Joerschke, who has allowed me to share my words with others; I am indebted to Philip Cafaro and Simon Ortiz for their thoughtful reading of the manuscript, to Kaelin Broaddus for her graceful cover design, and to Barbara Wojhoski for copyediting the manuscript. Moreover, this book could not have been written without the influence of Janisse Ray, Terry Tempest Williams, and Linda Hogan. I am blessed to count each of them as a friend and colleague. They have given us a great gift in their writing. I am especially indebted to Linda Hogan for the title of my book, which I borrowed from her essay "Walking."

I would like to recognize Donna Price Henry, who was my dean during the time that much of this book was written; her generous spirit and kind ways nurture all of those who are under her care. I deeply appreciate the assistance of my friend and colleague Nicolette Lucia Costantino, who assisted with research, proofreading, typing, and sorting through ideas; her companionship while I was the associate dean helped me make it through many difficult days. I wish to thank the Circle of Eleven, an embrace of love and acceptance; every person should be so lucky to have such friends.

I also acknowledge the support of my family: my parents, Pam and Al; my brother and sisters, David, Heidi, Bridgett, and Kathryn, who have walked the journey of my life with me; and my children, Zachary James and Kathryn Keene, who are also my best friends. This book has been written with Zach and Kat in my mind and my heart.

Finally, and most fully, I must acknowledge my wife, Sasha Ree Linsin Wohlpart, who is my bedrock. She is light and love and makes the world around her dance with a brilliant radiance. This book would never have happened if she had not joined me on my journey across our beautiful and fragile Earth.

I am blessed beyond measure.

# A NOTE ON DOCUMENTATION

The following literary works are referenced in the text:

Hogan, Linda. *Dwellings: A Spiritual History of the Living World*. New York: Touchstone, 1995.

Ray, Janisse. *Ecology of a Cracker Childhood*. Minneapolis: Milkweed Editions, 1999.

Williams, Terry Tempest. *Refuge: An Unnatural History of Family and Place*. New York: Vintage, 1991.

*Walking in the*
*Land of Many Gods*

# CHAPTER ONE

# Introduction

## A Mind of Sky and Thunder and Sun

I remember walking on a dirt road that crossed a steep hillside somewhere in Switzerland. I was with my Opa, my German grandfather. I must have been about four years old. Opa had on his characteristic gray fedora with a blue jay feather stuck in the band. He had removed his shirt, retaining his starch-white A-shirt, so that the sun could warm his bare shoulders. We had left the rest of the family—my parents, an older brother, two sisters, and my Oma—back at our cabin. Opa and I had gone in search of *Gemüse*, in this case, wild spinach. Earlier in our stay, the whole family had walked together, and Opa had shown us the thick, broad-leafed, deeply green plant growing alongside the road. But this journey was just for us. I remember keenly the sun shining on the hill that rose to our left out of sight, melting into a porcelain-blue sky. Up the green hillside, yellow flowers danced in a gentle breeze. We walked slowly, meditatively, collecting just enough *Gemüse* for dinner.

The memory stops there, arrested on that hillside. I don't remember eating the spinach; indeed, in my youth, I don't remember caring for spinach at all. What was significant was the act of mindfully walking, of searching for and gathering the spinach, of being fully present and fully engaged.

It is that moment of collecting that is etched in my mind, the quiet and slow walk under that pale blue sky and warm sun on that green and yellow hillside, led by my grandfather's kind and generous hands.

I didn't know it at the time, and it is likely that I barely understand it now, but the significance of that four-year-old's experience, a memory that still shines over forty years later, may have been the result of a connection to other species I experienced that day, what Edward O. Wilson calls biophilia, and perhaps more than that to something deep in my biological and evolutionary past.[1] Knowingly or unknowingly, my grandfather was guiding me in a kind of ritual, honoring our Earth, which sustains us physically and spiritually. In her essay "The Feathers," Linda Hogan describes the importance of such ceremonies in our lives:

> Perhaps there are events and things that work as a doorway into the mythical world, the world of first people, all the way back to the creation of the universe and the small quickenings of earth, the first stirrings of human beings at the beginning of time. Our elders believe this to be so, that it is possible to wind a way backward to the start of things, and in so doing find a form of sacred reason, different from ordinary reason, that is linked to forces of nature. In this kind of mind . . . is the power of sky and thunder and sun, and many have had alliances and partnerships with it, a way of thought older than measured time, less primitive than the rational present. (19)

Hogan suggests that ceremonies connect us to primal creation, expanding our awareness outward to the plants and animals and rocks and hills that surround us and to the forces that quicken these things, as well as backward in time to the originary, creative forces of the universe. To be connected to this energy is to have a different way of thinking and acting in the world than the one handed to us by Western civilization, to have a mind that holds the "power of sky and thunder and sun." Such a mind participates in the ecology of life, the "forces of nature," and is thus regarded as a form of "sacred reason," different from the calculative and scientific reason that we have come to accept in our time as the only access to truth or reality.

Martin Heidegger names this form of calculative reason, which has its essence in a technological way of being in the world and has come to dominate our Western worldview in the twentieth and twenty-first centuries,

*Ge-stell* (Enframing). For Heidegger, Enframing is a way of seeing and thinking about the world that conceives of all objects, humans included, as something waiting to be used, a resource for advancing some technological aim.
Rather than participating in the unfolding of truth, what Heidegger calls
the act of "revealing" or "unconcealing" (to bring what is concealed out
into the open) of beings, humans have relegated the world around us to
the "standing-reserve."[2] More insidiously, humans have become oblivious to
the facts that our way of thinking and acting is only one way that can allow
things to be revealed, one mode of disclosing truth or reality, and that this
mode allows things to show up in only one manner, as resources, as objects
to be used in technological production. Kevin Aho offers a nice summary of
the results of this way of being in the world: "The technological age is vio-
lent, according to Heidegger, because it 'sets upon' (*stellt*) nature and forces
beings to show up or reveal themselves in *only one way*, as an object-region
available for use. Caught up in the technological worldview, our lives have
become increasingly frantic, sped up with machines and institutions that
allow us to consume, produce, and exchange beings at faster rates."[3] As a
result of this way of being, we have lost our connection to a deeper truth
or reality; Heidegger notes that "the rule of Enframing threatens man with
the possibility that it could be denied to him to enter into a more original
revealing and hence to experience the call of a more primal truth."[4] As Hogan observes, our calculative and scientific reason is more "primitive," that
is, less rich and fertile and generative, than sacred reason, which allows access to the forces of nature, to a way of thinking that predates our historical
consciousness, which is "older than time."

Yet Heidegger also offers an alternative to our scientific, objectifying
reason based on his exploration of how we dwell on Earth. For Heidegger,
dwelling's fundamental character is that of caring for the world, an attitude
that allows us to perceive the world as holy and sacred, as a land filled with
many gods, and that ultimately opens us as humans to becoming guard-
ians of truth or reality, of the revealing of the world on its own terms rather
than relegating the world to objects for our use. For Heidegger, the idea of
dwelling is connected to what he calls "the fourfold," which includes Earth
and sky, divinities and mortals. The first two, Earth and sky, comprise the
natural world and the forces of the universe that guide creation; the latter two, divinities and mortals, comprise our culture or the community in
which we are embedded.[5] Heidegger explains that humans as mortals, as

those aware of their own death, *"are* in the fourfold by *dwelling*. But the basic character of dwelling is to spare, to preserve. Mortals dwell in the way they preserve the fourfold in its essential being, its presencing." In a long passage, Heidegger explains what it means to dwell in the fourfold:

> Mortals dwell in that they save the earth. . . . Saving does not only snatch something from a danger. To save really means to set something free into its own presencing. To save the earth is more than to exploit it or even wear it out. Saving the earth does not master the earth and does not subjugate it, which is merely one step from spoliation.
>
> Mortals dwell in that they receive the sky as sky. They leave to the sun and the moon their journey, to the stars their courses, to the seasons their blessing and their inclemency; they do not turn night into day nor day into a harassed unrest.
>
> Mortals dwell in that they await the divinities as divinities. In hope they hold up to the divinities what is unhoped for. They wait for intimations of their coming and do not mistake the signs of their absence. They do not make their gods for themselves and do not worship idols. In the very depth of misfortune they wait for the weal that has been withdrawn.
>
> Mortals dwell in that they initiate their own nature—their being capable of death as death—into the use and practice of this capacity, so that there may be a good death. To initiate mortals into the nature of death in no way means to make death, as empty Nothing, the goal. Nor does it mean to darken dwelling by blindly staring toward the end.
>
> In saving the earth, in receiving the sky, in awaiting the divinities, in initiating mortals, dwelling occurs as the fourfold preservation of the fourfold. To spare and preserve means: to take under our care, to look after the fourfold in its presencing.[6]

For Heidegger, then, dwelling depends on allowing the things around us to come into being on their own terms rather than objectifying them and subjugating them for our use, on taking an attitude of "care" toward the world so that everything can show up, can be revealed to us, in its radiant holiness.

While Heidegger's fourfold might seem similar to Hogan's sacred reason, Heidegger remains firmly grounded in Western civilization. Indeed, his notion of divinities is not in any way pantheistic or polytheistic, as it might be construed in Hogan, but rather is a way of capturing "the fundamental *ethos* of a community" as lived by exemplary members of that community.[7] Heidegger locates an authentic form of dwelling in the ancient Greeks, in their concept of leisure and their recognition of the importance of ritual and ceremony. Kevin Aho suggests that leisure and play, which occur in festivals, rituals, and ceremonies, can engender a sense of awe and wonder in the world around us. For Heidegger, this sense of wonder is not about regarding the unusual but rather about setting the commonplace before us and assisting us in perceiving the sacredness of everything that surrounds us. Aho concludes: "Leisure . . . is an active embodiment of wonder over the fact that 'there is something rather than nothing, that there are beings and we ourselves are in their midst.'"[8] Heidegger's ideas thus provide a beginning for a deeper remembering, but as I've noted, his ideas remain firmly embedded in Western history.

To broaden this notion of dwelling—to move it outward to embrace all species and the landscape that we inhabit and backward to acknowledge our deep history—and connect it to Hogan's sacred reason is the project of this book. I explore three works of contemporary environmental literature—Janisse Ray's *Ecology of a Cracker Childhood*, Terry Tempest Williams's *Refuge: An Unnatural History of Family and Place*, and Linda Hogan's *Dwellings: A Spiritual History of the Living World*—in order to suggest possibilities for an alternative way of thinking and acting in the world. I hope to show that sacred reason is ecological and restorative in nature, based on interdependence, interrelationship, and healing. In this sacred reason, time is circular rather than linear, allowing us to exist in a mythical, eternal present, and we experience a constant flowing together of self and other rather than a divided or dualistic world. Thus, while we have an awareness of our own limitations as finite and mortal beings, we also understand that all things are connected and that the physical components of our selves live on in the other beings that our dead bodies nurture. Sacred reason is based on our connectedness to place, to an understanding of the entwinement of our internal and external landscapes, a melding of the inner and the outer. Sacred reason causes us to act with great humility and a sense of terrible responsibility, for we know that what we do to our place, we do to ourselves, and so we learn to act with care, sparing and preserving the world. Finally, sacred reason opens our eyes to the holy, the divine, the sacred that surrounds us on a daily basis, allowing us to live lives of awe and wonder. The literary works discussed here open a pathway to a deeper remembering, one that takes us back to and reconnects us with the primal forces of creation, one that honors the sacredness of the world that surrounds us and our oneness with that world.

In what follows, Martin Heidegger's later philosophy provides a theoretical foundation for my thinking, but I will not overwhelm my discussions of the literary works with this background. Chapter 2, "Remembering Deep Space and Deep Time: Heidegger, the Pleistocene, and Native American Philosophy," offers a deeper engagement with the theoretical context for my project, first discussing Heidegger's essays and then building on these discussions, moving them outward to embrace other species and backward to include prehistorical humanity through the ideas of deep anthropologists, contemporary environmental philosophers, and Native American writers. Chapter 3, "Restor(y)ing the Self: Ecological Restoration in Janisse Ray's *Ecology of a Cracker Childhood*," and chapter 4, "The Long Migration Home: Listening to Birds in Terry Tempest Williams's *Refuge: An Unnatural History of Family and Place*," engage literary works of two authors who reside firmly within the technological worldview but who work to expose that worldview's limitations, while offering an alternative way of thinking and acting in the world. Ray does so by thinking of her life and her landscape as a kind of palimpsest, with a connection to nature as the erased text that she works to reassert. Williams's dual narrative, that of Great Salt Lake's rise and that of her mother's cancer, reveals the way in which a technological worldview not only provides certain answers but also only allows us to ask certain questions. Ultimately her journey, which moves through the death of her mother and the near ruination of the Bear River Migratory Bird Refuge, is one of learning to listen to alternative voices, those of birds, which offer her a different way of being in the world. Chapter 5, "Healing the Severed Trust: Linda Hogan's *Dwellings: A Spiritual History of the Living World* as Native Ceremony," most fully offers an alternate worldview, one based on sacred reason that critiques and deconstructs our technological way of being in the world and offers glimpses of the sacred and mysterious Earth. Along with the theoretical foundation outlined in this chapter and explored more fully in the next, each of these main chapters has its own additional theoretical framework—autobiographical theory for Ray, ecofeminist theory for Williams, and discussions of ritual and ceremony for Hogan.

Because of the way in which all three literary works that I discuss negotiate the boundaries between the natural world and human culture, they might be considered works of restoration—both ecological restoration and cultural restoration. William Jordan defines restoration in *The Sunflower Forest* as "*everything we do to a landscape or an ecosystem in an ongoing attempt to compensate for novel or 'outside' influences on it in such a way that it can continue to behave or can resume behaving as if these were not present.*" Significantly, Jordan insists on a very narrow definition of restoration, where all the elements and processes of an area of land or ecosystem are engaged, not just those that we might consider "beautiful, interesting, or useful but also those that we consider uninteresting, useless, ugly, repulsive, or even dangerous."[9] Jordan situates his understanding of restoration within a paradigm of values creation that allows humans to engage and mitigate their sense of shame for the destruction and degradation of the land. In a similar vein, the literary works analyzed here both describe our embeddedness in a technological horizon of disclosure, Enframing, and seek to offer alternatives. Jordan asserts that our relationship with the natural world is necessarily complex and troubling and that the act of restoration in particular instigates a psychological sense of the limitations of our actions as humans and of any attempt at reparation; we come to understand, when we engage this complexity, that "our relationship with the rest of nature, as with anything, is not really an equation or a problem to be solved. It is a mystery."[10] Ecological restoration then becomes a performative act, a ritual or ceremony founded on an acceptance of our complicity in the destructive forces of the universe. Through the ritualized act, ecological restoration fosters a new set of values, a new way of thinking and being in the world, an act similar to that performed in environmental literature.

As noted, ecological restoration begins with an understanding of our limitations as humans—not only the limitations evinced by our destruction of habitats but also the limitations apparent in our ability to put those habitats back together. Jordan acknowledges that any act of restoration is necessarily incomplete, that it is an ongoing and failing process, a gift we give back to the natural world but that in no way compensates for what we have taken. In restoration, we work to reassert a past that we do not always know, to use technology to erase the signs of human and technological impact, always reminded in these acts of the limitations of our effectiveness as restorationists and thus of our limitations as humans. Yet the restorative act itself, if it unfolds in an attentive and caring way such that the performance of the act attains dignity and a heightened sense of meaning, becomes an act of values creation in which we find our way through the psychology of shame to a place of healing. Ultimately, if the restorative act is pursued as a ritual meant to heal the divide between humans and nature, the subject and the object, then the interior landscape and the exterior landscape become one. Jordan notes that "the distinction between subject and object is a modern one. In the archaic mind, as in the virtual space created by ritual, the two realms are inseparable. The world is what we make of it through performative interaction with it, redeeming it from chaos into cosmos by rituals that renew our ability to order the world, make sense out of it, and experience beauty in it."[11] When ecological restoration is pursued as a way of remaking our values and beliefs and placing ourselves on the land in a new way, we come to perceive the natural world—and our relationship to that world—with new eyes.

Such an understanding of restoration has parallels in Heidegger's conceptions of the fourfold and dwelling. Both an awareness of our mortality, our limitations as finite beings, and a remembering of our past are central to Heidegger's conception of dwelling deeply on Earth. Aho concludes that to live an authentic existence, one must "own up to one's being *as a whole*, and this means coming to grips not only with Dasein's future ('being-towards-death') but also with the communal past ('being-towards-the-beginning')." Aho continues: "Authenticity, in this regard, involves a retrieval or 'repetition' (*Wiederholung*) of Dasein's beginnings, what Heidegger calls authentic 'historicality' (*Geschichtlichkeit*), referring to the cultural possibilities that belong to our shared history but have largely been forgotten, covered over by the conformist assumptions and prejudices of the modern world."[12] As noted, the common heritage that Heidegger was interested in retrieving was found in Greek life and coalesces around the concept of leisure. Counteracting the busyness of our technological age and its concomitant mood, boredom, leisure leads to a mood of awe and wonder, to "a disposition that does not flee from the enigmatic event of being but celebrates it."[13] Such leisure occurs in festivals, ceremonies, and true holidays ("holy-days") that connect us to our place, that remind us how we dwell on Earth, and ultimately that remind us to dwell differently, to engage in "communal or solitary acts of resistance" that connect us to an "ancient temperament."[14] Julian Young notes that the role of the festival was paramount to inducing the "saving power"; through festival, the average everydayness of our lives is disrupted so that we can remember the extraordinary nature of the common and the ordinary.[15]

Yet in our time, we cover over our mortality and our sense of shame and thus lose the possibility for an authentic connection to the natural world, one dependent on rituals and ceremonies that help heal the divide between us and the rest of creation. We have lost the authentic holiday, for we take vacations to ignore our plight as limited human beings or to relieve the stress of our workaday lives in order to prepare ourselves to return to those lives. Interestingly, what I didn't remember about my childhood experience in Switzerland, what I didn't know but discovered much later, was that the place we visited as a family was a place that the government reserved for lower-income Swiss families to vacation. As a part of Swiss culture, both the government and businesses understood the need for leisure, for a break from the routinized nature of work, not to prepare workers to return to the grind of their everyday lives but as a ritualized act intended to engender an attitude of awe and wonder in the world around them. Heidegger, according to Young, was interested in the "ecstatic state—ecstatic in both the ordinary sense and in the literal sense of 'standing out from' the ordinary—in which everyday experience of the world is transformed into something quite different."[16] This ecstatic state is born of an attentiveness to the world around us and can be found most fully, according to Heidegger, in the Greeks. In this project, I extend Heidegger's thinking to suggest that our remembering goes back even further than the Greeks, into our evolutionary roots, where our emplacement on Earth depended on an inextricable entwinement of the inner and the outer, of self and world, and to suggest that a similar emplacement occurs in the performative act of ecological restoration, which implicates us in all aspects of creation, both the positive and the negative.

What is interesting to me, what I certainly did not know then and perhaps what I have grappled with in writing this book, is that my experience on that hillside in Switzerland as a four-year-old provided me with a foundation for a way of thinking and being on Earth that continues to resonate with me.[17] In this memory, I am reminded of a moment when I felt a connection to place in which the entire landscape, the green grass and yellow flowers, the blue sky and bright sun, hummed with a vibrant energy that electrified my own interior landscape, my "self." In her preface to *Dwellings*,

Linda Hogan notes that her writing "connects the small world of humans with the larger universe, containing us in the same way that native ceremonies do, showing us both our place and a way of seeing" (12). As a kind of ceremony, my walk across that hillside led by my Opa, an elder who mentored me in his generous and gifted way of being on Earth, connected me to something much larger, and offered me a way of thinking about and seeing the world that is at odds with much of the rest of my life. Hogan explains that ceremonies help us "remember that all things are connected," a remembering that allows for "a healing and restoration . . . a mending of a broken connection between us and the rest" (40). She continues: "The intention of a ceremony is to put a person back together by restructuring the human mind. This reorganization is accomplished by a kind of inner map, a geography of the human spirit and the rest of the world. We make whole our broken-off pieces of self and world. Within ourselves, we bring together the fragments of our lives in a sacred act of renewal, and we reestablish our connections with others. The ceremony is a point of return. It takes us toward the place of balance, our place in the community of all things. It is an event that sets us back upright" (40). When I return in my mind to that hillside under that sky and warmed by that sun, I feel whole again, whole in a way that this life of everydayness, of things presencing only for our use, does not offer.

We need more ritual and ceremony in our lives. We need artists and healers who remind us of our place in the midst of this grand universe, who allow us to remember how to dwell deeply in our places so that we experience, once again, the divinity of the landscape. Hogan notes that the ceremonial act "is not a finished thing. The real ceremony begins where the formal one ends, when we take up a new way, our minds and hearts filled with the vision of earth that holds us within it, in compassionate relationship to and with our world" (40–41). Although we have lost our connectedness to Earth, we can reestablish our relation through rituals, ceremonies, and acts of restoration and through reading works of literature that assist us in understanding how we are placed on Earth and how we might be placed differently. What I have learned, and what I suggest here, is that while we have forgotten our connection to the creative and originary forces of the universe, we can find our way back to these forces through dialogue and conversation. If we can relearn the sacred art of listening—to plants and animals, to mountains and valleys, rivers and streams, to sky and thunder and sun—we can remember the creative force that language is and begin to speak, again, in a way that honors our being, that allows us to fully realize our humanness as the ones who care for the world and thus participate in the unfolding of the infinite mystery of Earth.

CHAPTER TWO

# Remembering Deep Space and Deep Time

## Heidegger, the Pleistocene, and Native American Philosophy

Around the middle of the 1930s, Heidegger's thinking took a turn away from an analysis of human being, or Dasein (which found its expression in what is often considered his most important work, *Being and Time*), to considering the unfolding historical movement of Being in general.[1] His exploration of the phenomenon of Being yielded the insight that being becomes manifest through humans, that being is dependent on the linguistic and sociocultural practices of humans (a word shortly about upper-case and lower-case usage). William Lovitt states that in his early philosophy Heidegger "is centrally concerned with the relation between man and Being, with man as the *openness* to which and in which Being presences and is known."[2] His later work, while shifting to an exploration of the history of being, builds on this early work by considering the various manifestations of being throughout Western civilization, starting with the pre-Socratic Greeks. Heidegger suggests that each era in human history manifests a particular way of thinking and acting in the world, what Heidegger calls a horizon of disclosure. Our horizon of disclosure allows things to be revealed, to show up in our daily lives, and to make sense in the course of everyday conversation; significantly, this horizon of disclosure also conceals, for at the same time that it provides a lens through which we see the world, this lens only allows us to see things in a certain way, like an intricately designed kaleidoscope.[3] In his later work, Heidegger was interested in tracing the horizon of disclosure that has provided humans in the Western world a relationship to the things surrounding us over time.

Heidegger concluded that the particular mode of revealing that has come to dominate our Western worldview is technological in nature, that our way of thinking is calculative and scientific, what Heidegger terms "Enframing."[4] According to Lovitt, "man's arrogation to himself of the role of subject in philosophy; his objectifying of nature, life, and history in dealing with them in the sciences; and his calculating and cataloguing and disposing of all manner of things through machine technology—all these alike are expressions of that essence and of that revealing."[5] Most importantly, Heidegger demonstrates that through metaphysics, the history of philosophy from Plato through the twentieth century, we have come to mistake our technological horizon of disclosure for truth or reality. That is, we have mistaken our way of thinking (calculative, scientific) and being (technological), along with the reality or truth that this way of thinking and being discloses, for the *only* way to think or act, the *only* truth or reality, the *only* way that things can reveal themselves. Lovitt concludes that "in this 'oblivion' that blocks the self-manifesting of Being, man's danger lies. The danger is real that every other way of revealing will be driven out and that man will lose his true relation to himself and to all else."[6]

Heidegger calls a particular mode of disclosure such as ours "world," a complex term that encapsulates both the totality of beings that are revealed to us (the ontic sense of "world") as well as the transcendental horizon of disclosure in which we are embedded (the ontological sense of "world") that makes it possible for us to understand and make sense of beings. The horizon of disclosure in which humans of a particular era are embedded is not optional; it arises from the context of language—understood as the expressive medium of sociocultural practices, beliefs, rituals, and institutions—that we have been thrown into and that guides our existence. Julian Young explains that "language, as Heidegger puts it in the *Introduction to Metaphysics*, is not something man has as an attribute. Rather, language is 'the happening that has man,' the 'process through which man first enters history as a being.'"[7] Any horizon of disclosure is dependent on a historical epoch; it is transcendental because we cannot get outside it or beyond it, yet it is a horizon because it is still only one way that beings can be disclosed. Young explains that

> to suppose the limits of intelligibility for my historical-cultural epoch to be also the limits of intelligibility *per se* would be the height of irrational epistemological chauvinism. Once one understands the notion of a transcendental horizon and sees its historically and culturally relative character, the conclusion presents itself that in addition to what is intelligible to us, reality possesses an indefinitely large number of aspects . . . which would be disclosed to us were we to inhabit transcendental horizons other than the one we do, horizons which, however, we can neither inhabit nor even conceive. Truth, then, is concealment, ultimate truth concealment of the, to us, *ineluctably* mysterious.[8]

Thus we can access truth within our own horizon, but we must remember that this access to truth is at the same time a concealment, for it does not allow other truths to be revealed.

And there are, according to Heidegger, a plenitude of truths. This Heidegger terms "earth." Young has made an interesting distinction in his use of the terms "beings," "being," and "Being," which I will adopt in my own discussion and which will help to distinguish "world" and "earth."[9] According to Young, "beings" (lower case, plural) are the things that reveal themselves to us—that which is noticeable, that which shows up in our daily lives, using Heidegger's terms, that which is lit up and comes into the clearing. According to Heidegger, in the twentieth and twenty-first centuries what shows up for us in our technological age are the things that are useful, things that allow us to do our work. For Young, "being" (lower case, singular) is the underlying ground of beings, the way in which beings show up, the presence or presencing of beings. In Heidegger's thought, "being" is the same as the horizon of disclosure of a particular epoch, the ontological sense of "world," that which is embodied in that epoch's linguistic or sociocultural practices. Young concludes that "it is for this reason that Heidegger says that being exists only through human (by which [Heidegger] means language-using) being."[10] Thus, "being" determines how "beings" will show up and is, therefore, human dependent. World, then, in both its ontological and its ontic fullness, is comprised of "being" and "beings"—a mode of disclosure or way of thinking along with the things that show up as a result of that worldview.

Finally, "Being" (upper case, singular) is that which is, in its infinite plenitude, the underlying ground of "being," indeed that which enables a horizon of disclosure to manifest in the first place. Young defines "Being" as that which presences for us (beings) and the mode of disclosure that enables that presencing (being) along with all other modes of disclosure that lie beyond our horizon of intelligibility.[11] For Heidegger, this generative ground of being/beings is "earth."[12] Heidegger describes a globe of Being with a lit side (world, that which is lit up, which presences) and a dark side (all the other possible worlds, which our mode of disclosure conceals). "Earth," then, is the undisclosed in its infiniteness, that which is unmastered and unintelligible in the truth surrounding us, a mysterious plenitude.

Heidegger suggests in his later philosophy that other ways of thinking exist beyond the calculative, scientific way that has dominated Western culture since the Enlightenment. In particular, Heidegger offers meditative or poetical thinking as alternatives to traditional scientific modes of disclosure; significantly, these other ways of thinking would reveal different worlds to us in that beings would show up in different ways and would lead to different ways of acting. For Heidegger, "earth" is the holy, the sacred, that which has been lost to us because our technological horizon of disclosure has become totalized or absolutized—it has become "Truth" or "Reality" to the complete exclusion of other modes of disclosure. This totalization of the calculative way of thinking in the twentieth and twenty-first centuries has not only cut us off from mystery—from the holy and the sacred, from a divine world radiant with many gods—it has also brought us to the brink of the abyss. Heidegger defines the abyss as "the complete absence of the ground," that is, the loss of the foundation for or connection to Being, the "ground that grounds" the world.[13]

Yet Heidegger also suggests, as I've noted, that humans have access to Being through dwelling, through preserving the fourfold of Earth and sky, divinities and mortals. Heidegger refers to this state of remembering the interconnectedness of all things as "mirror-play," a concept that he explores in his essay "The Thing." He explains that in the unity of the fourfold, "each of the four mirrors in its own way the presence of the others. Each therewith reflects itself in its own way into its own, within the simpleness of the four"; yet, he continues, "this mirroring does not portray a likeness. The mirroring, lightening each of the four, appropriates their own presencing into simple belonging to one another." Initially, Heidegger insinuates that in the unity of the fourfold each of the four, Earth and sky, divinities and mortals, reflect the other three. Yet because each element is reflected in the others, which then reflect it back, each not only has the likeness of the others directed toward it but also has its own likeness reflected back—but a likeness that has been appropriated by the others. This play of mirroring, of elements reflecting off one another in a constant change and interchange, depends on a willingness to relinquish a sense of individuality and the experience of separation: "None of the four insists on its own separate particularity. Rather, each is expropriated, within their mutual appropriation, into its own being. This expropriative appropriating is the mirror-play of the fourfold."[14] Although each of the elements in the fourfold appropriates the others, they do so only through relinquishing their own nature to the others so that the others may in fact engage in the act of appropriating as well.

Heidegger's "expropriative appropriating" finds a nice parallel in N. Scott Momaday's definition of Native American ethical perspectives on the physical world as "a matter of reciprocal appropriation." Momaday explains that this paradoxical ethic of appropriation occurs when "man invests himself in the landscape, and at the same time incorporates the landscape into his own most fundamental experience."[15] Significantly, Heidegger's use of the word "play" emphasizes that this mirroring is not a static thing but rather a dynamic happening of giving up and taking in. This mirroring is world for Heidegger, not the world as a spatial entity but world as a happening, as an event, a "worlding." And the role of humans in this happening of being is to "step back from the thinking that merely represents—that is, explains—to the thinking that responds and recalls."[16]

Heidegger's understanding of language lies at the heart of this concept of co-responding. For Heidegger, true language names things in such a way that they are "called," bringing "the presence of what was previously uncalled into a nearness."[17] As a result, the "things that were named, thus called, gather to themselves sky and earth, mortals and divinities. The four are united primally in being toward one another, a fourfold. The things let the fourfold of the four stay with them. This gathering, assembling, letting-stay is the thinging of things. The unitary fourfold of sky and earth, mortals and divinities, which is stayed in the thinging of things, we call—the world."[18] Through language, then, humans have the opportunity to dwell, to allow things to be called in such a way that this calling unites the fourfold, what Heidegger calls "world." While world, which occurs through the happening of the thinging of the thing, and the thing itself are intimately interwoven, they remain disparate, which Heidegger denotes through the term "*dif-ference*."[19] He explains that "the way in which mortals, called out of the dif-ference into the dif-ference, speak on their own part, is: by responding. Mortal speech must first of all have listened to the command, in the form of which the stillness of the dif-ference calls world and things into the rift of its onefold simplicity. Every word of mortal speech speaks out of such a listening, and as such a listening." Authentic human speech becomes a responding to the call of Being, which begins through listening: "Mortals speak insofar as they listen."[20] But the listening is of a certain kind—it is a listening to the stillness of world and thing, to a granting that is a preserving and a caring. Stillness is not something human but is rather the staying of things on Earth, the allowing of things to presence in themselves; through this staying, which becomes a responding, language speaks through humans: "What is important is learning to live in the speaking of language. To do so, we need to examine constantly whether and to what extent we are capable of what genuinely belongs to responding: anticipation in reserve."[21]

While Heidegger offers a pathway back to Being through the concepts of dwelling and the fourfold, he insists that we must first understand the nature of our Western worldview and the way in which an important forgetfulness lies at the heart of this worldview. For Heidegger, this forgetting is in fact a double forgetting: the first occurs as a result of the nature of revealing itself, which is, as has been noted, also a concealing; the second occurs as a result of our forgetting that our mode of revealing, our horizon of disclosure, is only one mode among many possible modes. Guignon notes,

> If unconcealment results from an event within being and so is not something humans do, it follows that the concealment running through the history of metaphysics is *also* something that happens within being itself. Concealment inevitably accompanies every emerging-into-presence in this sense: just as the items in a room can become visible only if the lighting that illuminates them itself remains invisible, so things can become manifest only if this manifesting itself "stays away" or "withdraws." This first-order

concealment is unavoidable and innocuous. But it becomes aggra-
vated by a second-order concealment that occurs when the original concealment itself is concealed. That is, insofar as humans are
oblivious to the fact that every disclosedness involves concealment,
they fall into the illusion of thinking that nothing is hidden and that
everything is totally out front.[22]

Heidegger suggests that the danger confronting us, which is the worst danger that could confront us, results from this double forgetting, where Being
withdraws from us, where the world is defined as a collection of items to be
used or discarded and where Earth, in all its mystery and possibility, withdraws.[23] This danger must be confronted and engaged if a healing of the resulting rift between humans and the world is to occur.

For Heidegger, because our worldview is not determined by humans
but rather by Being, humans cannot through their will overcome the danger, but they can enact other ways of thinking and being in the world that
would nurture a new horizon of disclosure. Guignon notes that "only by
coming to experience fully the distress of this abandonment of being can
we begin to move beyond the mode of understanding dominated by technology and metaphysics. . . . By bringing us face to face with the concealment itself, the transition to a new beginning will lead us to experience exactly what was forgotten in metaphysics: the *truth* of being."[24] This is where
philosophers and poets come in, and where I want to situate my analysis of
works of literature. Guignon observes, "A great work of art . . . can inaugu-
rate a new beginning for a community. What before had been humdrum
and self-evident suddenly stands forth as strange and challenging as a result
of this reconfiguration of the world."[25] The literary works selected for discussion here both engage the technological worldview that dominates our
thinking, revealing it for a limited and constraining horizon of disclosure,
and suggest new ways of thinking and being, offering new possibilities for
opening up new horizons. That is, these works both reveal "world" in its ontological and its ontic fullness and provide a glimpse of "earth" in its mystery and holiness.

But Heidegger's great strength, I suggest, is also one limitation among
many.[26] Germane to my own work is a recognition that Heidegger's thinking has a narrowness of scope that gives it its great strength but that also de-
limits what is discussed. Heidegger focuses on Western civilization, starting

with the pre-Socratic Greeks and tracing the results of Greek thinking into the twentieth century. Although several scholars, and even Heidegger himself, have drawn important connections between his later philosophy and Eastern thought, his thinking remains firmly embedded in Western civilization and culture.[27] For Heidegger, the turn in his thinking that began in the 1930s was an attempt to transcend the anthropocentric nature of his earlier philosophy. Again, his early philosophy focused on the importance of humans in the revelation of being—the way in which, as Michael Zimmerman puts it, "human existence is the openness, clearing, or nothingness in which things can manifest themselves."[28] The shift in the later philosophy deemphasizes humans, suggesting that humans receive Being as a free gift. Zimmerman explains that "later Heidegger emphasized that human existence is appropriated as the site for the self-disclosure or being of entities. Instead of conceiving of being from the perspective of human Dasein, then, Heidegger began thinking of being in its own terms."[29] Dorothea Frede notes that the "transcendental anthropocentrism" of Heidegger's early work is only part of the story, for as Heidegger came to recognize and investigate in his later thinking, humans "do not create our own universe, not even its meaning. The intelligibility resides as much in the 'things' encountered themselves as in the understanding residing in us, and this 'fittingness' is not due to any merit of ours. *Enlightenment* (*Lichtung*) is something that simply *happens* to us, and in this sense 'being' is quite out of our control. It is an 'opening,' a 'free gift,' as Heidegger liked to say later in his life; all we can try to do is 'appropriate it' in an authentic understanding."[30] Yet even with this turn, Heidegger's thinking remains quite anthropocentric—it is to humans that Being is a gift, not animals, not rocks or plants or sky. Kate Rigby suggests that even in Heidegger's later philosophy "an arrogant assumption of human apartness" persists because of the connection between Being and language and the role of humans in "speaking things, as it were, into Being."[31] Certainly there is a great deal less pridefulness in this view where humans become the recipients of the gift of Being rather than the ones who guide or control Being, but humans still remain special and different and central to Heidegger's thinking and project.

The continued anthropocentric strain in Heidegger's thinking largely results from the parameters of his project, which focuses, as I've noted, on an investigation of the disclosive movement of Western history. Heidegger categorically rejects Darwinism and thus excludes prehistorical humans and our evolutionary heritage, the 2 million years since the appearance of the genus *Homo* and the 150,000 to 200,000 years since the appearance of *Homo sapiens*, a time period in which our brains tripled in size from about 400 cubic centimeters to 1,350 cubic centimeters.[32] Heidegger does so with good reason since he has defined world or being as the context of linguistic and sociocultural practices that we move through and that give our lives meaning on a daily basis. For Heidegger as for many others, such a definition of being precludes any consideration of prehistory and thus provides distinct parameters to his thinking. Yet recent humans are not the sole proprietors of language, which likely dates back to 65,000 years ago or more.[33] Indeed, if we broaden our conception of language to include our interaction with the external world, our use of language or protolanguage (if we must) dates back to the beginning of time. As David Abram observes, "To our indigenous ancestors, and to the many aboriginal peoples that still hold fast to their oral traditions, language is less a human possession than it is a property of the animate earth itself, an expressive, telluric power in which we, along with the coyotes and the crickets, all participate."[34]

In my analysis, I would like to build on Heidegger's work, asking two central, related questions. First, how are we placed on Earth?[35] That is, how do we dwell, and how does our dwelling lead to a particular way of thinking and acting? Heidegger's philosophy greatly helps in answering this question and will provide a framework for my investigation of our placedness on Earth in the three literary works that I have selected for my reading. Second, how might we re/place ourselves on Earth in more meaningful ways?[36] That is, how might we reconstruct our dwelling, offering other ways of thinking and acting so that our physical placedness on Earth provides us with a deeper spiritual, emotional, and psychological experience? Again, Heidegger points the way for this second question with his emphasis on art, festival, and ceremony, though I believe a richer foundation for this question lies in a remembering that goes beyond the Greeks back into an ancient wisdom of prehistorical humans and their predecessors, what Paul Shepard calls a homecoming to our Pleistocene roots, and that considers the ancient wisdom of Native Americans.[37] As Heidegger rightly notes, I believe, how we dwell determines how—and even whether—we receive Being. If this is correct, then a markedly different relationship with Being (not being as a particular horizon of disclosure but Being as the foundation of being, that which makes being possible in the first place) existed for our hunter-gatherer forebears and exists for many Native American cultures that have a different way of thinking and acting in the world. Significantly, some have suggested that this 200,000 years (or even 2 million years) provides the foundation for who we are as humans, for our relationship to Earth, for how we dwell, think, and act, a foundation that has not been eliminated in the last 10,000 years of recorded human history, but certainly one that has been forgotten, erased, written over, and ignored. In many respects, Native American philosophy retains an understanding of our embeddedness in the landscape that characterizes our Pleistocene roots.

I would like to explore two main avenues for building on and expanding Heidegger's ideas.[38] The first, which I pursue primarily through the works of Paul Shepard and David Abram, considers our biological heritage in the Paleolithic period, the long trajectory of time in which the genus *Homo* was shaped, our brains slowly expanding and the foundation of our modern selves created, and considers our bodily, sensuous experience of the world. The second, which I undertake by exploring various Native American cultures, considers a different worldview than the one we experience in the Western world, a worldview that does not understand the separation between interior and exterior landscapes and thus sees the human as embedded within the physical world, a world mysterious and sacred in nature. Such an expansion of Heidegger's ideas moves his thinking outward in space to embrace our interconnectedness with other species and the land and backward in time to embrace prehistory and provides a broader foundation for considering the literary works that I explore here. Such an exploration reveals both world (the totalizing horizon of disclosure that we experience in our time) and Earth in its fullest plenitude, Earth conceived as the interconnectedness and interdependence of humans with all species and the landscape, the animate and what we have come to see in the Western world as the inanimate. Such a vision is in actuality a remembering of an ancient wisdom that understands the world around us as sacred, as a divine landscape that glimmers and shines in a radiant holiness.

At the heart of the worldview that Heidegger critiques, the totalized framework that he calls Enframing, is the separation of the subject from the object such that the subject manifests as a master controller of the external world. René Descartes has often been described as one of the primary thinkers who nurtured our sense of interiority and our separation from the natural world. Scholars have suggested that his *Discourse on Method*, published in 1637, reveals the nature of the dualistic thinking that can be found in his work. In an oft-cited passage that sets up the opposition of the mind and the body, Descartes begins by "reject[ing] as if absolutely false everything in which [he] could imagine the least doubt" and then concludes: "Immediately I noticed that while I was trying thus to think everything false, it was necessary that I, who was thinking this, was something. And observing that this truth '*I am thinking, therefore I exist*' was so firm and sure that all the most extravagant suppositions of the sceptics were incapable of shaking it, I decided that I could accept it without scruple as the first principle of the philosophy I was seeking." Descartes continues: "Next I examined attentively what I was. I saw that while I could pretend that I had no body and that there was no world and no place for me to be in, I could not for all that pretend that I did not exist. I saw on the contrary that from the mere fact that I thought of doubting the truth of other things, it followed quite evidently and certainly that I existed; whereas if I had merely ceased thinking, even if everything else I had ever imagined had been true, I should have had no reason to believe that I existed." Descartes derives his evidence for the existence of a thinking self from the fact that he can doubt his body but cannot doubt a thinking self and still exist. He then concludes: "I knew I was a substance whose whole essence or nature is simply to think, and which does not require any place, or depend on any material thing, in order to exist. Accordingly this 'I'—that is, the soul by which I am what I am—is entirely distinct from the body, and indeed is easier to know than the body, and would not fail to be whatever it is, even if the body did not exist."[39] Descartes's thinking being, displaced (or, more accurately, no-placed) and bodiless, is completely independent of the material world. Elizabeth Grosz notes that "since the time of Descartes, not only is consciousness positioned outside of the world, outside its body, outside of nature; it is also removed from direct contact with other minds and a sociocultural community."[40]

Although scholars have recently argued that the dualistic thinking attributed to Descartes is misplaced, a misreading of Descartes's ideas and his intentions, we have nevertheless come to think of the nature of our philosophical orientation in the West as deriving in large part from his works.[41] Regardless of the correctness of the attribution, "Cartesian dualism" comprises several components: "(*a*) that the self is most fundamentally a contingently embodied point of consciousness transparently knowable to itself via introspection, (*b*) that its contents are knowable immediately by contrast to all outward mediated knowledge (and that self-knowledge is thus non-evidential), (c) that first-person thought and experience is invariably private, thus presenting as a brute first fact of human existence an other-minds problem, and (d) that language is the contingent and *ex post facto* externalization of prior, private, pre-linguistic, and mentally internal content."[42] Max Oelschlaeger observes that Descartes proposed a new metaphysical schema that separated mind from matter and viewed the natural world mechanistically. The individual consciousness, disembodied, becomes of prime importance and was set over and against the natural world, which, as a result of the scientific revolution, became viewed increasingly as a machine.[43] Descartes notes that through the philosophy he is developing, "we could know the power and action of fire, water, air, the stars, the heavens and all the other bodies in our environment, as distinctly as we know the various crafts of our artisans; and we could use this knowledge—as the artisans use theirs—for all the purposes for which it is appropriate, and thus make ourselves, as it were, the lords and masters of nature."[44] With the separation between our "inner self" and the "external world," we lost a sense of embodiment, of what I have termed placedness, of an intimate and integral interdependence with the natural world that surrounds us and sustains us and became instead the "lords and masters of nature."[45]

Carolyn Merchant's *The Death of Nature: Women, Ecology and the Scientific Revolution* traces the shift that occurred in the sixteenth and seventeenth centuries from an organic metaphor for understanding the relationship between the self, society, and the natural world to a mechanical metaphor. She notes in her preface: "Between the sixteenth and seventeenth centuries the image of an organic cosmos with a living female earth at its center gave way to a mechanistic world view in which nature was reconstructed as dead and passive, to be dominated and controlled by humans."[46] Merchant details the way in which the organic model of the universe failed in the seventeenth century as a result of advances in science. The sighting of a comet and the discovery of a new star in the 1570s, combined with Galileo's discoveries of craters on the moon, spots on the sun, and the moons circling Jupiter, "provided evidence of the corruptibility of the unchanging heavens above the moon."[47] For thinkers such as Francis Bacon, the disorderly state of nature (which, Merchant observes, was compared to certain female attributes) needed to be analyzed through new scientific methods, which in turn gave rise to an attitude of control and domination of nature and ultimately to a "new mechanical philosophy . . . [that] achieved a reunification of the cosmos, society, and the self in terms of a new metaphor—the machine."[48] French thinkers in the 1620s and 1630s, including most notably Descartes, expanded this thinking such that reality was redefined through the metaphor of the machine—the universe becomes a watch and God a watchmaker. Merchant concludes: "As the unifying model for science and society, the machine has permeated and reconstructed human consciousness so totally that today we scarcely question its validity. Nature, society, and the human body are composed of interchangeable atomized parts that can be repaired or replaced from outside."[49] This is the double-order forgetting lying at the heart of our worldview, both the concealment that occurs with any mode of disclosure and the forgetting of the fact that this is only one mode of revealing reality among many possible modes.

Over time, this worldview led to the commodification of the natural world such that all objects became valued for their resource use, the "standing-reserve" in Heidegger's terms. In recent times, this view of the living world as a machine that humans manipulate and control for our own benefit has led to the valuation of natural ecosystems not on their own merit but rather in terms of the services that they provide to human beings. Bryan Walsh notes that both some environmentalists and a growing number of business people "are arguing that nature in its own right provides economically valuable services that underpin business."[50] While such a view might be misconstrued as accepting the inherent value of natural systems, deep ecologists and many environmentalists would disagree. As Walsh notes, these systems attain their value based on the translation of their services into dollars for businesses and corporations, not on some inherent value of the things themselves. In a 1997 article in the journal *Nature*, "The Value of the World's Ecosystem Services and Natural Capital," the authors estimate the value of the entire planet's ecosystem services in 1997 US dollars to be approximately $33 trillion, though they state that this should be considered a minimum estimate, partly because their calculations do not fully account for the interdependent nature of ecosystem functions and the current unmarketed values of some of these functions.[51] The authors note that "the chains of effects from ecosystem services to human welfare can range from extremely simple to exceedingly complex. Forests provide timber, but also hold soils and moisture, and create microclimates, all of which contribute to human welfare in complex, and generally non-marketed ways."[52] Similarly,

Walsh observes that a "virgin forest is pleasant to look at, of course, but it also prevents soil erosion and improves water quality at no cost—valuable if you happen to own a beverage plant downstream that depends on clean water."[53] The acceptance of a monetary valuation of ecosystems may seem to some environmentalists a necessary tactic, a desperate attempt to convince soulless corporations not to degrade the planet for short-term monetary gain, though there is little evidence that such a tactic is working.[54]

In any case, such a view of Earth and the plants and animals, hills and valleys, sky and sun and, more widely, the ecosystems that support not only our physical bodies but also nurture our imaginations and spirits would be completely antithetical to our hunter-gatherer forebears. Paul Shepard, in *Coming Home to the Pleistocene*, reveals that prehistoric humans lived deeply in their place and through their traditions of oral storytelling passed along a knowledge, derived from their ancestors, of an interconnectedness to the landscape. He describes these peoples as living "within a 'sacred geography' that consisted of a complex knowledge of place, terrain, and plants and animals embedded in a phenology of seasonal cycles. But they were also close to the earth in a spiritual sense, joined in an intricate configuration of sacred associations with the spirit of place within their landscape. Time and space as well as animals—humans—gods—all life and nonliving matter formed a continuum that related to themes of fertility and death and the sacredness of all things."[55] For hunter-gatherers, such a thing as "wilderness" did not exist, for they were embedded in a landscape that became part of their interiority through the lived experience of "sacred associations" with their places. The reciprocity and continuity between the human and the nonhuman consisted in a sacred relation to time that was cyclical and that recognized the interplay of life and death and in an understanding of the spiritual as manifested in the physical landscape. Significantly, they lived in a world populated with many gods, a sacred and divine place that provided a foundation for a heightened sense of responsibility that often became manifest in ceremony.

Shepard describes, in detail, the ontogeny of human beings from an evolutionary perspective, noting that childhood is central to our ultimate maturation as adults, for it is during this phase of our existence that we learn to associate with the other, to fully develop our sense of embeddedness in the landscape. This process begins with the infant's relationship with the mother, which, as Shepard observes, exists within a wider context: "For the infant as person-to-be, the shape of all otherness grows out of that maternal relationship. Yet, the setting of that relationship was, in the evolution of humankind, a surround of living plants, rich in texture, smell, and motion." He continues: "The unfiltered, unpolluted air, the flicker of wild birds, real sunshine and rain, mud to be tasted and tree bark to grasp, the sounds of wind and water, the calls of animals and insects as well as human voices— all these are not vague and pleasant amenities for the infant, but the stuff out of which its second grounding, even while in its mother's arms, has begun. The outdoors is also in some sense another inside, a kind of enlivenment of that fetal landscape which is not so constant as once supposed."[56]

Shepard's investigation of the development of our prehistoric forebears from early childhood through adulthood demonstrates the way in which hunter-gatherers formulated their sense of self in connection with other beings and the landscape around them.

> Mentally and emotionally, children, juveniles, and adolescents move through a world that is structured around them following a time-layered sequence of mother and other caregivers, nature, and cosmos. Infants go from their own and their mother's body to exploring the body of the earth to the body of the cosmos. Our basic human intuition tells us that these bodies comprise a "matrix," that is, "mother." The significance of perceiving environments through a series of different but perpetually "motherly" matrices or contexts is that the world is prototypically organic, feminine, and maternal. The study of nature among primitives begins in childhood but is a lifelong preoccupation.[57]

The maturation of hunter-gatherers depended not only on bonding with their physical mother but also on coming to see the world around them as a mother figure who cared for them and whom they must care for in return. Their "lifelong preoccupation" becomes, in Heidegger's terms, the creation of a space where other beings can emerge-into-presence.

As noted, childhood becomes especially important in this process of maturation, for this is the period in which the initial relationship to the world is developed. According to Shepard, the child in hunter-gatherer societies engages the natural world in an experiential rather than an abstract manner, providing the foundation for an entwinement with that world that becomes central to the child's maturation. As a hunter-gatherer moves into adolescence

> he will learn that his childhood experiences, though a comfort and joy, were a special language. Through myth and its ritual enactments, he is once again presented with that which he expects. Thenceforth natural things are not only themselves but a speaking. He will not put his delight in the sky and the earth behind him as a childish and irrelevant thing. The quests and tests that mark his passage in adolescent initiation are not intended to reveal to him that his love of the natural world was an illusion or that, having seemed only what it was, it in some way failed him. He will not graduate from that world but into its significance.[58]

Thus, in adolescence the hunter-gatherer comes to deepen his relationship with the world around him, understanding the way in which an inextricable interdependence exists between humans and that world. Shepard concludes that "with the end of childhood, he begins a lifelong study, a reciprocity with the natural world in which its depths are as endless as his own creative thought. He will not study it in order to transform its liveliness into mere objects that represent his ego, but as a poem, numinous and analogical, of human society."[59] The natural world, then, is reflected in human culture, just as human culture is dependent on the natural world, and the dance of reciprocity between the two becomes central to the very being of human. In adulthood, our hunter-gatherer forebears came to live fully the intimate interrelationship of self and landscape. Shepard argues that "this Me in a non-Me world is the most penetrating and powerful realization in life. The mature person in such a culture is not concerned with blunting that dreadful reality but with establishing lines of connectedness or relationship. Formal culture is shaped by the elaboration of covenants and negotiations with the Other."[60]

For the hunter-gatherer, the relationship between the surrounding world and language is especially important. For Heidegger, language is the house of Being, the nexus through which Being becomes manifest. A similar notion is captured in the hunter-gatherer relationship to language. Shepard observes: "The most crucial human experience is childhood—its bonding, socializing, and exploration of the nonhuman world, its naming and identification. Speech emerges according to an intrinsic timetable. Language must be taught. But nature is the child's tangible basis upon which symbolic meanings will be posited. The naming and recognition of plants and animals of the home range is the primary function of speech in childhood and the basis for later metaphorical meaning."[61] As the foundation for passing down culture from one generation to the next, language, and especially oral storytelling, plays a key role in maintaining an understanding of the entwinement of humans and the natural world, of humans' connection to things in their own right. In the case of hunter-gatherer societies, language originates from the landscape, from the beings that surround them in their youth, and provides a sense of identity and health as they mature. In childhood, the world is filled with stories told from a wide variety of voices that originate from both cultural and natural contexts. Shepard notes that "voices last only for their moment of sound, but they originate in life. The child learns that all life tells something and that all sound—from the frog calling to the sea surf—issues from a being kindred and significant to himself, telling some tale, giving some clue, mimicking some rhythm that he should know."[62] Significantly, the ability to maintain this connection between themselves and the land through language also assists in maintaining the health of the land: "The ability to read the landscape or the environment, later in life, grows from establishing natural things as its anatomy, keys to the wholeness and well-being of the habitat."[63]

For Heidegger, an authentic response to Being depends on a willingness to listen to the call of stillness, to allow human language to act as a co-responding. As Shepard explains, for our hunter-gatherer forebears, the world of sound is as important as the world of sight in the development of placedness in children. He states: "Not only separately but together, things have a voice. The Voice of life is made up of calls, drums, songs, musical instruments, moving wind and water; they tell us of the livingness of the world in a surprisingly coherent milieu. Vision discovers parts but sound links them."[64] Embedded in the voice of the natural world that surrounds them, hunter-gatherers develop a sense of self connected to other beings. Shepard explains that while they have a sense of self-consciousness, of an identity distinct from others, their understanding of self exists within an "enhanced complexity of relationships." He continues: "A healthy personal development proceeds through a corresponding process that emphasizes relationships to others, so that intensified separateness does not maroon but establishes the self as ever more unique and yet more fully bonded to non-selves by chains of interaction, kinship, dependence, cooperation, and compliance."[65] In Heidegger's terms, then, our hunter-gatherer forebears lived in a matrix of reciprocity, interconnectedness, and entwinement with other beings, perpetually acting as a space within which these other beings could emerge-into-presence on their own terms. And this dance not only allowed other beings to emerge into the clearing but also allowed humans to constantly maintain a connection to themselves, to their role as the ones who provide the space for the clearing to happen.

In his work *In Search of the Primitive*, Stanley Diamond elaborates the sense of integration that exists in primitive cultures. He notes: "Between religion and social structure, social structure and economic organization, economic organization and technology, the magical and the pragmatic, there are intricate and harmonious correlations."[66] He provides an interesting example of a family's relationship with the land that is tilled to provide sustenance: "The land cannot be alienated or sold because the primitive living within the system views the earth as the dwelling place of his ancestors; it is *terra sancta*. Thus, we can trace a functional connection between religion and land tenure, an economic factor."[67] For prehistoric humans, the separation between the self and an objectified external world, which lies at the heart of our current worldview, did not exist. Our evolutionary heritage has attuned us to something that we have forgotten: a negotiation between humans and the landscape that created a living matrix between self and other.

Of the many contemporary environmental philosophers who have engaged our traditional conception of mind, David Abram has offered the most far-reaching analysis in terms of the need to reconnect our understanding of mind, of our internal world, to our sensuous, bodily experience of the external world. He suggests that "mind is not at all a human possession, but is rather a property of the earthly biosphere—a property in which we, along with the other animals and the plants, all participate." For Abram, then, the understanding that our minds comprise some interior space set over and against an exterior, objectified world belies our experience: "The apparent *interiority* that we ascribe to the mind would . . . have less to do with the notion that there is a separate mind located inside me, and another, distinct mind that resides inside you, and more to do with a sense that you and I are both situated *inside it*—a recognition that we are bodily immersed in an awareness that is not ours, but is rather the Earth's." Ultimately, Abram connects our sense of self—our psyche or spirit—to the atmosphere that invisibly surrounds us: "The awareness that stirs within each of us is continuous with the wider awareness that moves all around us, bending the grasses and lofting the clouds. Every organism partakes of this awareness from its own angle and place within it, each of us imbibing it through our nostrils or through the stomata in our leaves, altering its chemistry and quality within us before we breathe it back into the surrounding world."[68]

Interestingly, Abram's analysis suggests that the apparent disjunction between our internal and external landscapes occurred because of the scientific revolution, and he cites the advent of the telescope as one element in this alteration of our understanding of our place in the world. Before we had the capacity to view the universe from a perspective apart from that universe, as happened when Copernicus and Galileo overturned the Ptolemaic cosmology, we saw the world around us and the heavens above us as a great interior. Abram argues: "It's likely that our solitary sense of inwardness (our experience of an interior mindscape to which we alone have access), is born of the forgetting, or repressing, of a much more ancient interiority that was once our common birthright: the ancestral sense of the surrounding earthly cosmos as the voluminous *inside* of an immense Body, or Tent, or Temple."[69] He concludes: "The mind is not ours alone, nor the imagination. With the other animals, as with the crinkled lichens and the river-carved rocks, we're all implicated within this intimate and curiously infinite world, poised between the tactile landscape underfoot and the visible landscape overhead, between the floor and the ceiling, each of us crouching or tumbling or swooping within the same vast interior. Inside the world."[70] Abram's investigation into our bodily sensation of the world and the way in which those felt experiences connect, in a reciprocal and binding fashion, the mind and the world surrounding us offers a different worldview than the one we know in the West, which is founded on an understanding of interiority that relegates the self to a valorized inner landscape, thus setting up the possibility for objectifying the external world and turning all objects into resources to be used.

A similar understanding of the intimate and integral relation between interior and exterior landscapes can be found in Pueblo thinking. In her essay "Interior and Exterior Landscapes: The Pueblo Migration Stories," Leslie Marmon Silko explains that Pueblo artists and storytellers "never conceived of removing themselves from the earth and sky. So long as the human consciousness remains *within* the hills, canyons, cliffs, and the plants, clouds, and sky, the term *landscape*, as it has entered the English language, is misleading. 'A portion of the territory the eye can comprehend in a single view' does not correctly describe the relationship between the human being and his or her surroundings. This assumes the viewer is somehow *outside* or *separate from* the territory she or he surveys. Viewers are as much a part of the landscape as the boulders they stand on." For the Pueblo, then, no distinction exists between our interior and exterior worlds as it does for those of us in the Western world. Indeed, as Heidegger notes, the objectification of the external world occurs largely because of our representational thinking—something quite foreign to the Pueblo. Rather than objectifying and then re-presenting the world around them, the Pueblo people perceive connections between themselves and the natural world. Such an intimate connectedness can be discerned in the concept of the clan:

> There is no high mesa or mountain peak where one can stand and not immediately be part of all that surrounds. Human identity is linked with all the elements of Creation through the clan; you might belong to the Sun Clan or the Lizard Clan or the Corn Clan or the Clay Clan. Standing deep within the natural world, the ancient Pueblo understood the thing as it was—the squash blossom, grasshopper, or rabbit itself could never be created by the human hand. Ancient Pueblos took the modest view that the thing itself (the landscape) could not be improved upon. The ancients did not presume to tamper with what had already been created.[71]

Unlike that of the Pueblo, our horizon of disclosure in the West, as a representational form of thinking and experiencing the world, has separated us from the beings that emerge-into-presence, and thus the landscape necessarily exists separately from the subject who views it.[72]

Significantly, many Native American cultures such as the Pueblo and the Western Apache, like our hunter-gatherer ancestors, maintain an intimate relation between the interior and the exterior through oral storytelling. Indeed, the Pueblo perceived the world—and themselves within the world—as a continuously unfolding narrative: "The oral narrative, or story, became the medium through which the complex of Pueblo knowledge and belief was maintained. Whatever the event or the subject, the ancient people perceived the world and themselves within that world as part of an ancient, continuous story composed of innumerable bundles of other stories."[73] Two particular forms of oral narrative—migration stories and emergence tales—describe the migration of the Pueblo people across the landscape to their home after their emergence into the fifth world. These stories are intimately connected to particular places in the landscape and foster their sense of unity with that landscape. Silko explains that the journey described in the migration story "marked with boulders, mesas, springs, and river crossings, [is] actually a ritual circuit or path that marks the interior journey the Laguna people made: a journey of awareness and imagination in which they emerged from being within the earth and all-included in the earth to the culture and people they became, differentiating themselves for the first time from all that had surrounded them, always aware that interior distances cannot be reckoned in physical miles or in calendar years."[74] As I understand it, then, the Pueblo people existed in total connection to and undifferentiated from Earth and all their animate and inanimate surroundings; in the emergence, the Pueblo became aware of themselves as distinct, as a people. Tales of the journey of emergence into distinction and differentiation rely on imagination and remind listeners of their source: the landscape.

Indeed, the purpose of these stories, which are always connected to special features of the landscape, is to maintain this interconnectedness, to constantly remind listeners of their interdependence with the land. According to Silko, "the journey was an interior process of the imagination, a growing awareness that being human is somehow different from all other life—animal, plant, and inanimate. Yet, we are all from the same source: awareness never deteriorated into Cartesian duality, cutting off the human from the natural world." As noted, the connectedness of the Pueblo to Earth was reinforced through their clan names. According to Silko, the opening into the fifth world was originally too small for humans, so they relied on the antelope and the badger to widen the hole. Silko concludes:

> The human beings depended upon the aid and charity of the animals. Only through interdependence could the human beings survive. Families belonged to clans, and it was by clan that the human being joined with the animal and plant world. Life on the high, arid plateau became viable when the human beings were able to imagine themselves as sisters and brothers to the badger, antelope, clay, yucca, and sun. Not until they could find a viable relationship to the

terrain—the physical landscape they found themselves in—could they *emerge*. Only at the moment that the requisite balance between human and *other* was realized could the Pueblo people become a culture, a distinct group whose population and survival remained stable despite the vicissitudes of the climate and terrain.[75]

Significantly—and here Native American thought diverges greatly from Western thought—humans could emerge and differentiate only when they understood their interdependence, only when they fully realized in a lived, reciprocal way the interconnectedness, the unity between themselves and the world that surrounds them. Before this moment of emergence, the Pueblo were part and parcel of the landscape, beings among other beings, enfolded in Being; in order to emerge, they paradoxically needed to simultaneously understand themselves as distinct and different *and* as interconnected.

The tension existing in the Pueblo emergence as a culture, as distinct from the living world that nurtures and sustains them, can also be seen in the Western Apache. According to Keith Basso, storytelling among the Western Apache is always connected to the landscape, so much so that the storyteller is called a "place-maker." The purpose of telling stories is to re-member an ancient wisdom, the sacred reason of Linda Hogan, that reminds listeners of their origins in the wider community of life that surrounds them. Basso notes that "the place-maker's main objective is to speak the past into being, to summon it with words and give it dramatic form, to *produce* experience by forging ancestral worlds in which others can participate and readily lose themselves."[76] The significance of place in Apache and other Native American conceptions of history and storytelling cannot be overstated.[77] Basso explains: "For Indian men and women, the past lies embedded in features of the earth—in canyons and lakes, mountains and arroyos, rocks and vacant fields—which together endow their lands with multiple forms of significance that reach into their lives and shape the ways they think. Knowledge of places is therefore closely linked to knowledge of the self, to grasping one's position in the larger scheme of things, including one's own community, and to securing a confident sense of who one is as a person."[78] Significantly, the horizon of disclosure, the way Western Apache people think and presence the world around, is constantly being shaped and reshaped by an ancient wisdom recalled through veneration of their elders and, more importantly here, that is embedded in the places where they dwell. This wisdom reminds individuals of their relationship with the world around them, with not only their human communities but also the plants and animals, hills and valleys, lakes and fields to which they are intimately tied for their survival. Through these reciprocal relations, the individual exists in a dance of placedness and replacedness, a constant interplay of past, present, and future and interior and exterior landscapes.

Which brings us back to stories. For the Western Apache, as noted, storytelling connects individuals and communities to the landscape and to their elders in such a way that they are able to survive as a distinct culture; yet their differentiation, as we observed with the Pueblo, occurs only in harmony with its paradoxical opposite, interconnectedness and interrelationship. More specifically, Apache historical tales are at the heart of coming to an understanding of the self as placed in a community that includes the land. In a long explanation of the role of these tales in Western Apache culture, Nick Thompson, one of Keith Basso's mentors, says, "This is what we know about our stories. They go to work on your mind and make you think about your life." When an individual behaves inappropriately, an elder will tell a story about an event, always connected to a prominent place, that is intended to help the individual correct his or her behavior. These stories then "stalk" the individual, hitting the person like an arrow, making the individual think about his or her life. Nick Thompson explains: "Then you feel weak, real weak, like you are sick. You don't want to eat or talk to anyone. The story is working on you now. You keep thinking about it. The story is changing you now, making you want to live right. The story is making you want to replace yourself." Thompson acknowledges that living right is hard, but once you've been stalked with a story you are reminded how to live right—not only by the story but, more importantly, by the place that the story evokes. In this way, the individual's internal world is shaped by the physical world; Nick Thompson concludes: "If you live wrong, you will hear the names and see the places in your mind. They keep on stalking you, even if you go across oceans. The names of all these places are good. They make you remember how to live right, so you want to replace yourself again."[79]

The Western Apache evince a robust understanding of community and of our participation in society, one that engages the psychologically difficult and troubling aspects of our transactions with others. Such a rich understanding is explicitly part of the restorative work that Apache storytelling achieves. A similar conceptual framework for community is offered in William Jordan's *The Sunflower Forest: Ecological Restoration and the New Communion with Nature*. Jordan suggests that at the heart of an authentic understanding of community is "the experience of shame that arises from our awareness of the world and the sense of limitation and difference this awareness entails."[80] Shame is an essential aspect of any and all relationships because in engaging the other we become aware of difference and therefore of our own limitations. Among the Western Apache, shame is prominently though appropriately a part of their culture, while in the West we work diligently to avoid a sense of our own limitations, including death, and thus the experience of shame. As a result, in the West we have lost access to the performative rituals that allow for a productive and constructive method of dealing with shame and building a robust and resilient community. Jordan suggests that ecological restoration can become such a ritual for us, for restoration acknowledges the limitations inherent in our relation to the land and even in our response, our attempt to heal the land, which often falls short. In ecological restoration we presume to participate in the act of creation just as we acknowledge our complicity in destruction.[81] In Heidegger's terms, restoration, which acknowledges limitations and especially the inescapability of death, would allow us to dwell in such a way that the fourfold would become united in a onefold.

What I have suggested through my discussion of Heidegger's later philosophy is that Enframing, the totalized horizon of disclosure that has led to a double-order forgetting, has resulted in a particular way in which we in the West are placed on Earth, how we dwell, how we think and how we act, such that we have lost our connection to Earth, to the full plenitude of being (as potential horizons of disclosure) and beings (the many ways that things could emerge into presence). Indeed, we have lost our connection to Being itself. And so I have argued, through Heidegger, that we must re/place ourselves, that we must remember an ancient wisdom—that Enframing is only one mode of disclosure, that beings can presence in multifarious ways, that a plenitude of truths exists, that humans have the opportunity and indeed the responsibility to act as the clearing in which beings can emerge-into-presence on their own terms. Such a remembering, if it goes deeply enough, would remind us of something that we knew and indeed lived in our evolutionary past, that continues to be known and lived in many Native American cultures, and that might be reconstituted in the performative act of restoration: that we are one species among many, that as humans we exist in a delicate and fragile web of relations with the animate and the inanimate world.

In our evolutionary past, in Native American cultures such as the Pueblo and the Western Apache, and in turning restoration into a ritualized act, we can find models for how to remember this ancient knowledge and how to place ourselves differently on Earth. Through oral storytelling, the Pueblo and the Apache are continuously in the mode of re/placement. Their tales, grounded in the landscape, reach into the past to an event or happening, always connected to a particular place, and bring that occurrence into the present to remind community members how to live, thus allowing them to reshape their behavior in the future. According to Basso,

> As Apache men and women set about drinking from places—as they acquire knowledge of their natural surroundings, commit it to permanent memory, and apply it productively to the workings of their minds—they show by their actions that their surroundings live in them. Like their ancestors before them, they display by word and deed that beyond the visible reality of place lies a moral reality which they themselves have come to embody. And whether or not they finally succeed in becoming fully wise, it is this interior landscape—this landscape of the moral imagination—that most deeply influences their vital sense of place, and also, I believe, their unshakable sense of self.[82]

As a result of storytelling or, as William Jordan suggests, through the act of ecological restoration, the exterior landscape, the physical world, comes to dwell in the interior landscape—reshaping the mind or self—and in this way the individual comes to dwell differently on the land. I would suggest, then, that this transformation is not simply access to a new or different horizon of disclosure; it is, rather, access to Being, to Earth in its fullest plenitude. When wisdom is attained, the Western Apache does not merely remember that his or her way of thinking is one mode among many; rather, wisdom leads to and depends on dwelling on sacred Earth in its majestic mystery. Embedded in the natural world, the culture and language of these Native American peoples remember their entwinement with the landscape in such a way that the natural world becomes embedded in their minds.

Significantly, the integration between humans and the landscape, self and other, interior and exterior depends on a willingness to listen to the other such that our storytelling becomes a co-responding. The emphasis within Heidegger's later philosophy and within ecological restoration on listening, on a stillness that allows Being to erupt into language, finds a nice corollary in Okanagan thought. Jeannette Armstrong describes how a sense of lived reciprocity leads to the idea that the landscape, through the voice of the land, comes to reside within humans. She explains, "As I understand it from my Okanagan ancestors, language was given to us by the land we live within." She continues: "The Okanagan language, called N'silxchn by us, is one of the Salishan languages. My ancestors say that N'silxchn is formed out of an older language, some words of which are still retained in our origin stories. I have heard elders explain that the language changed as we moved and spread over the land through time. My own father told me that it was the land that changed the language because there is special knowledge in each different place."[83] The Okanagan view of language emphasizes the way in which the land contains a wisdom that humans can learn if they understand themselves to be embedded in their places. Constantly listening to and remembering this "special knowledge" becomes the ground of their being, a listening and remembering that occurs through language.

After explaining the way in which a special knowledge emanates from the land, Armstrong states:

> All my elders say that it is land that holds all knowledge of life and death and is a constant teacher. It is said in Okanagan that the land constantly speaks. It is constantly communicating. Not to learn its language is to die. We survived and thrived by listening intently to its teachings—to its language—and then inventing human words to retell its stories to our succeeding generations. It is the land that speaks N'silxchn through the generations of our ancestors to us. It is N'silxchn, the old land/mother spirit of the Okanagan People, which surrounds me in its primal wordless state.[84]

Armstrong provides a very nice gloss on Heidegger's concept of humans listening to a voice other than their own and out of this listening responding in such a way that the stillness, the "primal wordless state," is given voice. Armstrong elaborates this idea, emphasizing the way in which humans move through language, through the speaking of the land. She states: "It is this N'silxchn which embraces me and permeates my experience of the

Okanagan land and is a constant voice within me that yearns for human speech. I am claimed and owned by this land, this Okanagan. Voices that move within as my experience of existence do not awaken as words. Instead they move within as the colors, patterns, and movements of a beautiful, kind Okanagan landscape. They are the Grandmother voices which speak."[85] For the Okanagan people, the foundation of existence, Being, is experienced as a movement of the land within, an interesting twist on the idea that humans are embedded within the land. For this indigenous culture, the engagement with Being that Heidegger argues we have forgotten in the Western world always already occurs as central to their way of being in the world. The land is Being and as such is experienced as an internal state that speaks to the individual.

The worldview of the Okanagan, then, differs markedly from a worldview that separates the speaker from the object spoken about. Language for the Okanagan becomes inextricably intertwined with the land: "The language spoken by the land, which is interpreted by the Okanagan into words, carries parts of its ongoing reality. The land as language surrounds us completely, just like the physical reality of it surrounds us. Within that vast speaking, both externally and internally, we as human beings are an inextricable part—though a minute part—of the land language." Humans dwell within the land-language and have access to reality, to Being, only through this dwelling. Land and language are one and are the source of Being. Through inhabiting the land-language, humans inhabit their being, their essence. Armstrong continues: "All indigenous peoples' languages are generated by a precise geography and arise from it. Over time and many generations of their people, it is their distinctive interaction with a precise geography which forms the way indigenous language is shaped and subsequently how the world is viewed, approached, and expressed verbally by its speakers."[86] The Okanagan way of being and way of thinking is formed by the land through the language arising from the land. Like other Native American cultures and our hunter-gatherer forebears, the Okanagan meld the internal world and the external world, evincing a deeper understanding of both space and time.

And as I've noted, in my project I am similarly interested in broadening Heidegger's understanding of dwelling and the fourfold to embrace Hogan's sacred reason. Several works of ecocriticism have been influential in and provide a foundation for my work as they have moved in related directions.[87] In the introduction to what was in the mid-1990s a ground-breaking collection, *The Ecocriticism Reader,* Cheryll Glotfelty states: "In view of the discrepancy between current events and the preoccupations of the literary profession, the claim that literary scholarship has responded to contemporary pressures becomes difficult to defend. Until very recently there has been no sign that the institution of literary studies has even been aware of the environmental crisis."[88] Glotfelty explains that ecocriticism expands the notion of the world studied in literary theory from the social sphere to the "entire ecosphere," having "one foot in literature and the other on land" and thus negotiating "between the human and the nonhuman."[89] I will summarize key works of ecocriticism to give some idea of the context of my work, though this summary is not exhaustive.

Max Oelschlaeger's *The Idea of Wilderness: From Prehistory to the Age of Ecology* is the preeminent work of scholarship that considers literary works within a deep view of space and time. He states in his preface that he has three goals in his work: to "open up that Pandora's box of the Paleolithic," to advance the study of literature "that reflects both the rise of an evolutionary paradigm and nineteenth- and twenty-century evolutionary thought," and to write "a universal history organized around one steadfast theme—namely, the idea of wilderness, the study of an ever-changing yet constant relationship between humankind and nature." His approach, which is founded on Heidegger's view of reason, is "not of suspicion and deconstruction but of restoration and reconstruction."[90] *The Idea of Wilderness* begins with a discussion of prehistoric humans and their relation to the natural world, which sets the stage for an analysis of Western civilization demonstrating how we have become distanced from our evolutionary roots. He then discusses the development of agriculture in the Mediterranean, the rise of Yahwehism, the philosophy of the Greeks, and Judeo-Christianity. From this beginning, Oelschlaeger then traces the ascendance of an anthropocentric worldview in the Renaissance, the Reformation, and the Enlightenment, one that embraces interiority and reason and creates a dualistic mind-set, separating subject and object; this worldview casts humans as masters of the natural world and ultimately severs our ties to nature. Yet what is of most interest to me and my own project are the challenges to the modernist worldview that Oelschlaeger describes. These challenges occur in the realm of science (through such thinkers as Charles Darwin and George Perkins Marsh), philosophy (through such thinkers as Benedict Spinoza and Arthur Schopenhauer), and literature.

Ultimately, for Oelschlaeger, Henry David Thoreau is the prime example of a writer who understands the connection between humans and the natural world, grounding his ideas of the social and the cultural in the presocial, in an indigenous wisdom that allows access to the creative forces of the universe.[91] Oelschlaeger concludes that Thoreau

> becomes a man of Indian wisdom, a person-in-contact with wild nature, with the Great Mother. His genius is not that he turned his back on civilization—Thoreau is no hermit, no misanthrope—but that he affirms the reality of organic process and the vital importance of understanding that humankind, too, is part of this larger, enframing realm—life within nature. Thoreau is a natural classicist who argues that humankind is wild nature grown self-conscious and that creativity—that is, evolutionary response to changing cultural circumstances—depends essentially on systematically acting upon this insight: in wildness lies the preservation of the world.[92]

Oelschlaeger follows his analysis of Thoreau with discussions of John Muir, who embraced a biocentric worldview and suggested that this broader wisdom should compel our ethical notions, and Aldo Leopold, who built on these notions by suggesting that ecology was a normative science that should be used to create values, norms, and ethics.[93] Oelschlaeger concludes his analysis with a discussion of two modern poets, Robinson Jeffers and Gary Snyder, revealing the way in which the language of these poets unconceals the Paleolithic and is thus "ontogenetic" or "world making."[94] His final two chapters consider contemporary wilderness philosophy before offering a postmodern wilderness philosophy. He concludes:

> Humankind is an interloper, a newcomer to a splendid evolutionary process writ large across the tens of thousands of millennia. We can, if we dare loosen the strictures of convention—of the logos that obscures the reality of the bios beneath—think like a mountain, and thereby grasp that palpable reality of the source. To think like a mountain demands that we break free of our Abrahamic concept of the land. For Western culture has forgotten the source of life, the point of origin from which wells up all that is good and free and beautiful, and has turned the land into environment, into re-source.

By thinking like a mountain—truly a Thoreauvian trope of gargantuan proportion—our species might rediscover its grounding in cosmic process.[95]

Oelschlaeger's monumental work, then, follows the trace of a more primal, sacred reason in Western thinking and works to reassert an "old-new way of being."[96] I am greatly indebted to his approach and his great wisdom and knowledge.

If Oelschlaeger presents the most comprehensive analysis of literary and philosophical works from a perspective of deep space and deep time, Joseph Meeker is often credited with the origin of this type of literary scholarship. In his seminal work *The Comedy of Survival: Studies in Literary Ecology*, Meeker suggests that the literary comedy, which "depicts the loss of equilibrium and its recovery" and parallels the inner workings of ecosystems, challenges humans to create a more complex civilization, one where "allowance would have to be made for the welfare of all the plants, animals, and land of the natural environment" and where humans would need "to cultivate a new and more elaborate mentality capable of understanding intricate processes without destroying them." He outlines the nature of his own project: "The comic mode of human behavior represented in literature is the closest art has come to describing man as an adaptive animal. Comedy illustrates that survival depends upon man's ability to change himself rather than his environment, and upon his ability to accept limitations rather than to curse fate for limiting him."[97] Meeker's book analyzes works of Shakespeare and Dante, as well as other works in the pastoral and picaresque modes, demonstrating his groundbreaking thesis. More recently, Glen Love, in *Practical Ecocriticism: Literature, Biology, and the Environment*, has taken this study of literature and the environment to its extreme through his emphasis on the use and relevance of the scientific method, relying especially on the sciences of biology and ecology, for gaining access to truth.[98] Ultimately, Love, following ideas in E. O. Wilson's *Consilience*, suggests that evolutionary biology could act as a bridge between the humanities and the sciences.[99] Love's analysis begins with the pastoral tradition, connecting this tradition to Wilson's concept of biophilia, before analyzing the works of Willa Cather, Ernest Hemingway, and William Dean Howells.[100]

Like Oelschlaeger, Lawrence Buell, in *The Environmental Imagination: Thoreau, Nature Writing, and the Formation of American Culture*, uses Thoreau as a touchstone in his analysis of American literary nonfiction. Buell's

central claim is that the environmental crisis is a "crisis of the imagination the amelioration of which depends on finding better ways of imag-
ing nature and humanity's relation to it."[101] Such a reimagining could occur through an exploration of environmental texts with "biota rather than
homo sapiens as our central concern"; this exploration is intended to help
us understand how our perceptions of the world have been informed by
these texts and how they might be reformed.[102] John Elder's *Imagining the
Earth: Poetry and the Vision of Nature* extends this type of argument, stating
that poetry "makes possible a more balanced culture, concentric with the
planet. In their imaginative passage from estrangement to transformation
and reintegration, poets enact a circuit of healing." His analysis of writers
such as Robinson Jeffers, Gary Snyder, Denise Levertov, and A. R. Ammons
demonstrates that "America's poetry of nature arises from the fever of cultural dividedness—man against nature, past against present, intellect against
senses—but discovers grounds for reconciliation in the inextricable wholeness of the world."[103] The three sections of Elder's book are each separated
by a literary essay describing his own experiences in the Vermont landscape,
the place from which he writes.

The three works that I discuss in the following chapters provide us with
a similar opportunity to gain insight into our place on Earth and to remember sacred reason, an ancient wisdom of Earth and elders. In concluding
this theoretical introduction, I would like to return to the two central questions that I posed earlier in order to connect them to the concept of sacred
reason and the way in which I have broadened Heidegger's central concepts through deep anthropology and Native American philosophy. The
first question, "How are we placed on Earth?" might be considered a question of how we dwell, how we think, and how we act. In the twentieth and
twenty-first centuries, we exist within a totalizing horizon of disclosure, a
mode of revealing beings that has excluded all other modes such that we
no longer even see that our horizon is exactly that—one way of presencing beings. Instead, we have taken it for "truth" or "reality," "the way things
are." Land is a site for shopping malls and gated communities. The sky is air
space that we move through (and thus demarcate and regulate) and exhaust
our factory and automotive effluent into (within what we have determined
are reasonable limits). Animals and plants are things to be manipulated and
modified in the most efficient ways to produce the largest quantities of eat-
able goods (that can withstand packaging and transportation halfway across

the globe). Longleaf pines are so many board feet (to be replaced by faster growing slash pine once they have been used up). The Great Salt Lake is a nuisance to be dammed, channeled, drained, or controlled (depending on what best suits our economic needs at the time). In our rushed and frenzied lives bent on accumulating more and more things, we have forgotten that another, more primal relation to Being exists for us. Thus, our placedness has become technological, our thinking calculative and scientific. And in this technological placedness, we have lost our place as beings who have the opportunity and responsibility to act as a clearing, an opening for beings to emerge-into-presence, and our place as beings connected to the land on which we dwell. In the end, these two understandings of our relation to place are the same thing, for we become the space for Being to become manifest when we are inextricably and interdependently connected to our landscapes.

The three writers discussed here, Janisse Ray, Terry Tempest Williams, and Linda Hogan, depict this technological placedness in their works. Ray's *Ecology of a Cracker Childhood* explores the nature of our destitute time by depicting a life lived on a junkyard, what would be the full measure of an existence founded on calculating reason, a life that is the endpoint of all our producing and consuming and discarding. She details her entrapment within Enframing, a truly totalizing horizon of disclosure that does not provide her with the opportunity to be, or, as she says, "to be able to be." Terry Tempest Williams's *Refuge: An Unnatural History of Family and Place* describes two parallel changes that confront her ability to find peace: the rise of Great Salt Lake, which endangers the Bear River Migratory Bird Refuge, and the rise of cancer in her mother's body. Williams recounts what appears to be the natural and only possible response to both changes: a technological fix, a complete surrender to a scientific and calculative way of thinking and being. Likewise, Linda Hogan's *Dwellings: A Spiritual History of the Living World* offers several anecdotes of the way in which we in the West have become disconnected from and objectify the natural world, though her work, from a Chickasaw perspective, most fully offers a remedy to our technological placedness on Earth.

We must remember, however, that Heidegger asserts that Enframing is not only the danger but also the saving power. Enframing, like all horizons of disclosure, is a granting, a gift from Being that allows humans to participate in the emerging-into-presence of things. We must remember, then, something that our hunter-gatherer forebears and our Native American brothers and sisters know, that Enframing is one mode of disclosure among many and that as humans we have access to the mysterious plenitude of Earth and a responsibility to care for, to spare and preserve, this plenitude. Which leads to my second question, "How might we re/place ourselves in more meaningful ways?" This question asks us to consider how we might dwell differently, how we might engage new ways of thinking and acting in the world that would allow us to remember sacred reason, the ancient wisdom of the Western Apache. My exploration of our Pleistocene heritage and of contemporary and Native American philosophy as well as my understanding of ecological restoration provide an avenue for answering this question. Within these other paradigms, we must maintain an awareness of our interdependence with the world around us, of the way in which the landscape lives in us as much as we live in it, of the unity of the fourfold. We must learn to listen to the stillness of Being, allowing things to thing and world to world, in Heidegger's terms; for Native cultures such as the Western Apache, doing so means to be in a constant mode of re/placement that occurs through storytelling and place-making. The self becomes entwined with the land, the mind mirrors the landscape, and language, when it ushers forth from the stillness of the mind-land matrix, speaks Being. Language becomes a co-responding, a listening that responds to things thinging and world worlding in an endless dance of reciprocity.

Heidegger suggests that writers are the ones who can lead us back to a more primal relation to Being, to Hogan's sacred reason. To do so, they must reach into the abyss, into the depths of our destitution, and through their engagement with our situation they can offer us a turning that will provide the foundation for a new mode of consciousness, based not on the logic of reason but on the logic of the heart. Ray's story, her autobiography of a life lived in the detritus of Western civilization, becomes the foundation for a recovery, a deeper remembering. Her narrative strategy of intercalating chapters on natural history with chapters on her family history disrupts her autobiography in order to demonstrate that Enframing is one mode of disclosure, of revealing, and that there are other modes. In the retelling of her life, Ray describes the opening of her heart as a counterbalance to the logic of the mind, an occurrence that opens her life to a new trajectory allowing for the restoration of her identity and her ecosystem, a healing of the rift between humans and the natural world. In Williams's memoir, the remembering of the atom bomb provides her with an understanding of the significant differences in the two changes that confront her life and provides a foundation for her voice and the telling of her story. Through this remembering, she learns to differentiate between change that is patterned and cyclical and change that is unnatural, an understanding that becomes the foundation for her activism.

Janisse Ray's narrative structure manifests the way in which her life becomes a listening to the landscape, to the stillness, and thus her narrative becomes a co-responding. In Williams's work, the listening and co-responding is central to the unfolding of the narrative; birds become a guide for the narrator as she encounters change and, ultimately, mortality. For Heidegger, animals do not participate in Being in quite the same way as humans, for they are *"poor in world,"* whereas *"man is world-forming."*[104] Heidegger suggests that the difference lies in the fact that humans have the capacity for *"comportment"*—for apprehending other beings as beings—while animals only have the capacity for "behavior."[105] The fundamental nature of the animal's behavior is that of "captivation," through which the animal has access to other beings through instinctual drives that create an "encircling ring" around the animal, but not to other beings *as* beings.[106] Such a conception of animals and the world around us (Heidegger goes even further with the "inanimate" world, calling it *"worldless"*) differs greatly from our Pleistocene heritage and many Native American cultures, as I've already demonstrated, as it does for Williams, who takes birds as her mentors.[107] Through the dual journeys of her narrative, Williams is able to inhabit both land and language and, through a deep and respectful listening, give voice to the land, to language, to Being. The journey that Williams takes in the narrative guided by the voice of the birds, a journey that includes an encounter with and acceptance of mortality, is a kind of migration, a returning home to a forgotten knowledge of interrelatedness and interdependence, of circularity and wholeness, a re/placing of herself on the land in order to heal both herself and the wider culture that surrounds her.

In her essay "First People," Linda Hogan describes how Earth, poisoned as it is with toxins and degraded with a vast extinction of species, is out of balance. She concludes: "We are hoping for, in need of, a ceremony that will heal this. In a changed world, we are in need of an ancient way of being."[108] William Jordan notes that ritual, and ceremony by extension, "though often understood as a sign of concord and harmony, are perhaps more accurately understood as the means by which a society manages discordant and divisive elements, both within the individual and among individuals, in order to achieve a measure of harmony."[109] Thus ceremony heals us, first, by acknowledging the ills that confront us and, second, by reminding us of our intimate connection with the world surrounding us, allowing us to re/place ourselves—that is, to become new people who reinhabit our landscapes. Linda Hogan's *Dwellings: A Spiritual History of the Living World*, the final work that I discuss, can be read as a ceremony of healing that describes the ills confronting us in Western society and that then brings us back into relation with the organic world surrounding us. Hogan's narrative structure mirrors a Native ceremony, first revealing our limited horizon of disclosure, the way in which we have separated ourselves from Earth, before working to heal that divide. The relationship that we recover at the end of her work is founded on reciprocity and humility, which restore to both the narrator and the reader an ancient way of thinking and open the door to a forgotten way of being. At the heart of this remembered knowledge is an awareness of the interdependence and interrelatedness of all things, a profound mirror-play integrating all beings into the oneness of the fourfold.

Like other Native American writers and philosophers, Hogan often emphasizes the importance of storytelling and connects stories to ceremonies. In "First People," she notes: "The stories that are songs of agreement and safekeeping, and the ceremonies that are their intimate companions, tell us not only how to keep the world alive, they tell us how to put ourselves back together again. In the language of ceremony, a person is placed—bodily, socially, geographically, spiritually, and cosmologically—in the natural world extending all the way out into the universe."[110] For Hogan, then, as in many Native American cultures, ceremony reminds us of our intimate interrelationship with the animate and the less-than-animate world around us, a remembering of sacred reason. In this way, all three works discussed in this project might be considered, more generally, as ceremonies, for they seek to heal the rift between humans and the natural world that is a central component of Western civilization. And more than simply describing the ills and the healing that needs to occur, these works, on some important level, enact our participation with the beautiful and fragile Earth surrounding us, accomplishing that healing through re/placing us on the land and bringing us into the fulfillment of our being.

# CHAPTER THREE

# Restor(y)ing the Self

## Ecological Restoration in Janisse Ray's
### *Ecology of a Cracker Childhood*

In *The Sunflower Forest*, William Jordan defines ecological restoration as "the attempt, sometimes breathtakingly successful, sometimes less so, to make nature whole. To do this the restorationist does everything possible to heal the scars and erase the signs of disturbance or disruption."[1] He explains that the work of the restorationist is to restore all aspects of an ecosystem or landscape, including those elements, such as fire or flooding, that might seem dangerous or nonproductive; he concludes that restoration "is a deliberate attempt to return *all* the features of the system to some historic condition, defined ecologically and with a studied disregard for human interests."[2] Restoring the land, then, becomes a way of reconsidering how we dwell on Earth, of how we think about the landscape around us and how we act toward that landscape. Although humans become implicated further in the land through the act of restoration—an act that paradoxically is about attempting to diminish the human impact on the land—they do so by relinquishing their own interests and listening to the stillness of the land. Although the ideal end result of the restorationist may be clear, the outcome is "paradoxical. The aim of the restorationist is to erase the mark of his own kind from the landscape. Yet through the process of restoration he enters into a peculiarly profound and intimate relationship with it."[3] In this way, restoration of the land becomes a means to restoration of the self, for the land becomes a part of us.

In a similar way, Janisse Ray's *Ecology of a Cracker Childhood* intimately connects a discussion of the degradation of the landscape and Ray's dream of restoring the land to a discussion of her life as it evolves in the telling of her story. As her autobiography unfolds and she describes a life lived on a junkyard in south Georgia, Ray intercalates chapters on the natural world surrounding her, including both elaborate depictions of the degraded land of her time and glimpses of the historic longleaf pine ecosystem that once covered much of the South. The intercalated chapters, interrupting the narrative of her life as they do, have the effect not only of revealing how the human community dwells on the land but also of suggesting how the land dwells in us. This autobiographical act becomes, then, not only an act of ecological restoration, metaphorically or textually restoring the land, but also an act of self-restoration, allowing the author to re/place herself in fundamental ways; that is, in *Ecology*, Ray considers how she dwells on Earth, and through an analysis of the technological horizon of disclosure that has become her worldview, she uncovers the possibility for a renewed emplacement on the land, one ecological in nature that reveals the human interdependence with the landscape. Ultimately, the writing of *Ecology* offers an opportunity for remaking her conception of self and reshaping the values of the human community in which she is embedded.

Significantly, William Jordan's central concern in exploring the act of ecological restoration is to unfold the way in which this act is also, like the writing of an autobiography such as *Ecology*, a means to the creation of values, a necessary step in the process of developing an ethical system that guides our individual and communal behavior. He reconfigures restoration, which is often undertaken as a scientific or technological pursuit, as a ritual, a ceremony, a performative act that allows us to examine our values, to criticize those values, and to open the possibility of shifting or redefining them. Ultimately, such a process allows a society to "change the deepest structures of its worldview and system of values and relationships."[4] Ecological restoration, when it becomes a ritualized performative act, affects the restorationist and the entire human community, reshaping our ideas and placing us differently on the land so that we become new beings who are "effective, knowledgeable, loyal, and responsible members of the biotic community."

Jordan concludes: "Crucially, what really has to be renewed is not the land-scape at all, but the human community's *idea* of the landscape, on which the well-being of the landscape ultimately depends."[5]

Jordan's conception of ecological restoration and our relation to the landscape offers the possibility for a conception of reality that differs from the one we enjoy in the Western world. If through the act of restoration as ritual we reconfigure our perception of the external world, then that world is not a static, fixed object to be manipulated and controlled but rather is dependent on our ideas of and our relationship to the land. As David Abram suggests, our bodily experience and our internal perception of the external world become an act of exchange, where the interaction that we have with the land reshapes our understanding of the land. Restoration, then, would allow things to presence in their ownness, to use Heidegger's terms, and humans to take up residency in their essence as the beings who create the space for presencing to occur. And the extension of this thought through Native American cultures such as the Pueblo and the Western Apache is that the stories we tell of the land, when they originate from the stillness of the land, reinforce the reciprocity existing between our internal and external landscapes and thus create our sense of reality. As N. Scott Momaday notes, "At the heart of the American Indian oral tradition is a deep and unconditional belief in the efficacy of language. Words are intrinsically powerful. They are magical. By means of words can one bring about physical change in the universe."[6] I would suggest that when words are chosen carefully, not only in oral but also in written forms, stories can become an important element in the ritual of restoration, can in fact become an alternate form and perhaps the basis of restoration, even if only a metaphorical restoration that reshapes our ideas and beliefs, thus reforming our understanding of and relation to the land.

Such a conception of storytelling finds parallels in autobiographical theory.[7] In *Fictions in Autobiography*, Paul Eakin suggests "that autobiographical truth is not a fixed but an evolving content in an intricate process of self-discovery and self-creation."[8] For Eakin, the act of writing the autobiography becomes a process whereby an identity is established and a life is made meaningful. Similarly, in his own autobiography, *So Long, See You Tomorrow*, William Maxwell asserts that memory—"a moment, a scene, a fact that has been subjected to a fixative and thereby rescued from oblivion—is really a form of storytelling that goes on continually in the mind and often

changes with the telling. Too many conflicting emotional interests are involved for life ever to be wholly acceptable, and possibly it is the work of
the storyteller to rearrange things so that they conform to this end."[9] Just
as strict preservation of the land is never possible, for there is always some
human influence on the land, no matter how remote the land, strict historically accurate autobiography is never possible for the self—our identity, our
sense of who we are in the world—is not some object that is carried with us
throughout our lifetime, isolated, pure, and preserved.[10] Eakin explains that
autobiographers in the twentieth century "no longer believe that autobiography can offer a faithful and unmediated reconstruction of a historically
verifiable past; instead, it expresses the play of the autobiographical act itself, in which the materials of the past are shaped by memory and imagination to serve the needs of present consciousness."[11] Thus, the stories we tell
of our lives are subject to our perceptions and values at the time of considering our autobiography, values that are in some sense reformulated in the
very act of reconsidering our lives.[12] Indeed, the values enunciated in the
autobiography may not have provided an explicit self-conscious foundation
for the unfolding of the self, but the performative act of writing—like the
act of ecological restoration—elicits these values from the act of storying
the self.[13]

Significantly, this act, which occurs in the nexus of memory and writing, becomes an exploration of self, the self of the writer at the time of
the writing as much as of the person who lived the life experience. As Kim
Barnes remarks about her own autobiographical writing, "To me the story
I want to tell exists in the conflict of memory. It's not *what* happened that's
most important to me but *why* I remember it the way I do."[14] Indeed, some
theorists have suggested that in autobiography such a journey into the self
becomes most fruitful when the writerly self discovers things that he or
she might not have known before embarking on the path of autobiography. John Sturrock notes that a "chronological narrative is a discipline which
greatly hampers the autobiographer's freedom. . . . A higher degree of candor . . . is reached when the autobiographer sets off in pursuit of the unlit
portions of his past rather than the lit ones and produces revelations that
were revelations for himself too."[15] Sturrock suggests not only that the act
of writing the self is an exploration of discovery but also that a narrative disrupted in its chronology can assist in revealing these deeper truths. Another
such method of disruption used in place-based writing is to find associations

between the self and the land that expand the understanding of the lived experience. Kim Barnes connects her own journey toward "self-discovery" to place; she asks: "'Who am I, and why?' I cannot answer this without looking to the land."[16] For Barnes, then, as for Ray, the exploration of self through the act of writing becomes intimately connected to an exploration of her past relation to the landscape.

In the introduction to *Ecology of a Cracker Childhood*, Janisse Ray sets up just such a complex interrelationship between the natural landscape and her autobiography. The opening passage describes the landscape of her homeland as a kind of palimpsest: "In south Georgia everything is flat and wide. Not empty. My people live among the mobile homes, junked cars, pine plantations, clearcuts, and fields. They live among the lost forests" (3). The dominant text—the junkyards, clear-cuts, and pine plantations—has erased the original text of the lost longleaf pine forest that once covered the area. In many respects, the project of *Ecology* is to recover that lost landscape; that is, the book is a metaphorical or textual attempt to restore the erased text of the longleaf pine ecosystem that once covered 85 of 156 million acres in the Southeast. Yet Ray's autobiography operates on another level that connects the landscape to her life. Ray goes on to note in the introduction that in south Georgia you see everything coming: "That's because the land is so wide, so much of it open. It's wide open, flat as a book, vulnerable as a child. It's easy to take advantage of, and yet it is also a land of dignity. It has been the way it is for thousands of years, and it is not wont to change" (4). Here Ray connects her concern for the land not only to a book, thus further advancing the image of the palimpsest, but also more importantly to her own autobiography, that of the vulnerable child. *Ecology of a Cracker Childhood* becomes, then, a lament for the lost forests and for her lost childhood—two suppressed texts that become restored in the writing of the book.

Because of the unique form of *Ecology*, with chapters that alternate between her autobiography and her native landscape, critics have offered interesting and diverse readings of Ray's relationship to the natural world. Jay Watson, in his essay "Economics of a Cracker Landscape," focuses on "how conditions of economic stress and deprivation work not only to inhibit environmental awareness . . . but also, perhaps surprisingly, to create it."[17] In his reading of *Ecology*, he concludes that "as a result of her family's comparative [economic] stability, Janisse's relationship with the pine forest, her sense of mystery and delight in the nonhuman landscape, begins early in life and is able to develop over many years."[18] Similarly, in Sarah Robertson's "Junkyard Tales," she suggests that a contradiction exists in Ray's text between the "need to promote ecological awareness and the desire to raise her family, particularly her father, above the definition of 'otherness.'"[19] Robertson asserts that Ray merges the junkyard and the natural landscape, which leads to a "divided sense of self" that cannot reconcile the two.[20] Finally, in their review of *Ecology*, Carolyn Kindell, K. C. Smith, and Andi Reynolds state that Ray "learned a fierce self-reliance and love of nature in her childhood home."[21] Yet a close reading of *Ecology of a Cracker Childhood* suggests that Ray did not develop such a deep and intimate connection to the landscape in her youth; just as she had no contact with or even knowledge of the lost longleaf pine forests that once covered south Georgia, she herself had a rather tenuous connection to the natural world.[22] As she says, rather emphatically, toward the end of the book: "When I pick up my childhood like a picture and examine it really closely, I realize that I left home not knowing how to swim, not knowing the name of one wild bird except maybe crow, and that I couldn't identify wildflowers and trees . . . [and] couldn't tell a weasel from a warthog. I never knew a naturalist or that there was such a thing as an environmentalist" (211).

Although Ray may not have experienced a longleaf pine ecosystem in her childhood, the story of her life—the close examination of her lived experience—becomes intimately intertwined with the story of that ecosystem. She states in her introduction that her ancestors "settled the vast, fire-loving uplands of the coastal plains of southeast Georgia, surrounded by a singing forest of tall and widely spaced pines whose history they did not know, whose stories were untold. The memory of what they entered is scrawled on my bones, so that I carry the landscape inside like an ache. The story of who I am cannot be severed from the story of the flatwoods" (4). Two erased texts exist in *Ecology*—the text of a lost childhood, one without the deep connection to the natural world that the adult author has come to value, and the text of the lost forests—both of which have been supplanted by junkyards, clear-cuts, and pine plantations. In this way, *Ecology of a Cracker Childhood* becomes a dual project in ecological restoration and the (re)formation of a self intimately tied to the landscape. Through (re)writing her life, Ray is able to revisit moments in her childhood and invest those moments with a richer significance than they might have had in the original

lived experience. Simultaneously, her revisioning, her ability to tell the untold stories of the singing forest, allows for a metaphorical reestablishment
of the longleaf pine ecosystem. Through the insertion of intercalated chapters depicting elements of the lost forest into her autobiography, Ray is able
to disrupt that autobiography and fashion a self embedded in the landscape;
that is, as she restores the lost forests of south Georgia through listening to
and telling the story of the land, a kind of textual restoration, she simultaneously recovers her lost childhood.

The first two autobiographical chapters in *Ecology* establish the paradoxical nature of the autobiography, at once asserting Ray's origins in a
junkyard and at the same time insinuating a potential intimacy with the
landscape of south Georgia. In "Child of Pine," the first autobiographical
chapter, she describes the way in which, in early February 1962, her parents "went out searching among the pinewoods through which the junkyard had begun to spread" (5). They trace the sound of a "bleating cry" to
"a clump of palmettos beneath a pine" and find, cradled in pine needles, a
baby: "And that was me. . . . I came into their lives easy as finding a dark-
faced merino with legs yet too wobbly to stand" (6). Ray, her older sister,
and her two younger brothers all have such creation stories that connect
them to the land, that insinuate their origin from the natural world that surrounds them. Yet Ray concludes this episode stating flatly: "If they'd said
they'd found me in the trunk of a '52 Ford, it would have been more believ-
able. I was raised on a junkyard on the outskirts of a town called Baxley, the
county seat of Appling, in rural south Georgia" (7). The creation story that
has been handed down to Ray and her siblings is just that—a story, one that
seemingly contradicts a lived experience where being found in a wrecked
automobile is more likely than being found in a cabbage patch, a grapevine,
a huckleberry bush, or a clump of palmettos. Yet, as I've noted, the telling
of the story has a profound impact on reality, and Ray early asserts that her
storytelling will allow her to restore her lost heritage.

"Child of Pine" along with "Shame," the second autobiographical chapter, offer contrasting images of her home place as a junkyard filled with
the detritus of Western civilization and as a locus for trees that connect her
to Earth. She notes that one of her favorite activities was to climb a chi-
naberry tree: "I would sit in the tree and wait, listening for something—a
sound, a resonance—that came from far away, from the past and from the
ground" (8–9). Ray's waiting and listening recall Heidegger's insistence that

humans must learn to allow language to speak through a listening that becomes a co-responding, and beyond that, her listening to something "from
the past and from the ground" recalls the Native American view of remembering sacred reason, of listening to Earth and elders. Yet this insinuation
of landscape is quickly juxtaposed with the reality of her surroundings: "I
could unhook the chain from the nail on the post and leave the yard, but I
wasn't allowed to go far. The junkyard was dangerous, strewn with broken
glass and shards of rusty metal. A rusty nail could send a streak of inflam-
mation into the bloodstream, Daddy warned, causing lockjaw that might
clamp your mouth shut like a beaver trap" (9), symbolically enforcing a silence that would prevent Ray from telling the story of her life. Likewise, in
"Shame," Ray provides a detailed description of the "swales of scrap" and
broken-down automobiles strewn across the land and concludes, succinctly,
"ten acres of failed machines" (22–23). She then contrasts this description by
noting that the red maple that grows at one end of the pond "was considered [her] tree" (24); yet she also acknowledges that at the time she "didn't
know its name," suggesting again that her connection to the natural world
in her youth was tenuous at best.

Ray concludes the chapter "Shame" with a reflection on her early life.
She recalls, "Away from home we were ashamed of the junkyard. Our
daddy was a junk dealer, but when we filled out his occupation on forms
from school we wrote 'salesman'" (29). Because Ray and her siblings were
not allowed to socialize with other kids or visit their homes, "the junkyard . . . was all [they] knew." She continues, "We knew nobody else lived
like we did, but we didn't know how they lived. We knew they were waste-
ful and threw perfectly good things in the garbage, which ended up at our
house. We thought that meant they were better than we were" (29). Ray
thus exists within a circumscribed space, placed in the midst of the discarded waste products of Western civilization. She carries her shame with
her into her adult life, a shame that could not be ameliorated in her youth,
and attempts to reconcile this feeling through the act of writing her life:
"Turning back to embrace the past has been a long, slow lesson not only
in self-esteem but in patriotism—pride in homeland, heritage. It has taken
a decade to whip the shame, to mispronounce words and shun grammar
when mispronunciation and misspeaking are part of my dialect, to own
the bad blood" (32–33). Her story, then, must embrace her past, not only
the past of her youth but also, more importantly, of her homeland and her

heritage. And while this more distant past entails a great deal of shame, as
we shall see, it also provides the foundation for renewal, for restoration of
the land and the self. In Heidegger's terms, the danger becomes the saving
power. Ray concludes this chapter: "What I come from has made me who
I am" (33), and *Ecology* becomes an exploration of everything that has made
her—the good, the bad, the ugly, and the way in which all these things offer possibilities for the future.

Having provided her creation story and a description of the junkyard in
which she was raised, Ray turns to tracing her heritage through her male
ancestors in the remainder of the autobiographical chapters in the first half
of the book. Again, in these chapters, she paradoxically provides a depiction of both her tenuous connection to the natural world and the disruption of that connection. In the chapter "Iron Man," she describes the life of
her paternal grandfather, Charlie Joe Ray, who suffered from acute mental
illness, perhaps bipolar disorder, but who also "knew the woods by heart"
(39). Whenever he had an onset of his illness, her grandfather took refuge
in the floodplain swamps and pine flatlands: "Because he withdrew often to
the woods for safety and comfort and for shelter and food, he knew them
like nobody I've ever known. All his life he never loved a human the way he
cherished woods; he never gave his heart so fully as to those peaceful wild-
land refuges that accepted without question any and all of their kind. He
was more comfortable in woods than on any street in any town" (40). Charlie Joe Ray symbolizes a deep and meaningful connection to the landscape
that Ray desires, identifies with, and values later in her life. She notes that
"he possessed a sort of magic when it came to nature" (41), a magic that she
covets and that guides the journey of restoration in the book. Her grandfather provides Ray a palpable awareness of what was possible in terms of
a lived connection, of an interdependence and reciprocity with the natural
world.

At one point during Ray's youth, Charlie Joe takes her and her siblings
to a special place hidden in the woods. They pick buckets full of berries that
"grew in deep blue profusion" (63). In reflecting on this incident, Ray acknowledges the lost opportunity for intimacy with the natural world that
marked her childhood: "Charlie could've tutored me, had he been able, in
the swamp's secrets—how to survive as an orphan there and how to survive in general. Even as a young girl I desired this unwrought knowledge
and knew it unreachable, fenced as it was by Grandpa's anguish, which had

driven him toward the solace of the wild in the first place and hindered as it was by Daddy's canon, which restricted daughters to the household and made them mistresses of domesticity and which prohibited an intemperate tramping about" (64). Significantly, from Ray's later adult point of view, she recognizes that incidents such as the gathering of berries in a hidden forest could have provided the foundation for a connection to the natural world. Yet she emphasizes that knowledge of such a relationship, even though desired as a young girl, was unwrought and unreachable at that time; that is, although Ray may have experienced a certain kind of fulfillment in these experiences, she was unable to translate this vague feeling into a conscious and deliberate way of being.

In concluding this important chapter on her paternal grandfather, Ray reveals the depth of this missed opportunity. She acknowledges her debt to her grandfather in a long passage: "Grandpa Charlie had a profound effect on me, and often I understand, when I'm in the woods, that I am looking for his secret copse of huckleberries. Something in me seeks the pure amazement I had that day as a girl: the sweet-faced wonder of enough berries to feed Appling County, a plenitude advertised by our purple-stained mouths, amid a beauty too reckless for return. What is left of this mythic terra incognita is a map I cannot follow. I have not stopped trying to go back" (64). In writing her autobiography, Ray returns to the hidden copse of berries and attaches meaning to this experience, a significance it may not have had in her childhood. Her life has become a journey to return to a mythic land, the mysterious plenitude of Earth, of Being, that failed to attain meaning in the original lived experience, in order to provide it with a significance that can ground her life as an adult and provide a value system for her relationship to the land.

Ray's relationship with her father, who also suffers from mental illness, is just as complex as that with her grandfather. She notes in her chapter "Native Genius" the distinct contrast between the two in their response to this shared illness: "Although my grandfather took to wilderness for solace to ease his wracked mind, my father turned to machines, and somewhere, between the two of them, the thread of nature was lost" (96). When Ray asks her father about his father taking him into the woods, he describes an incident when Grandpa Charlie intentionally frightened all his children, severely inhibiting their desire to enter the woods: "And that was that. So much for tradition. So much for a long line of outdoorspeople. So much for the woods. What my grandfather planted in my father was a crazy fear and mistrust of being lost in a wilderness alone" (97). She concludes with the image of a journey just as she did at the end of her chapter on Charlie Joe: "I search for vital knowledge of the land that my father could not teach me, as he was not taught, and guidance to know and honor it, as he was not guided" (97). The thread of living a life intimate with the land was broken with her father, and she recognizes that this thread cannot easily be mended.

While her father's mental instability is one primary reason for the lost connection to the natural world, his fundamentalist religion is another. In the chapter "Heaven on Earth," Ray describes the Apostolic Church that her family attended and the way in which religion functioned to isolate her from the world. She notes that even though she was provided all the necessities in life, "sometimes [she] felt discontent, not an overwhelming unhappiness, but an absence of lightness." She admits, "I was bewildered. I would feel as if something dreadful had happened, and I carried the burden and grief of it" (115). Her loss was the result of an ideology that promoted the afterlife over this life, heaven over Earth: "When I was growing up, the world about me was subverted by the world of the soul, the promise of a future after death" (120). She recounts her nightly prayer and her strong desire "to be better . . . to measure up, to keep my knees covered by my dress, to tell the truth" (120). She asks, "Did I want to burn for eternity, separated from my family who loved me?" (120–21). She concludes from these experiences that for her, "the chance to be simply a young mammal roaming the woods did not exist" (121). Ray's experience, focused as it is on some transcendent and spiritual afterlife, separates her not only from Earth but also from her own biology, from her bodily engagement with the physical world.[23] While the autobiographical chapters leading up to "How the Heart Opens" in the middle of *Ecology* largely demonstrate Ray's disconnection from the natural world, a separation that seems to originate from her male ancestors, they also provide glimpses of a different set of values than the ones that have constrained her and thus of the possibility for restoration of the self.

Just as the autobiographical chapters in the first half of *Ecology* describe the lost opportunity for an intimate relation with the landscape, the intercalated chapters in the first half of the book chart the destruction, the objectification and control, of that landscape. To provide a sense of both the

original landscape that has been erased and the landscape that Ray knew
as a child, which now dominates, she sets up a contrast very early in *Ecology*. In "Below the Fall Line," she observes: "My homeland is about as ugly
as a place gets. There's nothing in south Georgia, people will tell you, except straight, lonely roads, one-horse towns, sprawling farms, and tracts
of planted pines. It's flat, monotonous, used-up, hotter than hell in summer and cold enough in winter that orange trees won't grow" (13). The pine
plantations and one-horse towns that now cover south Georgia have created
a sense of ugliness that is readily apparent, dominating the perspectives of
those who live there. The land has been dissected and placed into neat grids,
the once-diverse ecosystem of south Georgia replaced with neat rows of
pine plantations, an objectification and commodification of the land, turning it into Heidegger's "standing-reserve." She adds, however, "Unless you
look close, there's little majesty" (13). Ray here suggests that, upon close in-
spection, a majestic beauty can be found hidden beneath the surface, that if
we can still for a moment our incessant need to control, if we can remember
the mysterious Earth that presides in the "here and now and little things," as
Heidegger reminds us, we can find our way back to sacred reason, to a wisdom that transcends our technological and commercial worldview.[24]

Indeed, Ray turns from describing the desecration of the landscape
to invoking the once-lost forests. She asserts, after describing the lack of
beauty in the current landscape: "It wasn't always this way. Even now in
places, in the Red Hills near Thomasville, for example, and on Fort Stewart
Military Reservation near Hinesville, you can see how south Georgia used
to be, before all the old longleaf pine forests that were our sublimity and
our majesty were cut. Nothing is more beautiful, nothing more mysterious,
nothing more breathtaking, nothing more surreal" (13–14). In this passage,
Ray recaptures the erased text of the once-dominant longleaf pine forests
through describing the remnants of that ecosystem. She continues, in a very
long passage:

> Longleaf pine is the tree that grows in the upland flatwoods of the
> coastal plains. Miles and miles of longleaf and wiregrass, the ground
> cover that coevolved with the pine, once covered the left hip of
> North America—from Virginia to the Florida peninsula, west past
> the Mississippi River: longleaf as far in any direction as you could
> see. In a longleaf forest, miles of trees forever fade into a brilliant

salmon sunset and reappear the next dawn as a battalion marching out of fog. The tip of each needle carries a single drop of silver. The trees are so well spaced that their limbs seldom touch and sunlight streams between and within them. Below their flattened branches, grasses arch their tall, richly dun heads of seeds, and orchids and lilies paint the ground orange and scarlet. Purple liatris gestures across the landscape. Our eyes seek the flowers like they seek the flashes of birds and the careful crossings of forest animals. (14)

Ray's use of verb tense in this passage, as it fades from present tense ("Longleaf pine *is* the tree") to past tense ("longleaf and wiregrass . . . *once covered*") and then back into present tense ("The trees *are* so well spaced"), reveals her project of ecological restoration as she chants the longleaf pine ecosystem into being, into the present, allowing it to presence. She concludes: "You can still see this in places" (14).

After these long lyrical passages, Ray steps back and provides a more objective and historical description of the loss of the original forests. Just as she does in the autobiographical chapters in the first half of *Ecology*, although she offers hints of a landscape and a self made whole, the reality of that landscape always dominates. She explains: "Forest historians estimate that longleaf covered 85 of the 156 million acres in its southeastern range. By 1930, virtually all of the virgin longleaf pine had been felled. Now, at the end of the twentieth century, about two million acres of longleaf remain. Most is first- and second-growth, hard-hit by logging, turpentining, grazing, and the suppression of fire" (14). She concludes: "Less than 10,000 acres are virgin—not even 0.001 percent of what was" (14). Although she has provided a hint of her restoration project in this early chapter, as noted, the first half of *Ecology* focuses on the degradation of the landscape. Here, she makes it clear that while remnants of the original forest still exist, the predominant text of the south Georgia landscape is not longleaf pine but rather the junkyards and pine plantations of her childhood. Indeed, Ray concludes this chapter by connecting her discussion of the lost forest to her discussion of her lost childhood. She notes, after detailing the historical loss of forest: "This was not a loss I knew as a child. *Longleaf* was a word I never heard. But it is a loss that as an adult shadows every step I take. I am daily aghast at how much we have taken, since it does not belong to us, and how much as a people we have suffered in consequence" (15). Ray explains, again, the lack of knowledge of and connection to the natural world that plagued her childhood, revealing that her understanding of this world only arrived in adulthood. The erased text of the longleaf pine forest, which can still be experienced if she looks closely, is connected to the text of a childhood that had a tenuous relation to the natural world. In the parallel projects of ecological restoration and reformation of the self—of restoring the land and her life—the lost forests must be reestablished before her life can be rewritten.

Significantly, the next two intercalated chapters, "Built by Fire" and "Forest Beloved," work to reestablish the erased text of the longleaf pine ecosystem. In the first of these two chapters, Ray tells a mythical story of the close relationship between longleaf and lightning, providing a kind of origin story for this ecosystem. "Forest Beloved" then gives voice to the longleaf pine forest:

> What thrills me most about longleaf forests is how the pine trees sing. The horizontal limbs of flattened crowns hold the wind as if they are vessels, singing bowls, and air stirs in them like a whistling kettle. I lie in thick grasses covered with sun and listen to the music made there. This music cannot be heard anywhere else on the earth.
>
> Rustle, whisper, shiver, whinny. Aria, chorus, ballad, chant. Lullaby. In the choirs of the original groves, the music must have resounded for hundreds of miles in a single note of rise and fall, lift and wane, and stirred the red-cockaded woodpeckers nesting in the hearts of these pines, where I also nest, child of soft heart. (67–68)

The forgotten language of the natural world—the silenced voice of the forests—finds expression in Ray's lyrical passage. Through the act of telling a story about the origins of the ecosystem, the natural world, even if only metaphorically in the text of *Ecology*, is restored to its once majestic and mysterious beauty. But only momentarily. Ray concludes this long passage: "Now we strain to hear the music; anachronous, it has an edge. It falters, a great tongue chopped in pieces" (68). The forest, which had recaptured its voice, has been silenced.

As an important chapter early in *Ecology*, "Forest Beloved" not only brings the lost forest back to life but also connects the reassertion of the forest's voice to the establishment of Ray's identity and voice. The chapter opens: "Maybe a vision of the original longleaf pine flatwoods has been endowed to me through genes, because I seem to remember their endlessness. I seem to recollect when these coastal plains were one big, brown-and-tan, daybreak-to-dark longleaf forest. It was a monotony one learned to love, for this is a place that, like a friend, offers multiplied loyalty with the passing years. A forest never tells its secrets but reveals them slowly over time, and a longleaf forest is full of secrets" (65). Ray's act of remembering displaces her lived experience, which did not include an encounter with the longleaf pine ecosystem until later in her adult life. She becomes placed in a landscape that engenders loyalty and is marked by mystery, an emplacement that occurs through the act of telling the story of her life and of the land. Indeed, she describes this emplacement in detail: "Something happens to you in an old-growth forest," she begins, before unfolding the way in which entering such a forest rearranges her bodily until she feels a "strange current of energy running skyward, like a thousand tiny bells tied to your capillaries, ringing with your heartbeat" (68). She continues: "You sit and lean against one trunk—it's like leaning against a house or a mountain. The trunk is your spine, the nerve centers reaching into other worlds, below ground and above. You stand and press your body into the ancestral and enduring, arms wide, and your fingers do not touch. You wonder how big the unseen gap" (68–69). Becoming placed in an old growth forest offers a deeper remembering, back to a time when humans and trees knew their common ancestry and experienced a common rootedness, one that connects us with Earth and sky.

The end of the chapter expands Ray's description of becoming placed, adding the divinities and the mortals to Earth and sky, uniting all four in the fourfold. She states:

> I drink old-growth forest in like water. This is the homeland that built us. Here I walk shoulder to shoulder with history—my history. I am in the presence of something ancient and venerable, perhaps of time itself, its unhurried passing marked by immensity and stolidity, each year purged by fire, cinched by a ring. Here mortality's roving hands grapple with air. I can see my place as human in a natural order more grand, whole, and functional than I've ever witnessed, and I am humbled, not frightened, by it. Comforted. It is as if a round table springs up in the cathedral of pines and God graciously pulls

out a chair for me, and I no longer have to worry about what happens to souls. (69)

Ray provides an interesting gloss on the concept of dwelling in this passage.
Rather than focusing on the homeland that humans have built, she emphasizes the way in which the homeland builds humans, that is, the way in
which humans access their essence through dwelling on the land in such a
way that Earth and sky, divinities and mortals become one. When we dwell
in this way, we become the space for beings to presence in their ownness
and we inhabit our rightful place. And in such an act of dwelling, the land
dwells inside us, replacing us and allowing us to speak the land. Significantly,
because passages such as this are inserted early in Ray's autobiography, readers have often misread the story of her life. The intercalated chapters, which
are told from a later, adult point of view, reveal a knowledge and a self that
come into existence only at the end of the journey. Here, her identity—and
as we will see later, her voice—is connected directly to the land. In this passage, the erased text of the lost forest is revealed, providing her with a place
in the world, human and nonhuman. By suggesting a connection to the natural world that was not fully experienced in her childhood, Ray begins the
project of rewriting her life.

The next three intercalated chapters, "Crackers," "Timber," and "Clearcut," which lead up to "How the Heart Opens" in the middle of *Ecology*,
most fully reveal the destruction of the south Georgia landscape. The first
of these three chapters focuses not only on natural history but also on the
history of her people and their encounter with the lost forests. In this way,
Ray revisits the originating site of destruction to reclaim what was once
there, entering the abyss and fully engaging the destitution of our time.
She explains that her lineage on her mother's side of the family goes all the
way back to the settling of Appling County, a fact that will become significant in the second half of the text, when she shifts from discussing her male
forebears to discussing her female ancestors. Between 1850, after the county
was first settled, and 1885, the longleaf pine forests were leveled. Ray observes: "Most important about the longleaf pine settlers was their attitude
toward nature, although this can only be inferred. They were great hunters
and fishers, great woodspeople. When they entered Appling County, it was
part of a rich wilderness stocked with fish and game, and it lay at their dis-
posal. They had no thoughts of a future—in America, as there had not been

in Britain, a great frontier lay beyond. They hunted; they fished; they slew natural predators. They shot passenger pigeons by the hundreds out of the skies" (85–86). The original settlers saw the land as a resource to be used without any awareness of the limits of that resource, for there was always a frontier beyond. She describes the destruction caused by the hogs brought over by the immigrants: "If they gave any thought to the environmental destruction wreaked by the introduction of armies of foreign beasts, it went unrecorded, dying as all conversations—over split-rail fences, on the drover's trail, at revival, at hoedown—died, forgotten or never said" (86). Ray recaptures the story of the original desecration of the land, giving it voice and thus providing a foundation for the restoration that will occur in the second half of the text. As William Jordan notes in *The Sunflower Forest*, owning the death and destruction is the first step in ecological restoration.

And the devastation—the erasure of the original landscape—is overwhelming. Ray reprints a letter from someone who had traveled through the area in 1858, when he first saw and described the intact forests, and then again in 1885. She notes: "By the time the traveler returned in 1885, the place was unrecognizable. Within a quarter of a century the grand woodlands were gone" (87). The letter exclaims: "Gone! . . . An invasion of a terrible army of axemen, like so many huge locusts, has swept over the whole face of the land, leaving nought of former grandeur but treeless stumps to mark the track of their tramp" (87). Within three decades, the once majestic and singing forests, the forests that had just been given a voice in earlier chapters, were leveled. Ray concludes this chapter: "More than anything else, what happened to the longleaf country speaks for us. These are my people; our legacy is ruination" (87). The language that Ray has inherited is one of commerce and trade, a language of neglect and abandonment, of beings presencing as resource-objects for our use. As a result, she finds herself disconnected from Earth, from the fullness and mystery of Being, in the midst of a ruination that she must embrace and fully engage if she is to offer an alternative voice and vision.

Significantly, the next two intercalated chapters, "Timber" and "Clearcut," do precisely that, bringing the devastation of the forests from the historic past into the lived present. Ray recounts the tale of her great-grandfather on her father's side, who came to the region during this time. According to Ray's father, Pun, as he was known, had no love for the woods; rather, he saw the forest as a place to be logged. Pun's ethics reveal a complete disconnection from the natural world: *"Don't take more on your heart than you can shake off on your heels"* (103), he is known to have said, reflecting his status as an exotic, in Neil Evernden's words, a being without a context or community that necessarily cannot care about the world around him.[25] Significantly, Ray responds to this way of being by asserting her own set of values, one not lived in her childhood but developed as an adult and enunciated through the act of writing her autobiography. She states:

> Of all lessons, that one I never learned and hope I never do. My heart daily grows new foliage, always adding people, picking up new heartaches like a wool coat collects cockleburs and beggar's-lice seeds. It gets fuller and fuller until I walk slow as a sloth, carrying all the pain Pun and Frank and so many others tried to walk from. Especially the pain of the lost forest. Sometimes there is no leaving, no looking westward for another promised land. We have to nail our shoes to the kitchen floor and unload the burden of our heart. We have to set to the task of repairing the damage done by and to us. (103)

In many respects, *Ecology* becomes an attempt to repair this damage, to seek and establish a new way of being in south Georgia. In order to engage such a project, Ray must reject the ethics and the way of being of her father and her father's ancestors and establish a new worldview, one founded on the alternative logic of the heart. Ray again asserts that the damage done to the land is also done to the individuals who inhabit the land, for the land dwells in us as much as we dwell on the land.

The first half of the book concludes with a poignant description of the loss of wild landscape. In "Clearcut," Ray returns to the lyrical mode, decrying the ethical view espoused by Pun. "If you clear a forest, you'd better pray continuously," she starts.

> While you're pushing a road through and rigging the cables and moving between trees on the dozer, you'd better be talking to God. While you're cruising timber and marking trees with a blue slash, be praying; and pray while you're peddling the chips and logs and writing Friday's checks and paying the diesel bill—even if it's under your breath, a rustling at the lips. If you're manning the saw head or the scissors, snipping the trees off at the ground, going from one

to another, approaching them brusquely and laying them down, I'd say, pray extra hard; and pray hard when you're hauling them away.

God doesn't like a clearcut. It makes his heart turn cold, makes him wince and wonder what went wrong with his creation, and sets him to thinking about what spoils the child.

You'd better be pretty sure that the cut is absolutely necessary and be at peace with it, so you can explain it to God, for it's fairly certain he's going to question your motives, want to know if your children are hungry and your oldest boy needs asthma medicine— whether you deserve forgiveness or if you're being greedy and heartless. You'd better pay good attention to the saw blade and the runners and the falling trees; when a forest is falling it's easy for God to determine to spank. Quid pro quo.

Don't ever look away or daydream and don't, no matter what, plan how you will spend your tree money while you are in among toppling trees. (123–24)

Having given voice to the singing forests of the past, Ray now gives voice to the act of eliminating those forests, thus engaging, even fully immersing herself in the destruction of the landscape, a destruction that ensues from a technological and capitalistic mind-set. The willingness to put greed over recognition of the sanctity and mystery of Earth necessitates praying, for we apparently do not have the ability to save ourselves from the destruction we wreak.

Ray concludes her critique of clear-cutting by explaining that the slow-growing longleaf pines were cleared and replaced with faster-growing slash and loblolly pines, all in neat rows. Because these trees are fire intolerant, the canopy closes overhead, darkness pervades, and the native vegetation and native species are lost. "Pine plantations dishearten God. In them he aches for blooming things, and he misses the sun trickling through the tree crowns, and he pines for the crawling, spotted, scale-backed, bushy-tailed, leaf-hopping, chattering creatures. Most of all he misses the bright-winged, singing beings he cast as angels. The wind knocking limbs together is a jeremiad" (125). She concludes: "God likes to prop himself against a tree in a forest and study the plants and animals. They all please him. He has to drag himself through a pine plantation, looking for light on the other side, half-crazy with darkness, half-sick with regret. He refuses to go into clearcuts at all. He thought he had given his children everything their hearts would desire; what he sees puts him in a quarrelsome mood, wondering where he went wrong" (125–26). The lack of light in the pine plantation that so disheartens God parallels Ray's own burden and grief and lack of "lightness" from her childhood. As an adult, Ray is able to understand and reflect on what has happened to the landscape and thus to her identity even though as a child she could not. Significantly, these final chapters in the first half of the book on the destruction of the forest are inserted between the final chapters that describe the loss of connection to the natural world that she experienced as a child because of her father's mental illness and fundamentalist religion.

Although remnants of the lost forest, the erased text of the landscape, exist for Ray to visit later as an adult and to use as a foundation for imaginatively restoring that landscape, the project of restoration in her life is more difficult. "How the Heart Opens," a significant chapter in the middle of the book, separates her lament for a lost childhood in the first half of *Ecology* from her recapturing—through rewriting—a life connected to the natural world in the second half of the book. She opens the chapter explaining that "one essential event or presence can save a child, can flower in her and claim her for its own. The French novelist and humanist Albert Camus said, 'A man's work is nothing but this slow trek to rediscover, through the detours of art, those two or three great and simple images in whose presence his heart first opened'" (127). By writing the story of her life, Ray discovers events that are given meaning, that flower in her now even though they may not have had the same significance in the lived experience. She continues: "For me, growing up among piles of scrap iron and glittering landmines of broken glass that scattered ivory scars across my body, among hordes of rubber tires that streaked my legs black, among pokeweed and locust, I attribute the opening of my heart to one clump of pitcher plants that still survives on the backside of my father's junkyard. I know it now to be the hooded species, *Sarracenia minor*, that sends the red bonnets of its traps knee-high out of soggy ground. In spring it blooms loose, yellow, exotic tongues" (127). The act of revisiting her relationship with the pitcher plant allows Ray to attribute meaning to this experience. Acknowledging later in the book that she left home knowing very little of the natural world, Ray makes clear here that the opening of her heart occurs as an adult who reflects back on events and invests them with meaning. Significantly, the central act providing the groundwork for the self created in this reflective process is the adoption of a worldview very different from that provided by a technological and calculating reason that can only see the forest as so many board feet to be used. Rather, the new worldview is based on the logic of the heart, a logic that will open the door to care and compassion, to sparing and preserving, to a reverence for the natural world and thus to a new set of values and beliefs.

In this central chapter, Ray describes a 4-H project on carnivorous plants that she completed in fifth grade, an experience that also begins the project of rewriting her life. At the judging, she shows the adults all the insects inside and explains how the plant gets nourishment from the insects, "but they weren't impressed" (128). She continues:

> The pitcher plant taught me to love rain, welcoming days of drizzle and sudden thundering downpours, drops trailing down its hoods and leaves, soaking the ground. In my fascination with pitcher plant, I learned to detest artificial bouquets of plastic and silk. Its carnivory taught me the sinlessness of predation and its columns of dead insects the glory of purpose no matter how small. In that plant I was looking for a *manera de ser*, a way of being—no, not for a way of being but of being able to be. I was looking for a patch of ground that supported the survival of rare, precious, and endangered biota within my own heart. (128)

As a child, she notes, the experience of the pitcher plant had not offered her "a way of being," that is, an understanding of how to dwell, of her reciprocity with the land. Rather, this experience creates in her a desire for a way "of being able to be," of being able to even consider the way in which she dwells on Earth and thus to begin to understand and fashion how she is placed. As a child, in her groundlessness she does not know enough about the natural world to search for a way of being connected to the landscape and the longleaf pine forests. Her connection is so tenuous that she desires something more fundamental, a ground or foundation for being. Significantly, Ray insinuates that her grounding, her emplacement, or, more poignantly, her re/placement, will come from paying close attention in the here and now to the little things, "no matter how small," all of which have a purpose. And the logic that will lead her to this place will not be the calculating reason of Pun but rather the alternate logic of the heart, a way of being founded on connection to community, which in turn will provide her with a context for being and thus for a sense of reciprocity and interdependence.

"How the Heart Opens," then, begins to offer a vision of self re/placed on the land, grounded and contextualized and in relation. Yet as in all the other chapters in the first half of *Ecology*, Ray very quickly reminds the reader that this revelation occurs later in life as she attributes meaning to her experiences that they may not have fully had in the lived childhood. After detailing all the work that she and her siblings were responsible for around the house and in the junkyard, she explains that there was no time for "hiking or camping or fishing." She concludes: "Nature wasn't ill regarded, it was superfluous. Nature got in the way" (128). Although her father deeply cared for animals, as she shows in the remainder of this chapter by describing how he tries to heal a squished toad or a heron's broken wing, his concern is for keeping systems—mechanical or natural—functioning smoothly. The first half of *Ecology*, then, depicts the destitution of our lives in the twentieth and twenty-first centuries, the way in which we are replacing once diverse and vibrant ecosystems with pine plantations and surrounding ourselves with discarded and used-up things. Although Ray offers glimpses of a different world—of Earth, in Heidegger's terms—early in her text, the first half of her autobiography, dominated as it is by the men in her family, demonstrates how we have come to regard the world as a resource object to be used and, worse yet, how we have forgotten that there are other ways that things can presence to us. As a result, we have lost our grounding, and we no longer know how to be. Significantly, in this central chapter, Ray indicates that any act of reconnecting with the natural world and thus re/placing herself on the land, providing a grounding and thus a connection to Being, will not come through her relation with her father.

In the second half of *Ecology*, Ray turns from her father's side of the family and her male ancestors to her mother's side and her female ancestors, thus providing a foundation for rewriting her life and revealing an intimate connection to the natural world. The first autobiographical chapter after "How the Heart Opens" describes the life—and death—of her father's parents, as if in recognition that this side of her family would not allow her the connection to the natural world that she desires. The next autobiographical chapter, "Poverty," first returns to a description of her father before providing one final glimpse of the socioeconomic conditions of Ray's lived experience. Ray explains that her father was a deeply caring man who took on the suffering of the world. In one example, her father invites a hobo into the house for a meal, a wayfarer with only one leg. She concludes: "Daddy had a kindness that belied his brusqueness. His heart was big enough for all of us and a world besides, and he put innocent children and very old people at the center of it" (159). Yet, she continues, his heart "was so big that most of the time he had to seal it off and pretend it wasn't there" (159). Ray again provides a glimpse into the possibility that her life might have been framed within a different worldview, one based on caring and compassion rather than the cold logic of reason. Yet just as she offers hints of a potential other life through the descriptions of her grandfather, who could have tutored her in the ways of the forest, here she makes it clear that the logic of the heart was closed off to her.

More importantly, "Poverty" depicts the deep poverty of the South in the 1950s, 1960s, and 1970s, one final time reminding the reader of Ray's lived childhood experience. She states, "In the rural South, the land of longleaf pine, these were the pictures travelers remembered: tarpaper tobacco shanties; bent-over women in the cotton fields; shoeless schoolchildren; chain gangs; bathrooms for whites only; Saturday afternoon towns spangled with mule farmers in faded and patched overalls and not a dime in their pockets" (164). She continues:

> Passing through my homeland it was easy to see that Crackers, although fiercely rooted in the land and willing to defend it to death, hadn't had the means, the education, or the ease to care particularly about its natural communities. Our relationship with the land wasn't one of give and return. The land itself has been the victim of social dilemmas—racial injustice, lack of education, and dire poverty. It was overtilled; eroded; cut; littered; polluted; treated as a commodity, sometimes the only one, and not as a living thing. Most people worried about getting by, and when getting by meant using the land, we used it. When getting by meant ignoring the land, we ignored it. (164–65)

Ray here explains the socioeconomic foundation for her own disassociation from the land. Although southerners have a deep rootedness in the land, they did not fully understand the biotic communities or the complex interrelationships within the ecosystems of that land. Without sufficient education or leisure time and burdened with a long history of racial injustice,

southerners did not have the opportunity to develop a more intimate connection to the land, which was either regarded as an object for commodification or not regarded at all.

After these two initial autobiographical chapters, however, Ray turns to
her mother's side of the family, which has its historical roots in the original
settlement of, and thus knowledge about, the ancient longleaf pine ecosystem. In "Beulahland," Ray describes visits to her maternal grandmother's
farm, where she experiences a freedom that does not exist in her daily life.
Grandmama Beulah, a lover of birds, is also a grand storyteller and thus
provides Ray with a model for a woman who has an established voice. At
her grandmother's farm, she plays outside under the water oaks: "The moss
was cool carpet, here a nook for the kitchen, a space between roots for a living room there. It was another world, one of the mind, and in that world
the trees were home" (179). The significance of these moments becomes
amplified when Ray contrasts her escape to the farm with her life at home:
"Although I was this junkyard daughter, it was easy for me to identify with
the country, its beauty, its normalcy. I loved the things a farm meant: shell-
ing peas, making plum jelly, cutting corn off the cob. In spring at Grandmama's the crabapples came into season; in summer the peaches and the
garden; and in fall the grapes, pecans, and pears. It was a shameless abundance. By Saturday morning, if Grandmama hadn't called us, we called
her" (184). At her grandmother's farm, Ray connects with the seasons and
the fertility of the land and its abundance as it revolves through those seasons. Although not the wildness of the longleaf pine ecosystem that she so
strongly aches for as an adult, the farm does provide a sense of normalcy in
her childhood and some connection to the natural world. Significantly, this
alternative worldview is offered to Ray not only through her connection to
the land but also through her grandmother's storytelling, which revolves
around the land and listening to it.

Ray then turns from her grandmother to her mother, Lee Ada, and sets
up a stark contrast between their characters. Ray's father and mother had
eloped in order to escape the disapproval of her mother's parents, thus de-
priving Ray of the possibility of a connection to the landscape that Beulahland offers. They marry under the eaves of a school: "Below their feet the
drip line etched a visible line of hollows, like those of ant lions, in the bare
sand. The line divided the world as surely as the desire to control our world
divides us from the wild, and Mama and Daddy stood on one side of the

line" (195). Lee Ada's decision to marry Franklin against her parent's wishes and without their knowledge is also a decision to leave the farm and all that it stands for, normalcy, the natural cycles of the seasons, and, significantly, a female voice. The traditional domestic relationship that Lee Ada enters, while filled with "virtue" and "wisdom" and "steadfastness," is also one without a clear and separate identity. Ray's mother, unlike her grandmother, who revels in storytelling, gives up her voice in her marriage. Ray states: "I was impatient with my mother's refusal to assert herself" (197), and exclaims that she "did not want to be like her. She had given up too much—her own opinions, even—to marry a strong man and be his helpmate. . . . The needs and desires of family eclipsed Mama's own" (203).

In the next autobiographical chapter, "Light," Ray offers the beginning of a new self, rewriting her life to include a lightness missing in the original, lived experience and re/placing herself on the land in order to develop an interconnectedness to the natural world. According to Ray, Lucia Godfrey, her fifth- and sixth-grade science teacher, "nurtured [her] interest in the living world" (211). On the playground one day, after Ray has been rebuffed by the boys who are playing football, she goes over to Mrs. Godfrey, whose first name, she explains, means "light." Her teacher points out the flowering pine trees, explaining that the flowers are the male part of the tree, while the cones are the female part. Ray discusses the significance of this event: "Out of all her science lessons, that one on the playground not only did I never forget but remember as vibrantly as if it happened last week. I learned that nature wouldn't ridicule you, would let you play. Oblivious, it went about its business without you, but it was there when you needed some gift, a bit of beauty: it would be waiting for you. All you had to do was notice" (214). The natural world, Ray suggests, even though ignored and pushed to the side, would be there waiting to be noticed, waiting to be understood and embraced. Ray brings the pitcher plant to school, and rather than describing how she was ignored as she did when she described her 4-H project, she recounts how her teacher is interested and explains the biological workings of the plant: "She said that because the plant needs more minerals than the soil provides, since they grow in infertile places, they found a way to utilize the nutrients of insect bodies. They adapted in order to survive" (215).

John Eakin in *Fictions in Autobiography* explains the way in which the act of writing the self becomes a reenactment of incidents that occurred in the lived experience such that the experience of writing the autobiography accrues meaning to these incidents. He conceives of "the autobiographical act as both a re-enactment and an extension of earlier phases of identity formation." He notes: "There is frequently a special order of experience in the life itself that for the autobiographer is inseparably linked to the discovery and invention of identity. Further, these self-defining acts may be re-enacted as the autobiographical narrative is being written." Thus the 4–H project described earlier in *Ecology* and the interaction with her teacher, both about the pitcher plant, become parallel incidents, but here, in the second half of the text, the incident is inscribed with a deeper significance, a true foundation for a connection to the natural world, with its exchange and flow of energy, its interdependence and reciprocity, its recognition and acceptance of death and mortality. Eakin observes that during the process of writing the self, "the qualities of these prototypical autobiographical acts may be re-expressed by the qualities of the act of *remembering* as distinguished from or in addition to the substantive content of the *remembered* experience."[26] As Ray notes at the beginning of this chapter, this episode is one that is remembered "vibrantly as if it happened last week," at once inscribing the event with deep significance and reinscribing it within the values of the adult autobiographer.[27]

However, Ray concludes this chapter true to form with a reflection on the lived experience of her childhood, reminding the reader that this experience included a tenuous association with the natural world. She states: "Perhaps something could have been different for me. Certainly not adulthood, for we become our heart's desires, but childhood—could the natural world I now revere have opened to me? Suppose someone had found my father the boy and said, *If you look closely, you will find palmetto bugs hardly bigger than apple seeds, and their iridescent black shells are walking onyx.* And, *A yellow-rumped warbler is in the wax myrtle. The eggs of fairy shrimp spread by wind.* Suppose. What then?" (215–16). Ray again explains that the landscape, the longleaf pine forest so dear to her as an adult, was not open to her as a child, that she did not have the opportunity to develop a close relationship with or knowledge of the ecosystems of her forebears. And significantly, she suggests that this lost opportunity is a result of her father's disinterest. Yet Ray's rewriting of the pitcher plant episode based on her interactions with Lucia allows her to recover a lost childhood that failed to open fully before her. In this way she relieves the burden, guilt, and darkness of her childhood, and by extension the darkness of the closed canopy of the pine plantation, and establishes a new way of being not only as an adult but also as a child, recovering a foundation of lightness that did not exist in her lived experience.

While the intercalated chapters on the landscape in the first half of *Ecology* conclude with a focus on the destruction of the longleaf pine forests, the intercalated chapters in the second half reassert those forests and their ecosystems, ultimately a necessary component to the reestablishment of Ray's identity and her voice. In "Longleaf Clan," the intercalated chapter immediately following "How the Heart Opens," Ray describes the fragile and intricate interrelationship between the longleaf pine forests and the animals that live there. She explains: "A clan of animals is bound to the community of longleaf pine. They have evolved there, filling niches in the trees, under the trees, in the grasses, in the bark, under ground. They have adapted to sand, fire, a lengthy growing season, and up to sixty inches of rain a year. Over the millennia, the lives of the animals wove together" (141). She then provides a long list of the names of animals, calling them into being and allowing them to presence in their ownness:

> *Yellow-breasted chat. Carolina and dusky gopher frog. Loggerhead shrike. Red-cockaded woodpecker. Brown-headed nuthatch. Blue-tailed mole skink. Striped newt. Prairie mole cricket. Pine barrens tree frog. Pine warbler. Pocket gopher. . . .*
>
> *Southern hognose snake. Arogos skipper. Carter's noctuid moth. Bachman's sparrow. Short-tailed snake. . . .*
>
> *Sandhills clubtail dragonfly. Pine snake. Tiger salamander. Florida mouse. Mitchell's satyr. Henslow's sparrow. Sand skink. Bobwhite quail. Buchholz's dart moth. Gopher tortoise. Ground dove. Indigo snake. Sandhill scarab beetle. Southeastern kestrel. Flatwoods salamander.* (141–142)

Naming the clan of animals becomes an important act as it works to reestablish the longleaf pine forest and thus provides the foundation for Ray's way of being, her identity. The exercise of naming is also evidence of having attained a voice, a necessary component to her identity. She concludes: "As Southern forests are logged, these species of flora and fauna, in ways as varied as their curious adaptations to life in the southeastern plains, suffer. All face loss of place" (142). Although she concludes on a negative note, these last two sentences do not proclaim that the end is here; rather they suggest that there is still time to save the forest ecosystem.

The next intercalated chapter in fact reasserts the lost forest, not merely

calling it into being but most fully describing its presence. In "Hallowed
Ground," Ray notes: "The first time I saw a red-cockaded woodpecker was
the first time I saw a real longleaf forest. I was grown. It was an April dawn
in the biggest tract of virgin longleaf left anywhere, a private quail-hunting
plantation embedded in the Red Hills of southwest Georgia" (151). She explains how forest fragmentation and the conversion to pine plantations will
lead to the extinction of the red-cockaded woodpecker. She concludes:
"Here was tree. Here was forest. Here was landscape. If left alone, it would
function like the children on the soccer field, spaces closing and opening
on a slow-ticking biological clock—a centuries-long game. A tree would fall
and in its vacancy in the puzzle of sky, a sapling would sprout" (156). Significantly, Ray's experience of an intact, old-growth longleaf pine forest comes
as an adult, but here she enfolds this description into the autobiography of
her childhood, thus symbolically allowing it to become part of her life, to
take root and grow there. This chapter thus plays a double role. First, it reasserts the lost forest over the dominant landscape of junkyards and pine
plantations, metaphorically completing the project of ecological restoration
of the land. Second, it provides the foundation for a new way of being, allowing Ray to rewrite her life both literally, since the insertion of this chapter into her autobiography disrupts the storyline of her disconnection from
nature, and metaphorically, since it offers a new vision, a new image and
perspective.

Significantly, the remaining intercalated chapters in the book focus on
the animals that can be found in the longleaf pine ecosystem, embodying
their presence and writing them into existence. In "The Keystone," Ray
describes the role of the gopher tortoise in providing habitat for other animals: "Of plants and animals native to the longleaf pine barren, the gopher tortoise may be most crucial, in the same way the keystone, or upper central stone in an arch, is thought to be most important in holding
the other stones in place. The tortoise is central in holding the ecosystem
together" (170). She recounts her first sighting of an indigo snake in the
wild in another chapter, and the plight of the Bachman's sparrow in yet
another: "Another bird distressed by the diminishment of longleaf pine
forests is Bachman's sparrow, small and nonmigratory, a bird so suited to
open pine savannas with little to no understory that it has been unable to
adapt to dense pine monoculture" (205). In "Flatwoods Salamander," she
explains that the decline in this species has occurred because of its need

to migrate for breeding and its inability to do so because of changes in the habitat: "Blindly the salamanders crawl, faithful to old processes lodged in their tiny skulls, faithful to the place of beginnings. A picture of that place is soldered into their brains, a map to it etched with the passing of millennia. Through time, this map does not weather but stays sharp and demanding inside them" (218). Unfortunately, with the control of fire in the forests, woody plants take over and fill the understory, and with the addition of roads and logging, "the map inside their heads no longer matches the terrain" (219). In "Pine Savanna," Ray describes a seepage bog, an area within the longleaf pine ecosystem that is "among the most botanically diverse on the planet. More than fifty species of flora have been counted in one square meter of savanna. Three of the world's four carnivorous plant families exist here. . . . Nowhere else on the continent can this diversity of carnivorous plants be found" (239–40).

In the penultimate intercalated chapter, "The Kindest Cut," she describes the work of Leon Neel, an "ecological forester" who logs in such a way that the forest ecosystem remains intact. Ray opens the chapter stating, "There is a way to have your cake and eat it too; a way to log yet preserve a forest" (251). According to Ray, "Leon applies ecology in such a way as to preserve a forest intact while extracting economic benefits. Known as single-tree selection or uneven-aged management, Leon's silviculture selects by hand individual trees to be harvested and leaves multigenerational or multispecies growth in a handsome, functioning grove" (251). She concludes: "It is an innovative alternative to clear-cutting, proving endangered species can exist in a working landscape" (251). Leon explains to Ray: "'You never terminate the forest; you terminate individual trees. . . . You never regenerate the forest; you regenerate individual trees'" (251). In many respects, then, Leon Neel's silviculture is an act of ecological restoration as William Jordan defines it, for it walks the middle ground between a *"colonial"* view of the land and a view of the land as a *"sacred place"*; instead, this view sees the relationship between humans and the natural world as "membership in a *community*."[28] Jordan suggests that ecological restoration is founded on a complex understanding of community, one that recognizes the emotional and cultural costs of interacting with an other in a nonegalitarian, hierarchical way and results in a state of *"relative* equality."[29] For Jordan, such an act leads to a sense of shame, for we recognize that we have taken more than we give back and we deal with this sense of shame through rituals and ceremonies. Ray notes that although most logging is dominated by "big industry, which is concerned only with making money," Leon Neel's silviculture is based on a "system that recognizes, in addition to timber production, the value of aesthetics, abundant wildlife, and a rich diversity of plants" (251–52). As a guide for a relationship with the land, such values indicate a balanced approach, one that implicates us in a community that has evolved over time and is maintained by the way we think and act.

Significantly, for Jordan, this is precisely the crux in ecological restoration, that a robust understanding of community must take into account the challenge of negotiating the relationship between the self and the other. He concludes that in making difficult decisions involving life and especially death, "we participate most fully in the monstrous and beautiful process of creation itself, and the inevitable foreclosing of possibilities it entails. This is naturally troubling and shameful. Yet it is a principle of creation and, properly handled, it too can be the source of beauty, community, and meaning."[30] Leon Neel provides exactly this type of understanding of his own relationship with the natural world, one that involves him in a community that is not about self-aggrandizement or self-perpetuation but rather that recognizes the necessary give-and-take between the self and the other. Neel explains: "You've got to think beyond your own life if you want to perpetuate the red-cockaded woodpecker" (253). Such an ethics is not only a direct rebuttal of Ray's great-grandfather Pun, whose ethical system allows him to take onto his heart no more than he can shake off his heels, but also a statement of the recognition that we must live beyond ourselves, both in terms of our own individual lives and the relationships we establish and in terms of our own time here on Earth and the way in which our actions affect generations yet to be born. We recognize, then, the way in which what we take from Earth is a gift and that, ultimately, our taking must come with some act of restoration.

The final autobiographical chapter of *Ecology*, "Leaving," describes Ray's time at North Georgia College and the way in which she first encountered and embraced the majesty of the natural world, thus creating the values that ultimately guide her existence and provide a foundation for rewriting her self. She recalls: "When I was eighteen and away from my town, I dived recklessly and surely into the world, not because it was a form of rebellion, as people might think, but as a form of healing and survival" (255).

Ray's endeavors at college allow her to escape from the narrow religious upbringing that she experienced as a child as well as from the confines of her father's and grandfather's mental illness. As a child, she yearned to leap from trees and soar through the air; she says, in an early chapter in *Ecology*: "I would sit in the [chinaberry] tree and wait, listening for something—a sound, a resonance—that came from far away, from the past and from the ground. When it came, the sun would hold its breath, the tree would shiver, and I would leap toward the sky, hoping finally for wings, for feathers to tear loose from my shoulders and catch against sweeps of air" (8–9). Desiring a lost knowledge from the past when longleaf pine forests abounded, Ray leaps into the air unsuccessfully: "The ground was hard, unyielding, but it wanted me, reaching out its hard, black arms and rising in welcome" (9). As an adult, however, she successfully soars through the air on a skydiving trip: "It was a magnificent journey back to earth, peaceful, floating above the hubbub of the world. I watched the fields and trees grow beneath me" (260). She lands far from the jump sight: "The closer I got to earth, the faster it rose, and I plummeted straight toward a pine. With some frantic tugging of the guides, I managed not to land in its crown. Nonetheless the tree reached out its arms and caught me: the parachute swept across its lower limbs and snagged enough to soften my fall, but still I landed hard against the ground—feet, knees, hips, shoulders" (260). Although this event clearly recalls the event described earlier in *Ecology*, here she concludes: "I was home" (260).

Ray calls her two years at North Georgia College studying literature "a stepping-stone into myself" (256), noting: "It was as if my spirit had suddenly been let free. Nature was the other world. It claimed me" (262). Ray's healing becomes a parallel act of restoration, one that occurs partly because of and through the ecological restoration of the land that she insinuates in the intercalated chapters in the second half of *Ecology*. Jordan notes that ecological restoration is "a way of communicating with other species and with the landscape, a mode of discovery and a means of self-transformation—a way of both discovering the natural landscape and discovering ourselves in that landscape. Any work, any kind of play, any experience naturally changes the participant."[31] The act of metaphorically or textually restoring the land in the autobiography becomes a means of re/placing the self on the land, of learning how to dwell differently, of providing a new way to think and to act. Through the act of writing the story of her life, Ray can attribute meaning to that life, investing it with significance and providing a foundation, a ground for her being.

The true turning point in her time at North Georgia College arrives when she encounters an episode of student activism—an attempt to save a tree from being cut down. She spots a sign on a maple in front of the Biology building: "'Woodman, spare that tree,' it read. 'For in my youth it shaded me. And I'll protect it now'" (263). Ray responds: "I knew George Pope Morris's poem, but in my history I'd not heard of a person who took it literally. The idea of caring for a tree for the tree's sake was so sentimental it was foreign, and the longer I thought about it, the more I admired whoever had lettered those words late at night in a biology lab and tied them furtively under cover of darkness to the threatened maple. One simple act turned my thinking, made me wish I knew myself better and wasn't gripped with fear when I spoke" (263). The episode recalls the newspaper account of the decimation of the longleaf pines in the 1860s described in the first half of *Ecology*. Here, however, the tree is spared from the ax men in a reversal of the earlier scene. Most significantly, the episode provides Ray with the foundation for a way of being—an identity and a voice based on care and compassion. She concludes: "What I learned at North Georgia was the direction my life would go. I also learned that I would never lose the tug of the past on my life" (263). She recognizes, finally, that her being, and the meaning of her being, would need to be drawn out of her past but that this past would not fully determine her pathway into the future. By returning to specific scenes in her lived childhood experience and investing those scenes with a meaning that they may not have originally had, Ray is able to rewrite her life and recover a lost connection to the landscape, much as she rewrites the longleaf pine ecosystem into existence in the second half of the book.

The final intercalated chapter before the afterword in *Ecology of a Cracker Childhood*, "Second Coming," most fully reveals the image of the palimpsest and the work of ecological restoration. After noting the lack of diversity of species in the junkyard where she grew up, Ray states: "Sometimes I dream of restoring the junkyard to the ecosystem it was when Hernando de Soto sauntered into Georgia, looking for wealth but unable to recognize it" (268). The cover of Ray's book materializes this dream, reasserting the lost text of the longleaf pine system over the junkyard of her childhood. The bottom half of the cover is a black and white photograph of Ray's childhood home, her mother standing in their yard next to their house holding one of Ray's younger brothers with Ray lying on a blanket. Surrounding the yard and fading off into the distance is the junkyard filled with abandoned cars, tires, and car parts. The top half of the book's cover is a drawing in color of longleaf pine trees soaring into a blue sky. Ray comments in "Second Coming": "It might take a lifetime [to restore the ecosystem], one spent undoing. It might require even my son's lifetime. And where would we find all the replacement parts for this piece of wasted earth? Yet, might they not come, slowly, very slowly?" (268). Ray's project in *Ecology* has been not only to reassert the lost text of the longleaf pine forest over the dominant text of junkyards and pine plantations but also to undo her own life and remake it by rewriting it.

Ray follows the chapter "Second Coming" with an afterword subtitled "Promised Land." She opens this chapter: "When we consider what is happening to our forests—and to the birds, reptiles, and insects that live there—we must think also of ourselves" (271). Ray asserts a close connection between the landscape and the people who inhabit it, broadening the scope of her restoration project beyond just herself and reminding us that how we dwell creates the people that we become. She continues: "Culture springs from the actions of people in a landscape, and what we, especially Southerners, are watching is a daily erosion of unique folkways as our native ecosystems and all their inhabitants disappear. Our culture is tied to the longleaf pine forest that produced us, that has sheltered us, that we occupy. The forest keeps disappearing, disappearing, sold off, stolen" (271). The loss of intimacy with the natural world that led to a loss of identity for Ray is extended to all southerners whose very culture and way of being is jeopardized by the disappearance of native ecosystems. She concludes her afterword by rewriting the South's history: "In a new rebellion we stand together, black and white, urbanite and farmer, workers all, in keeping Dixie. We are a patient people who for generations have not been ousted from this land, and we are willing to fight for the birthright of our children's children and their children's children, to be of a place, in all ways, for all time. What is left is not enough. When we say the South will rise again we can mean that we will allow the cutover forests to return to their former grandeur and pine plantations to grow wild" (272). Here Ray recasts the spirit of the South in terms that move beyond race and class and connects that spirit to the land from whence it originated. Rather than ignoring or glossing over issues of color

or economics, Ray reestablishes a common ground that unites all southerners, a foundation that existed before slavery or the separation between city
and country.

"Second Coming," the last intercalated chapter before the afterword,
concludes with a statement of Ray's dream of ecological restoration. She
says: "Pine lilies don't grow in the junkyard anymore, nor showy orchis, and
I've never seen a Bachman's sparrow flitting amid the junk. I'd like to. I have
a dream for my homeland. I dream we can bring back the longleaf pine forests, along with the sandhills and the savannas, starting now and that we can
bring back all the herbs and trees and wild animals, the ones not irretriev-
ably lost, which deserve an existence apart from slavery to our own" (270).
This passage recalls one early in *Ecology* where Ray reminds us that our
homeland builds us, for how we connect with the land determines the kind
of people we are. In this passage at the end of the book, Ray the restorationist stills the colonizing mind-set that she has inherited, the voice of calculating reason, and allows the land to presence on its own terms. Indeed,
Ray indicates that her desire to recover the lost text of the longleaf pine ecosystem and rewrite the historic landscape back into existence has become
intimately connected to her own identity and being. The act of ecological
restoration becomes a mutually appropriative act, for as we quiet the human will to dominate the land, allowing the land to unconceal itself, in Heidegger's terms, we open ourselves to the land's healing grace, which further
rearranges our values and beliefs. Ultimately, listening to the stillness of the
land and giving the land voice provides a foundation for our way of being in
the world, allowing humans to inhabit their essence as the ones who are the
clearing for things to presence.

Interestingly, Ray adds one final intercalated chapter after the afterword.
"There Is a Miracle for You If You Keep Holding On" fully envisions the
restored landscape: "I will rise from my grave with the hunger of wildcat,
wings of kestrel, and with possession of my granddaughter's granddaughter, to see what we have lost returned" (273). The long ancestral link running through her maternal grandmother—Grandmama Beulah—continues down four generations of women. Ray continues: "My heart will be
a cistern brimming with rainwater—drinkable rain. She will not know my
name, though she bears the new forest about her, the forest so grand. She
will have heard whooping cranes witnessing endless sky. While around her
the forest I longed all my short life to see winks and slips and shimmers

and thumps. Mutes and musks and lights. She will walk through it with the azure-bodied eagerness of damselfly" (273). Ray's female descendant, surrounded as she is by a forest that speaks its own language, manifests as a biological being, something Ray could never do as a child. Yet in the reestablishment of the forest—a project that initially allowed Ray to create an identity and a voice—her identity becomes hidden, invisible. She suggests that she may try to call out to her granddaughter's granddaughter but then concludes: "Perhaps I will not speak at all but follow her through a heraldry of longleaf, seeking for the course of a day the peace of pine warblers. And in the evening of that blessed day, I will lay to rest this implacable longing" (273). Not only has Ray's self become transparent but so, too, has her voice become silent—a voice not necessary in a reestablished and thriving ecosystem where the forests can sing for themselves. Because Ray has listened to the land and allowed the land and all the beings on it to presence, her language, her storytelling, gives voice to the land, becomes in fact landlanguage speaking. In this restorative act, Ray's voice and the voice of the land become one.

Ray's *Ecology of a Cracker Childhood*, as a dual act of restoration of the land and of the self, remembers the lost forests, metaphorically or textually reinscribing the longleaf pine ecosystem into existence. As an act of ecological restoration, telling the stories of the land—a performative and ritualistic act that honors the here and now and gives little things purpose and meaning—creates a new value system within the storyteller and, by extension, her community. In her review of Ray's work, Alison Hawthorne Deming notes that *Ecology* "paid its respects to Ray's family and the ecosystem of her nativity, suggesting through its structure that a life gains its meaning not only from familial history but also from the other-than-human creatures that surround it."[32] Significantly, the parallel journeys that arc through the book—that of the restoration of the landscape and that of the restoration of Ray's lost childhood—become intertwined, for the restoration of her self can only happen with the restoration of the lost longleaf pine forests. That is, through listening to the stillness of the land and allowing the land to speak, Ray offers glimpses of Earth in its fullest mystery and plenitude and thus offers an alternate worldview to the technological horizon of disclosure that we have all inherited. Jordan notes in *The Sunflower Forest* that "restoration forces us to become aware of aspects of our relationship with an ecosystem that we might otherwise have overlooked. In this way restoration amounts to the discovery and dramatization of the precise nature of our relationship with the ecosystems we attempt to restore."[33] In Heidegger's terms, the act of restoration allows us to consider, and more importantly to reconsider, how we dwell on Earth, how we think about the landscape in which we are embedded, and how we act toward that landscape.

As noted, such a reconsideration of how we dwell creates a new value system that embraces Earth in its plenitude and in turn provides Ray the foundation for rewriting her life. Jordan continues: "Properly and reflexively carried out, it [restoration] generates nothing less than an ecological definition of who we are—that is, a definition of our species, or of a particular human community, expressed in terms of how it has influenced and interacted with other organisms and with whole ecological systems over a particular period of time."[34] *Ecology of a Cracker Childhood* becomes exactly this—through the act of ecological restoration, Ray offers an understanding of who we are in ecological terms and of who we might become. Thus the values created in the autobiographical and restorative act allow Ray to remember a life connected to the land, a life she depicts through the narrative strategy of disrupting her autobiography with chapters on the natural history of south Georgia that insinuate a close intimacy to the historic longleaf pine ecosystem. In *Autobiography* Janet Gunn notes that the autobiographical act "involves a certain mode of self-placing in relation to the autobiographer's past and from a particular standpoint in his or her present," an act that occurs through language.[35] She concludes that such an act of placement also necessarily includes replacement: "Just as placement must be understood as *placing*, an ongoing rather than a settled process, the autobiographical effort at possessing one's life must be understood as a movement toward possibility as much as a turning around to the already achieved."[36] In this way, Ray's autobiography not only explores how we dwell in the world through our technological horizon of disclosure, Enframing, but also offers a new vision of dwelling, one that embraces the flow and exchange of energy through life and death and the necessity of our interdependence and reciprocity with the landscape, the melding of our interior and exterior worlds. Remembering the lost forests and restoring the land become, then, a way of projecting a possible identity, of remembering a lost self and restoring her childhood.

Which brings us back to the art of storytelling and the role of language in the restoration of the self and the land. Jordan notes that rituals, and I would suggest by extension performative acts such as the autobiographical act, "reflect an awareness that the conceptual and psychological ordering of the world achieved by culture is always running down and requires periodic renewal by a deliberate human effort. Being directed at the soul, this effort is not literal but figurative, involving rituals that do not affect the landscape directly, but do renew the conceptual, psychological, and spiritual structures on which the health of the landscape quite literally depends."[37] But if, as I have suggested, words have deep power, if language can (re)shape reality, then something more than a metaphorical restoration must be the end result of *Ecology*. This is indeed the crux. If ecological restoration, even if only metaphorical, creates new values, allowing us to be placed differently on the land, then such an emplacement must in turn replace us, creating a new sense of self. I have suggested that in a similar way the autobiographical act also creates a new person, replacing the individual through the act of telling the story of that individual's life. Gunn notes that it is "toward the future that the act of autobiography heuristically points. It is in the future that reality stands waiting to be *realized*; it is from the future that time comes"; she concludes: "Autobiography's arc of meaning projects forward where that meaning can be realized."[38]

This is precisely what occurs in the writing of *Ecology of a Cracker Childhood*. As Ray rewrites the longleaf pine ecosystem into (textual) existence, she rewrites her self. And the end result is a new self with new values and an adult autobiographer who then can act on these new values. Significantly, seventeen years after Ray left Baxley, Georgia, to begin the process of stepping into herself at North Georgia College, she returns to her homeland and takes up residence in her grandmother Beulah's home, the very place that allowed her some sense of normalcy, some connection to the natural world in her childhood, and that offered a space within which a female voice was paramount. She describes the process of moving into her Grandmama's home in a chapter titled "Restoration" in *Wild Card Quilt*, the sequel to *Ecology*. Her goal, she tells us, is to make "a life in a place that held [her] past, a place that as a young woman [she] had gladly left behind." The purpose of her return, and of writing *Wild Card Quilt*, is to "rejoin with place, land, kin, history, and neighbors in an attempt to gather the pieces of [her] life." She explains: "I wanted to live in a less fragmented, less broken, more meaningful way, to have more of what I loved around me, to say with my body, 'This is what matters.' I was looking for wholeness."[39] In returning to

Baxley and remembering her past, she seeks to dwell in a more authentic and meaningful way, in a way that allows her to re/place herself on the land and thus to achieve wholeness.

More importantly, *Wild Card Quilt*, unlike *Ecology*, describes Ray's participation in the physical preservation and restoration of longleaf pine forests. Although *Wild Card Quilt* has its share of lament for the decimated forest, it also describes a concerted effort to save Moody Swamp, a 3,500-acre piece of land along the Altamaha River that includes "one of the last pieces of virgin longleaf pine forest left anywhere, replete with fox squirrels and gopher tortoises."[40] Ray notes that in Moody Swamp, "all of the elements [of a fully functioning longleaf pine ecosystem], except fire, were present." She continues: "In that moment, I saw how I belonged. Across our Cracker history flows the signature of longleaf pine, the endless forests that greeted the first inhabitants. If a landscape could be returned to function, so could a family, and a community. I could be returned to a life rooted in the fullness of place."[41] When the owner of Moody Swamp passes away, the land descends to her nieces and nephews. Ray works with the Nature Conservancy and others to convince the new owners to sell the land, and ultimately they agree to place it in a silent bidding process. When all the bids are opened, the Nature Conservancy's is the largest, and the land is saved.[42] In this act of preservation, Ray not only connects with a community of activists who help her to understand her role, her place, in south Georgia, but she also becomes firmly placed on the land where she can take root and live a life of wholeness, thus counteracting the fragmentation surrounding her.

In addition to the preservation of Moody Swamp, Ray, with her parents' assistance, buys up three or four parcels of land that comprise her Grandmama Beulah's original homesite. She notes that some of the land "we decided to keep for food production. Some we would plant in cover crops. Some we would turn back to longleaf pine. We knew that we would never in our lifetimes see on the farm the kind of forest that survives on the Moody land, but maybe our offspring will."[43] This passage recalls the conclusion of *Ecology*, where Ray dreams of her granddaughter's granddaughter walking through a fully functioning longleaf pine ecosystem, but here the passage is no longer a dream, a hope inscribed in a story; rather, here the dream comes to life and the story becomes reality. Indeed, Ray goes on to describe the planting of thousands of longleaf pine seedlings and concludes:

It is our dream to rebuild community, human and wild, and it is earth's dream to have its forests back. We are making the dream of the earth come true, creating the possibility of wholeness around us, so that our lives can be of a piece. We are living the stories that for years we will tell, how the root of one of the saplings was split but my father planted it anyway, and it grew as well as the rest. How the trees began to take root and exhibit new growth and turn a bright, flourishing green. How over 90 percent of them lived.[44]

The story of the lost forest is replaced with an act of ecological restoration, and in the new story created in this act, the story of a lost childhood is replaced with a self and a community made whole.

# CHAPTER FOUR

# The Long Migration Home

## Listening to Birds in Terry Tempest Williams's
## Refuge: An Unnatural History of Family and Place

As a work of ecological restoration and the reformation of self, Janisse Ray's *Ecology of a Cracker Childhood* reinscribes the longleaf pine ecosystem into existence on a metaphorical or textual level. The restoration of the lost forest in turn creates a value system in the autobiographer such that she is able to rewrite her own childhood, insinuating a close intimacy with the natural world around her, including the vanishing longleaf pine forests. Telling the story of the forests and of the self provides a foundation for Ray's identity, a way of being that allows the landscape to presence in its ownness and that reconnects her with the mysterious plenitude, the sacredness of Earth. In *The Sunflower Forest*, William Jordan explains that sacredness derives from two sources, from an "apprehension of the unity underlying the manifest diversity of creation" and from acts that violate this unity, acts such as hunting or the felling of forests. He suggests that the second type of access to the sacred is the basis for our "*ecological* engagement with the world," for it recognizes a broader and more complex understanding of community, one that depends on an awareness of the necessary complications of engaging the other and the psychological difficulties that come with this transaction.[1] Ray's work moves through these complexities in order to develop a diverse and resilient community around her, one that can, in turn, move beyond metaphorical restoration and physically restore the lost forests. Jordan concludes: "If environmentalism is to succeed at its central task of providing the basis for a healthy relationship between ourselves and the rest of nature, it must . . . confront the difficult, emotionally challenging aspects of such relationships."[2]

Through the two intertwined narratives that comprise the work, *Refuge: An Unnatural History of Family and Place* also strives to broaden our understanding of community through developing an awareness of our mortality and the otherness that exists between ourselves and the rest of the world, including both humans and the land. According to Charles Mitchell, the stories of Williams's mother's cancer and of the rise of Great Salt Lake are "driven by a need to learn how to live with, and within, change: each searches for a metaphor that will allow one to remain rooted without being buried, broken, or swept away: How can we feel at home on a landscape that is always in flux? How do we belong to something—a family, a place— that refuses to stay put?"[3] Specifically, in *Refuge* Williams must learn to evaluate the nature of the changes that confront her—the loss of her mother from cancer and the loss of the Bear River Migratory Bird Refuge from the rise of Great Salt Lake—and to reconfigure these changes within her understanding of the self and the sacred. In the process of unfolding the stories of her mother and the lake, the two narratives of the memoir become parallel constructions in a search for acceptance of change and loss. Cheryll Glotfelty charts the correspondence between the rise of the lake and the climaxes of the story's plot; she notes that "with the skill of a fiction writer, Williams has arranged her factual material so that the highest lake levels correspond to turning points and personal transformations in the family narrative."[4] The connection between these narratives, the confluence between the rise of her mother's cancer and the rise of Great Salt Lake, allows Williams to explore the histories of two simultaneous and seemingly unnatural events that reveal an interconnectedness of family and place and complicate her understanding of self and community.

Although these two external events dominate the narrative, another narrative layer exists that provides a unifying thread in the stories of her mother's cancer and the rise of the lake. At the conclusion of her prologue, Williams suggests what her book is about: "Perhaps, I am telling this story in an attempt to heal myself, to confront what I do not know, to create a path for myself with the idea that 'memory is the only way home.' . . . I have been in retreat. This story is my return" (4). As I have explored in chapter 3, the autobiographical act—the remembering of a life and the capturing of that life in the act of storytelling—creates a sense of identity or self through the clarification of the values of the autobiographer, values that then become the basis for activism. Here the creation of identity is described as way of healing and returning home to one's essence. Williams notes: "Volunteers are beginning to reconstruct the marshes just as I am trying to reconstruct my life. I sit on the floor of my study with journals all around me. I open them and feathers fall from their pages, sand cracks their spines, and sprigs of sage pressed between passages of pain heighten my sense of smell—and I remember the country I come from and how it informs my life" (3). Williams here asserts not only that a close connection exists between the two narratives of life and land but, more importantly, that her narrative is one with the sand and feathers and sprigs of sage, that is, that the telling of her story gives voice to the land. Yet her narrative is not one of sentimental harmony, for it engages the limitations of human beings through her encounter with mortality and the pain and loss that come with death and the desecration of the land.

Interestingly, one of the more contested aspects of *Refuge* is the way in which the book is an ecobiography, defined by Cecilia Farr as a text in which "nature becomes an identifying canvas on which to write a self," and indeed the way in which it is a feminist ecobiography.[5] For instance, Glotfelty nicely describes the ecocritical nature of *Refuge*, which, she notes, "expands the boundaries of the nature-writing genre to encompass matters of gender, breaking the ground for natural-history writing to open itself to new methods and concerns." Yet, according to Glotfelty, "there is one boundary that not only remains intact but is actually reinforced: that is the division between the sexes."[6] Glotfelty notes that "throughout *Refuge* Williams highlights, not the similarities, but the differences between men and women, privileging the special bonds that exist among women."[7] Focusing especially on the concluding chapter of *Refuge*, Glotfelty asserts that Williams might have invoked gender in order to bridge differences rather than exaggerate them and thus advance rather than undermine an ecofeminist agenda. Other ecofeminist readings of *Refuge* have complicated this reading. For instance, Karl Zuelke suggests that "because male-dominated systems are responsible for painful environmental depredations that the author feels intensely, the linking of a female-nature linkage against a male-culture linkage arises as a dominant motif, with women and nature linked in ways that sometimes seem essentialist." Yet, he continues, Williams uses an essentialist strategy self-consciously "with the political objective of reimagining the categories of 'woman' and 'nature' in order to subvert the dominant patriarchal culture's demeaning notions of them." According to Zuelke, Williams's "constructed essentialism" allows her to create an identity based on telling stories that undermines the dominant political structures from within the establishment.[8]

Although Williams may use gendered and dualistic thinking only to undermine it in some rhetorical manner, critics generally agree that she reveals the dominant worldview that provides the foundation for the experiences captured in her memoir. One of the ways that she does this is by describing her religious upbringing, which locates all authority in men and relegates women to a subservient, even a silent role. Through expanding the Godhead to include the feminine, connected in the memoir to imagination, intuition, the land, and the female body, Williams seems at once to challenge and to reassert the engendered dualisms embedded in her time. Cassandra Kircher observes: "Throughout *Refuge* Williams moves randomly back and forth between . . . the confrontational, linear dichotomies (which she often problematizes [but which ultimately uphold a dualistic and gendered worldview]) and the circularity of the extended family [which undermines this worldview], not being quite able to let go of the former while she experiments with the latter." As a result, Kircher concludes, the memoir becomes so slippery that "ecofeminists committed to exposing the negative implication of linking women with nature . . . may be tempted to dismiss the book."[9] Yet I would suggest that one of the great strengths of Williams's *Refuge* is indeed the way in which it not only reveals the Western worldview—Enframing, our technological horizon of disclosure that relegates all beings, the land and women included, to resource objects for our use and sets up distinct binary oppositions between men and women, culture and nature—but also reveals Williams's own embeddedness, her emplacement within that worldview. Williams does not extract herself from the dualistic and gendered mindset that encompasses and indeed engulfs her during the unfolding of the intertwined narratives of the work; indeed, one of the points of the book is to demonstrate the way in which this worldview determines how we dwell on Earth, how we think and how we act, especially when we are confronted with otherness and mortality and with the desecration of the wild.

Yet, as I have suggested, the dual narratives of cancer and the rise of Great Salt Lake are not the only narratives in the text. Significantly, Williams offers both a prologue and an epigraph as a pathway into her work. The epigraph, Mary Oliver's poem "Wild Geese," reminds us that even in times of despair "the world goes on" and that while we are talking about our despair "the wild geese, high in the clean blue air / are heading home again" (ix). Oliver's poem reminds us that even in the midst of our own personal difficulties, which include pain and death, a grander order continues and everything returns to its place. To access or participate in that order would require a broadening of our relationships and our sense of community—here to include animals such as the geese, the sky and "the sun," "the landscapes," the "prairies and deep trees, / the mountains and the rivers." Moreover, to access the sacred requires not only an awareness of the unity underlying all life, as noted, but also acts that violate this unity. The poem concludes stating that the world is calling, "over and over announcing your place / in the family of things" (ix). The epigraph, then, like the prologue, suggests that beneath the two narratives of despair another journey is occurring, a migration home that returns the narrator to her rightful and forgotten place. This journey, Williams's journey, unfolds during the course of the writing and the reading of *Refuge*; that is, the story itself, and the telling of the story, is the journey—a telling and a journey that allow Williams to confront what she does not know or understand, including especially the relationship between life and death and the integral nature of mortality in our interaction with the world, creating a pathway through memory, a type of migration that returns her home to her family and her place.

On the one hand, the long migration home that unfolds in Williams's *Refuge* is about establishing an identity, a self, one that may be transitory and rooted in change. Significantly, this journey depends on revealing the technological horizon of disclosure of our culture, a worldview dependent on dualisms and binary oppositions that oppress and silence women and degrade the land. Williams poignantly reveals how all the beings around us, including the land and other human beings, presence for us in only one way, as resource objects to be used. The land is meant for development and the advancement of human society; as such, it should be mined, dammed, and controlled. Likewise, women are the helpmates of men and should be quiet, subservient, and domestic. Williams's journey toward self moves through this worldview, revealing the way in which we are all implicated in the double forgetting, the oblivion of Being, an oblivion that has cut us off from the sacred, the holy, from Earth in its mystery and plenitude. Yet *Refuge* does more than this. In addition to revealing our horizon of disclosure and the way in which we are all entranced by this worldview, a revealing that is then also implicitly a critique, Williams offers an alternative worldview that she learns through opening herself to the landscape and, specifically, to the voices of birds. Birds teach Williams about reciprocity and interdependence, the relation between life and death, and the circular nature of time and memory. Through this alternative worldview, Williams becomes re/placed, physically placed on the land in a new and different way that in turn leads to a new identity and way of being. She learns to dwell in a more authentic fashion that gives the land a voice, that allows land-language to speak.

Significantly, the journey toward self captured in *Refuge* climaxes with the establishment of a voice that ultimately gives birth to the final chapter of the book, a voice originating in Williams's homeland, embedded in her landscape, both physical and spiritual. Her identity and voice as revealed in the writing of *Refuge* demonstrate the way in which Williams can dwell in a more authentic way than we typically experience in our time, offering glimpses of the mystery and sacredness of Earth. Williams offers several important markers that reveal her progress in the long migration home that allows her to be re/placed so that she can listen to the stillness of the land and co-respond, to allow land-language to speak. She refers often to patterns and circles as providing a new way of thinking and being, one that challenges our Western linear consciousness, Enframing, our technological horizon of disclosure, one that is, ultimately, a remembered way of thinking and being. She also suggests in the first part of the book that the inner and the outer, the spiritual and the physical, are in opposition, again demonstrating her own embeddedness in a Western worldview; yet during the course of the journey and the establishing of a voice, the narrator works to transcend this dualism and unite the two. But most importantly, Williams describes her relationship with birds as the key to the unfolding of her journey, for it is the birds that teach her about the intimate and perhaps paradoxical relationship between the inner and the outer and provide her with a perception of the changes and patterns existing in the universe, patterns that take us home and provide us with meaning. Birds in *Refuge* become mentors on Williams's journey, teaching her to accept change, even certain kinds of abnormal and difficult change, as part of a greater pattern. They teach her to reconnect with Earth, with wildness, to remember a forgotten knowledge of intimacy, wholeness, and interrelationship, the sacred reason of Linda Hogan, which depends on and accepts such things as death and dying and ultimately erases the dichotomy between the inner and the outer and allows Williams to live in contradiction. Her journey, then, offers an alternate worldview to the dominant patriarchal—scientific and technological—horizon of disclosure, which constrains us and limits our relationship to the beings surrounding us.

"Burrowing Owls," the first chapter in *Refuge*, opens with a description of Great Salt Lake that introduces the motif of patterns. Williams explains that it is "a terminal lake with no outlet to the sea" (6). She observes that within the context of wide-ranging changes in the lake, there is some order, some pattern: "The water level of Great Salt Lake fluctuates wildly in response to climactic changes. . . . If rainfall exceeds the evaporation rate, Great Salt Lake rises. If rainfall drops below the evaporation rate, the lake recedes. Add the enormous volume of stream inflow from the high Wasatch and Uinta Mountains in the east, and one begins to see a portrait of change" (6). Many critics have suggested that adapting to change is a key theme in Williams's work. As already noted, Mitchell's analysis of the intertwined narratives focuses on Williams's "need to learn how to live with, and within, change."[10] Jeannette Riley argues that the changes confronting Williams threaten her identity: "In an effort to stabilize her self in the face of frightening changes, she turns to the land for inspiration, support, and solace."[11] Significantly, Williams delineates different kinds of change in *Refuge*—changes that are regular and cyclical, such as the annual rising and falling of Great Salt Lake or the migration of birds, and changes that are abnormal, such as cancer. Jordan asserts that ecological restoration, as an attempt to remember the past, leads to the development of wisdom about time and change. He notes that "by actually doing the work [of ecological restoration], confronting hard, present-day realities, the restorationist escapes sentimentality and nostalgia, and learns to discriminate between changes that are reversible and changes that are not."[12] This is precisely the dilemma facing Williams; in working to restore the foundation of her life through telling her story, she must learn to evaluate the different types of changes occurring around her. And through this discrimination, Williams learns about herself; Jordan comments that "since the changes a restorationist tries to reverse have usually been brought about by human beings, restoration is a powerful way to explore our own influence on the landscape, and in this way to gain a clearer idea of who, in ecological terms, we are."[13]

Generally, the changes that occur in the lake are seasonal, and thus they represent a sense of normalcy and provide the foundation for stability. Williams explains that "Great Salt Lake is cyclic. At winter's end, the lake level rises with mountain runoff. By late spring, it begins to decline when the weather becomes hot enough that loss of water by evaporation from the surface is greater than the combined inflow from streams, ground water, and precipitation" (6). What is described during the course of *Refuge*, however, is beyond the regular, cyclical patterns of the rising and falling of Great Salt Lake. After providing a naturalistic and scientific explanation for the abnormal rise in the lake, she explains that "the rise from September 18, 1982 to June 30, 1983, was 5.1', the greatest seasonal rise ever recorded" (8). She notes that her "interest lay at 4206', the level which, according to [her] topographical map, meant the flooding of the Bear River Migratory Bird Refuge" (8). The lake eventually peaks twice at 4,211.85 feet, well beyond the elevation of the refuge. In many respects, *Refuge* becomes Williams's attempt to navigate the physical and emotional effects that the flooding has on the bird refuge. While the memoir regularly reinforces a scientific horizon of disclosure through references to measurements of the lake level, Williams learns to engage this abnormal change just as she engages the abnormal change in her mother's body, through listening to and learning from birds, thus insinuating an alternative way of knowing. Immediately after her description of the abnormal rise of the lake, she turns to a description of burrowing owls. She says, "There are those birds you gauge your life by. The burrowing owls five miles from the entrance to the Bear River Migratory Bird Refuge are mine. Sentries. Each year, they alert me to the regularities of the land. In spring, I find them nesting, in summer they forage with their young, and by winter they abandon the Refuge for a place more comfortable" (8). For Williams, birds represent change, but change as part of a larger pattern. As *Refuge* progresses, Williams, by encountering, reflecting on, and accepting this type of change, learns to accept all change, even abnormal change. The goal, ultimately, is to learn to see even abnormal change as part of the overall system and to find meaning in it as well.

After describing the patterned regularity of the burrowing owls' seasonal movements, Williams introduces gender issues into her narrative. She
and a friend drive to the refuge to see whistling swans. On the way, they
discuss gender differences, the way in which men define intimacy through
their bodies and thus have developed a dominating attitude toward women
and the land. Williams's friend suggests that "many men have forgotten
what they are connected to. . . . Subjugation of women and nature may be
a loss of intimacy within themselves" (10). They arrive at the place where
the burrowing owls—those birds that Williams gauges her life by—usually
reside only to find the land razed and a new building, the Canadian Goose
Gun Club, in the place of the owls. She feels as if she is in "unfamiliar country" (11) and then comments, "I knew rage. It was fire in my stomach with
no place to go" (12). In *Refuge*, Williams makes a distinction not only between changes that are cyclical and those that are abnormal, but also between different types of abnormal change. While she learns about adapting to change from witnessing the patterns and cycles embodied in birds,
she also learns to differentiate what appears to be an abnormal change in
nature, such as the rise of Great Salt Lake, and abnormal changes wrought
by humans. Indeed, it is through the exploration of these various manifestations of change that she examines identity, engages issues of gender, and
encounters her mother's cancer and the rise of the lake, all of which ultimately leads to establishing a voice.

A significant part of Williams's journey with birds as her guide involves
reaching an understanding of the paradoxical interrelationship between the
inner and the outer, the spiritual and the physical. After describing the displacement of the burrowing owls, Williams provides a bit of her family
background, explaining that her family has "deep roots in the American
west" (13) and that she has known five of her great-grandparents well. She
concludes: "As a people and as a family, we have a sense of history. And our
history is tied to land" (14). She continues: "I was raised to believe in a spirit
world, that life exists before the earth and will continue to exist afterward,
that each human being, bird, and bulrush, along with all other life forms
had a spirit life before it came to dwell physically on the earth. Each occu-
pied an assigned sphere of influence, each has a place and a purpose" (14).
For Williams, as a result of her religious upbringing, the physical and the
spiritual become united in this life on Earth, though the spiritual takes pre-
cedence, for it exists before and after physical beings. She states: "It made

sense to a child. And if the natural world was assigned spiritual values, then those days spent in wildness were sacred. We learned at an early age that God can be found wherever you are, especially outside" (14). According to her Mormon upbringing, the physical world, the natural world, was also spiritual and thus sacred. Access to wildness, then, provides meaning above and beyond the mere physical encounter with the natural world, beyond perceiving the things that surround her as resource objects for her use.

The conclusion of "Burrowing Owls" returns to a discussion of birds and their role in her journey. She describes a childhood birding trip sponsored by the Audubon Society to the Bear River Migratory Bird Refuge with Mimi, her maternal grandmother. On the trip, they spot ibises, which are, according to Mimi, "companions of gods" (18). The ibis escorts Thoth, the "Egyptian god of wisdom and magic, who is the guardian of the Moon Gates in heaven" (18). The two colors of the ibis, white and black, are associated with birth and death. The length of their stride was used to determine dimensions by the builders of the Egyptian temples. In the middle of this childhood excursion, Williams reflects on her new knowledge: "I sat down by the rear wheels of the bus and pondered the relationship between an ibis at Bear River and an ibis foraging on the banks of the Nile. In my young mind, it had something to do with the magic of birds, how they bridge cultures and continents with their wings, how they mediate between heaven and earth" (18). The ibis, and birds in general, mediate between the physical and the spiritual, Earth and heaven, life and death, providing Williams access to wildness and the sacred, to a worldview other than the technological one dominating her culture and even her own sense of being in the world. As a child, these contradictory associations, the connection between the physical and the spiritual, life and death, were readily accepted and understood, yet as an adult such paradoxical relationships are more difficult to maintain. Because birds also represent regularity, order, and pattern, multiple layers of meaning accrue around birds as the narrative progresses and Williams's journey unfolds.

The next chapter, "Whimbrels," reinforces the connection between birds and patterns. She notes: "The Bird Refuge has remained a constant. It is a landscape so familiar to me, there have been times I have felt a species long before I saw it. The long-billed curlews that foraged the grasslands seven miles outside the Refuge were trustworthy. I can count on them year after year" (21). Significantly, the curlews represent constancy within change;

they provide a pattern that becomes familiar and trustworthy, grounding Williams and giving her meaning. Suddenly, six whimbrels join the curlews, something new in a familiar landscape: "Whimbrel entered my mind as an idea. Before I saw them mingling with curlews, I recognized them as a new thought in familiar country" (21). Birds thus represent both constancy and change, but not strangeness or unfamiliarity. She states: "The birds and I share a natural history. It is a matter of rootedness, of living inside a place for so long that the mind and imagination fuse" (21). By dwelling in a place, the mind (familiarity) and the imagination (newness) become one, just as being rooted in a landscape allows the inner (the spiritual) and the outer (the physical) to become one. Describing the many birds that migrate to the Bear River Migratory Bird Refuge, she concludes: "It is a fertile community where the hope of each day rides on the backs of migrating birds" (22). At this point, Williams explicitly introduces the idea of migration, the ultimate expression of a pattern within change. The birds that pass through the marshes of Great Salt Lake have allowed her to understand and accept newness and change because they were folded into familiarity and constancy. Most significantly, she then declares about the lake: "I could never have anticipated its rise" (22).

The next section of the chapter introduces Williams's mother's cancer, directly connecting the cancer to the rise of the lake. She says, "My mother was aware of a rise on the left side of her abdomen" (22). Connecting the cancer to the theme of change, she notes: "It's strange to feel change coming. It's easy to ignore. An underlying restlessness seems to accompany it like birds flocking before a storm. We go about our business with the usual alacrity, while in the pit of our stomach there is a sense of something tenuous" (24). Unlike the addition of whimbrels to the flock of curlews in the previous chapter, a change that was easily accommodated and even anticipated because it has occurred in a familiar landscape, her mother's cancer does not fit within her conception of her mother's body. Significantly, in order to attempt an understanding of the cancer, she makes a comparison between her unease and birds rising before a storm. Yet she has no place in either her mind or her imagination to put this abnormal change; like the rise of Great Salt Lake, her mother's cancer is an abnormal change that cannot be engaged in a comfortable manner; it cannot be folded into something familiar, a pattern, a rhythm, a migration.

After Williams's mother explains why she had waited a full month to tell her family about the cancer, a month that she spent in solitude floating down the Grand Canyon, Williams introduces a key concept in the book, the significance of listening to other voices as they provide her with guidance on her own journey. She says,

> I know the solitude my mother speaks of. It is what sustains me and protects me from my mind. It renders me fully present. I am desert. I am mountains. I am Great Salt Lake. There are other languages being spoken by wind, water, and wings. There are other lives to consider: avocets, stilts, and stones. Peace is the perspective found in patterns. When I see ring-billed gulls picking on the flesh of decaying carp, I am less afraid of death. We are no more and no less than the life that surrounds us. My fears surface in my isolation. My serenity surfaces in my solitude. (29)

Williams suggests most explicitly in this passage that her journey, her quest, is to learn to listen to a forgotten language, the language of "wind, water, and wings," of "avocets, stilts, and stones," and thus to open herself to a worldview other than the linear, scientific, and calculative one dominating our time. This language shows that the narrator perceives the patterns pervading the universe, the cycles of life and death that become one, the intricate and fragile interrelationship joining us all even when—maybe especially when—we enter our solitude and leave behind the noise and distractions of our culture. In the presence of this forgotten knowledge, the inner and the outer, the internal self and the life around us, become one, and we find ourselves at peace.

The reference to gulls in this key passage is picked up a few chapters later. In "California Gulls," Williams explores the way in which birds, which represent pattern and repetition, also represent resilience and adaptability. During a visit to the doctor, Williams's mother at first hears that her recovery looks promising. As a result, both Williams and her mother become optimistic, believing that the battle with cancer is over. Yet later in the afternoon, when the pathology report comes in, the doctor explains that she still shows evidence of cancerous cells. Williams then acknowledges: "I was heartsick. I had betrayed her. I felt as though I had killed her with my optimism and I was strapped with guilt. Why couldn't I have respected her belief that the outcome mattered less than the gift of each day. We had wanted everything back to its original shape. We had wanted a cure for Mother for ourselves, so we could get on with our lives. What we had forgotten was that she was living hers. I fled for Bear River, for the birds, wishing someone would rescue me" (68). Williams reveals in this passage her inability as an adult to accept—as she seemed to do so readily as a child, albeit in an abstract manner—the interconnectedness of life and death. Recognizing her inability to accept abnormal change, she flees to the refuge and watches the gulls. "While sitting on the edge of Great Salt Lake, I noticed the gulls flying in one direction. From four o'clock until dusk, with their slow, steady wing beats, they flew southwest. I pocketed this information like a small stone. The next day, I returned and witnessed the same pilgrimage. After all these years of cohabitation, the gulls had finally . . . seized my imagination. I had to follow" (70–71). Noticing a repetition in the gulls' movements from one day to the next, Williams decides she must track them and learn from them.

What Williams gleans from opening herself to the gulls allows her to begin to accept abnormal change such as the rise of Great Salt Lake. She sees that gulls embark on a daily pilgrimage from their nests on the islands in the lake to their feeding grounds. The gulls are joined by other colony nesters such as white pelicans, double-crested cormorants, and great blue herons (71). The populations of colony nesters fluctuate with lake levels and human disturbance. Some birds, such as great blue herons, are more sensitive than others and leave at the slightest disturbance. Others, such as gulls, stay and thrive: "The gulls never leave. They just fly around in circles screaming at the intruders" (71). As a result of the rising Great Salt Lake, "gull communities [are] on the rise. Gulls are more resilient to change and less vulnerable than other birds to environmental stresses" (71). In the midst of this abnormal rise of the lake, gulls are thriving and offer Williams the opportunity to learn how to accept this abnormal change.

In order to engage this new consciousness, Williams must first relinquish her cultural conditioning, her current way of thinking and being, the technological horizon of disclosure that relegates all beings to objects for our use. She walks into the midst of the gulls and observes: "To wander through a gull colony is disorienting. In the midst of shrieking gulls, you begin to speak, but your voice is silenced. They pull the clouds around you as you walk on eggshells. You quickly realize that you do not belong" (73). Williams's voice is silenced as an initial part of the process of opening herself to another language. She continues: "Hundreds of gulls hovered inches above my head, making their shrill repetitive cries, '*Halp! Halp! Halp!*' Several wing tips struck my forehead, a warning that I was too close to their nests. There were so many nests, I didn't know where to step, much less how to behave. Finally, I just stood in one place and watched" (73). Williams experiences a deep sense of disorientation, a loss not only of voice but of self. In response, she abandons her preconceptions, her culturally trained consciousness, and opens herself to a radically new experience. "I wondered in the midst of so many gulls and so many eggs, how the birds could differentiate between them. They do. Parental recognition. The subtle distinctions in patterning and coloration among individual egg clutches test my eye for discrimination. Each brood bears its own coat of arms" (74).

In the midst of this chaos, the rising lake's disruption of nesting sites, the cacophony and disorientation of the gulls, Williams encounters meaning in the most subtle of details, the intricate and distinct patterning of egg shells that allows the male and the female gulls to recognize their own eggs. Such a state parallels Heidegger's insistence that the saving grace lies in the "here and now and little things" and recalls Janisse Ray's assertion that meaning exists in every aspect, no matter how small, of the longleaf pine ecosystem. Williams directly connects this lesson to acceptance of her mother's condition: "I love to watch gulls soar over the Great Basin. It is another trick of the lake to lure gulls inland. On days such as this, when my soul has been wrenched, the simplicity of flight and form above the lake untangles my grief. '*Glide*' the gulls write in the sky—and, for a few brief moments, I do" (75). Her experience with the gulls in this chapter allows Williams to begin to accept change, even abnormal change. At this early stage in her journey, she has not yet begun to differentiate kinds of abnormal change, but her journey through the guidance of birds has been fully engaged.

She concludes the chapter "California Gulls" with a reflection on what she has learned and how this lesson will allow her to confront her mother's condition in a more accepting manner. She explains, "I go to the lake for a compass reading, to orient myself once again in the midst of change. Each trip is unique. The lake is different. I am different. But the gulls are always here, ordinary—black, white, and gray" (75). Significantly, her journey to the

refuge, even this journey, which involves an experience of dislocation, a loss
of self and voice, provides her with a reorientation, a new grounding and
foundation for the exploration of the significance of her experience. Only in
the loss of self, in the disruption of her current way of being and thinking,
can she find herself and be re/placed. She continues: "I have refused to believe that Mother will die. And by denying her cancer, even her death, I deny
her life. Denial stops us from listening. I cannot hear what Mother is say-
ing. I can only hear what I want" (75–76). Williams recognizes that she must
learn to accept change, even the change that comes with death and dying,
for these are important elements in a rich and complex community. Only
through such a willingness to accept can she open herself to another voice,
another language, one lost and forgotten as a result of her cultural train-
ing. She acknowledges that "denial lies. It protects us from the potency of a
truth we cannot yet bear to accept. It takes our hands and leads us to places
of comfort. Denial flourishes in the familiar. It seduces us with our own desires and cleverly constructs walls around us to keep us safe." She concedes:
"I want the walls down. Mother's rage over our inability to face her illness
has burned away my defenses. I am left with guilt, guilt I cannot tolerate because it has no courage. I hurt Mother through my own desire to be cured"
(76). Rather than engaging difference and change, Williams had remained
in sameness, in familiarity, in what is comfortable. In doing so, she had not
been open to the other—to her mother, to her mother's cancer, to the larger
order and pattern existing in the universe, which includes pain and loss. She
concludes this chapter reflecting on birds: "I continue to watch the gulls.
Their pilgrimage from salt water to fresh becomes my own" (76).

By engaging the changes that she witnesses around her, Williams begins to develop a new way of thinking and being, one less linear and scientific and practical. In the chapter "Pink Flamingos," she encounters what
she calls "accidentals," species "that have wandered far from their normal
range. They are flukes in a flock of predictable migrants. They are loners in
an unfamiliar territory" (88). Pink flamingos represent one such accidental,
as do roseate spoonbills and the European wigeon. Williams notes that the
manufacture of plastic flamingos, which grace our lawns, suggests that "we
have lost the imagination to place them in a dignified world. And when they
do grace the landscapes around us, they are considered 'accidental.' We no
longer believe in the possibility of such things" (89). Having focused on the
unnatural and made it familiar, we have lost touch with the grace and the

beauty of the natural, and even of the abnormal in the natural. She reflects at the conclusion of this chapter:

> How can hope be denied when there is always the possibility of an American flamingo or a roseate spoonbill floating down from the sky like pink rose petals?
>
> How can we rely solely on the statistical evidence and percentages that would shackle our lives when red-necked grebes, bar-tailed godwits, and wandering tattlers come into our country?
>
> When Emily Dickinson writes, "Hope is the thing with feathers that perches in the soul," she reminds us, as the birds do, of the liberation and pragmatism of belief. (90)

Up to this point in *Refuge*, Williams has demonstrated that birds, which represent regularity and pattern, can teach us to accept change. Here she makes it most clear that birds can also teach us to accept abnormal but natural changes. Significantly, she demonstrates that such a lesson depends on loosening ourselves from the shackles of our linear, scientific Western consciousness, that hope and belief arise from listening to different voices.

And because of her growing awareness of alternate ways of knowing, Williams begins to differentiate kinds of abnormal change, a key element in the final development of voice and the expression of an alternative worldview. She notes that the loss of wetlands is "one more paradox of Great Salt Lake. The marshes here are disappearing naturally. It's not the harsh winter or yearly spillover that threatens Utah's wetland birds and animals. It is lack of land" (112). Under normal circumstances, with the annual rising or falling of the lake—and even, as we find out later in the book, under abnormal circumstances such as the current rise—the birds adapt, relocate, survive: "In the normal cycle of a rising Great Salt Lake, the birds would simply move up. New habitat would be found. New habitat would be created" (112). The issue, according to Williams, is that this option is no longer available for the birds: "They don't have those options today, as they find themselves flush against freeways and a rapidly expanding airport. . . . Refugees" (112). While Williams has begun to work toward accepting abnormal changes, such as the sudden and accidental appearance of a pink flamingo or roseate spoonbill, she also has begun to differentiate abnormal changes that are natural and those that are inflicted by humans. By adopting a new consciousness, one of hope, intuition, and belief, she finds space in her imagination to accept pink rose petals floating down from the sky. But she also learns to look sideways at her culture, which insists on developing and controlling every last inch of land.

To further emphasize this point, Williams relates her discussion with her father regarding the West Desert Pumping Project, the approved plan to mitigate the rising lake. Originally, five plans were considered to make certain that Great Salt Lake would not rise above 4,202 feet, as required by Utah state law. The first option, to breach the causeway separating the two halves of the lake, has no real mitigating affect. The other options were deemed too costly or ineffective and so the legislature settled on the pumping project. This attitude most fully reveals a technological view of the world, where the world is to be monitored and controlled for the benefit of humans. Her father explains that the plan is ridiculous; when Terry asks what would happen if the governor did nothing, accepting the rise of the lake as a phenomenon to be adjusted to, her father says that the governor would be impeached (138–39). Yet Williams's family is implicated directly in this worldview, for they bid on and eventually participate in laying pipe for the project. Williams's own embeddedness in a calculative and scientific worldview is revealed here—and it disrupts her journey. She responds to the plan, acknowledging her inability to accept change: "I am not adjusting. I keep dreaming the Refuge back to what I have known: rich, green bulrushes that border the wetlands, herons hidden behind cattails, concentric circles of ducks on ponds. I blow on these images like the last burning embers on a winter's night" (140). Yet Williams's struggle, manifested in her desire to see the refuge whole, reflects more her inability to accept the human response to the rising lake than her ability to accept the abnormal change in the lake. She concludes the chapter, making this point: "There is no one to blame, nothing to fight. No developer with a dream of condominiums. No toxic waste dump that would threaten the birds. Not even a single dam on the Bear River to oppose. Only a simple natural phenomenon: the rise of Great Salt Lake" (140).

The next chapter, "Long-billed Curlews," which happens to be the middle of the book and recounts a turning point in Williams's journey toward self and voice, emphasizes the lessons she has learned from birds. She drives to Great Salt Lake, what used to be a fifteen-mile drive but which is now only three miles. It is May, yet it is snowing: "It is one of those curious days when time and season are out of focus, when what you know is hidden behind the weather" (141). The next day, when she returns, she describes the patterned mating dance of western grebes, the ordered process of cliff swallows' nest building, and notes: "The spinning of phalaropes. The court-ship of grebes. The growth of a swallow's nest. Each—a natural history un-folding" (144). She finds the breeding ground of the long-billed curlew and explains that the bill of this bird, shaped like a sliver of new moon, sym-bolically connects the bird to darkness and destructiveness, but also, para-doxically, to light and the new phase of a planting season. She comments: "Maybe it is not the darkness we fear most, but the silences contained within the darkness. Maybe it is not the absence of the moon that frightens us, but the absence of what we expect to be there. A wedge of long-billed curlews flying in the night punctuates the silences and their unexpected calls remind us the only thing we can expect is change" (146). The moon, which represents connection to cycles, offers a foundation for exploring a new way of being, just as the darkness offers the opportunity to explore the unfamil-iar. Like the addition of whimbrels to the flock of curlews early in *Refuge*, within this pattern of regular cycles something new is born. Williams sits on a boulder in the midst of the curlews, which are initially disturbed but slowly grow accustomed to her presence: "This too, I found encouraging— that in the face of stressful intrusions, we can eventually settle in" (147).

Williams then reflects on the desert and the meaning of this barren place, a lesson that she can engage because of her journey with birds. She observes that it is

> strange how deserts turn us into believers. I believe in walking in a landscape of mirages, because you learn humility. I believe in living in a land of little water because life is drawn together. And I believe in the gathering of bones as a testament to spirits that have moved on.
>
> If the desert is holy, it is because it is a forgotten place that allows us to remember the sacred. Perhaps that is why every pilgrimage to the desert is a pilgrimage to the self. There is no place to hide, and so we are found. (148)

In the middle of her journey, Williams reflects on key elements of what she has learned: that we should remain humble and open to alternative ways of knowing because our knowledge may not provide a complete or accurate picture of reality; that we should recognize the fragility and interconnected-ness of all life; and that life and death, the physical and the spiritual, Earth and heaven are one. This new way of thinking is actually a remembered knowledge that reattaches us to wildness and the sacred and, ultimately, to our self. She continues: "In the severity of a salt desert, I am brought down to my knees by its beauty. My imagination is fired. My heart opens and my skin burns in the passion of these moments. I will have no other gods before me" (148). Her imagination and her heart, allowing the exploration of a new way of thinking and being, explode, and her flesh burns. Returning to birds, she concludes this chapter: "I pray to the birds. I pray to the birds because I believe they will carry the messages of my heart upward. I pray to them because I believe in their existence, the way their songs begin and end each day—the invocations and benedictions of Earth. I pray to the birds because they remind me of what I love rather than what I fear. And at the end of my prayers, they teach me how to listen" (149). Williams here describes her relationship to birds as a kind of ceremony that honors Earth and the recurrent and interdependent elements of the natural world. She acknowledges that birds have taught her to listen to a forgotten language, to remember an ancient way of being, one dependent on the cycles of Earth and moon, that has provided a foundation for her identity and for a voice founded on listening, on a co-responding in Heidegger's terms.

Immediately following this chapter, the lake level, recorded at the beginning of each chapter, peaks at 4,211.85 feet for the first of two times. In this chapter, titled "Western Tanager," two important events occur that provide the groundwork for Williams's exploration of voice. The first is her mother's acceptance of cancer. When her doctor finds further evidence of cancerous cells and suggests a new round of chemotherapy, Williams's mother decides that she does not want the treatment, explaining: "It feels good to finally be able to embrace my cancer. It's almost like a friend. . . . For the first time, I feel like moving with it and not resisting what is ahead. Before, I always knew I had more time, that the disease was outside of myself. This time, I don't feel that way. The cancer is very much a part of me" (156). Accepting this intrusion into her body, she then tells her daughter: "I need you to help me through my death" (156). The second important and parallel event is the official closing of the Bear River Migratory Bird Refuge offices. The supervisor declares: "We have pretty well abandoned the sixty-five-thousand-acre refuge fourteen miles west of Brigham City, because it is impossible to second-guess the Great Salt Lake" (156). Significantly, after describing both of these occurrences, Williams reengages gender issues. She notes that her mother asks her for a blessing and explains: "In Mormon religion, formal blessings of healing are given by men through the Priesthood of God. Women have no outward authority. But within the secrecy of sisterhood we have always bestowed benisons upon our families" (158). She then lays her hands on her mother's head, "and in the privacy of women, [they] pray" (158). Ignoring cultural tradition and refusing to be relegated to the limited role ascribed by her religion, the two women rebel against a patriarchal system that has silenced their voices.

Yet Williams continues to struggle, even after her mother's request to let her go, to accept her impending death. Terry's mother says to her: "You still don't understand, do you? . . . It doesn't matter how much time I have left. All we have is now. I wish you all could accept that and let go of your projections. Just let me live so I can die" (161). As a child on the Audubon excursion with Mimi, Williams could imaginatively engage the interconnectedness of life and death, yet as an adult she is less able to do so. She wonders: "How can I advocate fighting for life when I am in the tutelage of a woman who is teaching me how to let go?" (165). She then leaves to join an archaeological dig, creating space between herself and her mother. She explains that while on the dig she feels "like a potter trying to shape [her] life with the materials at hand." She continues: "But my creation is internal. My vessel is my body, where I hold a space of healing for those I love. Each day becomes a firing, a further refinement of the potter's process" (168). She recognizes even in the midst of the despair surrounding her that the world goes on and that she is growing and learning. She reflects: "I must also learn to hold a space for myself, to not give everything away" (168). When her mother must suddenly be hospitalized for another operation to remove a blockage, Williams returns home. After a week in the hospital, her mother decides she is finished with the hospital and wants to go home to die.

Williams then describes a trip with her husband, Brooke, to Vancouver Island to watch whales in Telegraph Cove. She uses the telling of this story to engage the forgotten language of wildness that she had first encountered with the gulls and to recognize the power of the forgotten voice of women. She explains that whale communities have "a culture maintained by oral traditions. Stories. The experience of an individual whale is valuable to the survival of its community" (175). She then connects this forgotten language of interconnectedness and interrelationship with gender: "I think of my family stories—Mother's in particular—how much I need them now, how much I will need them later. It has been said when an individual dies, whole worlds die with them. The same could be said of each passing whale" (175). Williams asserts here the significance not only of the voice of wildness that reminds us of all our relations but also of the voice of women who hold families and communities together. She recounts a childhood memory with Mimi, who had shown her how to create a lens with her fingers through which she could view the world. She comments:

> My world was my own creation.
>> It still is.
>> Now if I take this lens and focus on Great Salt Lake, I see waves rolling in one after another: my mother, my grandmother, myself. I am adrift with no anchor to hold me in place.
>> A few months ago, this would have frightened me. Today, it does
> not. (177)

The oncoming repetitive waves represent the regular patterns that exist in the universe, which ground us and provide us with meaning. These waves become, significantly, the women of the family, who offer stability through their connection to the rhythmic patterns of the universe, such as the waxing and waning of the moon. Yet within this regularity, this pattern, Williams is adrift, an experience that she has come to accept, representing her newfound ability to live within the abnormal and the unfamiliar.

Williams then concludes the chapter with a passage that most fully and explicitly reveals the central nature of her own journey in this memoir. She comments, "I am slowly, painfully discovering that my refuge is not found in my mother, my grandmother, or even the birds of Bear River. My refuge exists in my capacity to love. If I can learn to love death then I can begin to find refuge in change" (178). While the despair of her mother's condition and the rise of the lake continues unabated, Williams recognizes that her own journey toward identity also continues and is shaped less by these outward occurrences and more by her own internal response to them. Because she had taken refuge, up to this point, in her mother, in her grandmother, in the birds, she was unable to locate or establish a sense of self. Taking refuge in love, and more specifically, in the capacity to accept the interconnectedness of life and death, Earth and heaven, the physical and the spiritual, allows Williams to accept change and opens her to an alternative worldview, not the logic of reason but the logic of the heart. What Williams learns is that her refuge cannot be an escape, a way of avoiding or ignoring reality with its lack of consistency. Rather, refuge becomes a way of being that fully engages the present in order to create memory—for memory is the only way home.

The next two chapters reinforce this lesson, connecting it to the motif of patterns. In "Greater Yellowlegs," she describes her exploration of an archaeological site with a friend. The Fremont people, who lived in the desert from 650 to 1250 AD, subsisted on irrigated crops and wild game. They lived in small bands, "closely tied to their immediate environment. They were flexible, adaptive, and diverse" (181). Most importantly, their lives flowed with the ever-changing landscape: "The Fremont oscillated with the lake levels. As Great Salt Lake rose, they retreated. As the lake retreated, they were drawn back. Theirs was not a fixed society like ours. They followed the expanding and receding shorelines. It was the ebb and flow of their lives" (183). Williams then contrasts these people, whose lives freely adapted to their changing environment, to her own culture: "They accommodated change where, so often, we are immobilized by it" (183). Williams's discussion of this ancient culture does several things. First, it demonstrates the way in which a human culture in the past was able to exist in ways that flowed with the changes and the patterns of the landscape, even, likely, unusual changes, very much unlike our own culture, which seeks to control these changes. Second, it shows her own incipient ability to comprehend an ancient way of being that contrasts thoroughly with the worldview in which she is embedded and which she moves through during the course of her journey. Last, it opens the door for imagining a connection between women of the present day with those of the past. She explains: "I wonder how, among the Fremont, mothers and daughters shared their world. Did they walk side by side along the lake edge? What stories did they tell while weaving strips of bulrush into baskets? How did daughters bury their mothers and exercise their grief? What were the secret rituals of women? I feel certain they must have been tied to birds" (184). Here Williams puts herself in the place of these ancient people in order to begin to piece together her own response to her current situation, a response driven by her relationship with birds.

Indeed, the next chapter returns directly to the role of birds in her journey and specifically to the image of migration. In the chapter "Canada Geese," Williams and her mother visit the Abbey of Our Lady of the

Holy Trinity, where the monks are singing the plea "Bring me back home." They go outside and witness autumn turning the cottonwoods golden. Williams notes: "[Mother] was quietly walking with the present. I knew she was tired. I also knew the power of this October afternoon. In another time, this moment would surface and carry me over rugged terrain. It would become one reservoir of strength" (191–92). At this point in her journey, Williams has learned that the pathway home, the pathway through despair and change, is through memory, and she works carefully to create moments that she can carry forward with her and return to. Previously, Williams had expressed an inability to accept change, to accept death as a part of life; now, she has come to a place of peace: "I saw in Mother's face the mature beauty that a woman in her fifties has earned. I also recognized her weight loss not so much as disease, but as a shedding of that which was no longer necessary. She was letting go. So was I" (192). Her mother then states, "Wild geese are my favorite birds. . . . They seem to know where they are from and where they are going" (192). Williams's telling of this moment at this point in her journey, with its explicit reverberations of Oliver's poem "Wild Geese" in the epigraph, connects it with the idea of finding her place in the universe, of learning to dwell in such a way that she can give voice to the land.

Indeed, at this point in the telling of her journey, a telling that creates self through returning her home, Williams reflects on the significance of migration and the way in which it offers an alternative way of knowing and being. She opens with a scientific explanation, one that fits within a technological horizon of disclosure: "One can think of migration as merely a mechanical movement from point A to point B, and back to point A, explain it in purely physiological terms: in the fall, the photoperiod is lessened, it correlates with a drop in temperature" (192). She then offers a less linear, less scientific description:

> Alongside the biological facts, could migration be an ancestral memory, an archetype that dreams birds thousands of miles to their homeland? A highly refined intelligence that emerges as intuition, the only true guide in life? Could it be that a family of Canada geese journey south not out of a genetic predisposition, but out of a desire for a shared vision of a species? They travel in flocks as they position themselves in an inverted V formation, the white feathers that separate their black rumps from their tails appear as a crescent moon,

reminding them once again that they are participating in another cycle. (192–93)

Migration, founded on an ancient knowing, connects birds and even people to the cycles of the universe that sustain us and offer the only true guide in life. Through intuition, not through analysis and scientific explanation, we reconnect to a broader, more primal way of knowing and being, to a sacred reason of Earth and elders. Through memory, an individual memory but more importantly a shared vision of a species, we return home. Williams's telling of her journey has allowed her to remember an ancient way of knowing of wholeness and interconnectedness that unifies life and death, the inner and the outer, Earth and heaven, the physical and the spiritual.

Interestingly, the next several chapters, although they mention birds, do not provide descriptions of the way in which birds are connected to patterns or cycles. Williams has learned to accept change and the interconnectedness of life and death; thus this part of her journey with birds as her mentor closes, and a new phase opens in which she helps her mother die. In the chapter "Sanderlings," Williams says, "Death is no longer what I imagined it to be. Death is earthy like birth, like sex, full of smells and sounds and bodily fluids. It is a confluence of evanescence and flesh" (219). Birth and death, the evanescent (the spirit) and the physical (the body) become united. As her mother's condition deteriorates and she becomes delirious, Williams kneels by her side, sobbing; "I tell her how much I love her and how desperately I will miss her, that she has not only given me a reverence for life, but a reverence for death" (226). Williams climbs into bed with her mother, breathing with her, telling her to let go. "There is a crescendo of movement, like walking up a pyramid of light. And it is sexual, the concentration of love, of being fully present. Pure feeling. Pure color. I can feel her spirit rising through the top of her head. Her eyes focus on mine with total joy—a fullness that transcends words" (231). Williams's father enters the room; his eyes meet the eyes of his wife, they smile, and she dies. Williams explains, "I felt as though I had been midwife to my mother's birth" (231). In this final passage, Williams most fully reveals the way in which she has learned that life and death are one, that the physical and the spiritual, Earth and heaven are not separate.

In being midwife to her mother's birth—not her death—Williams makes it clear how far along the journey to self she has come. Death becomes part of a larger process of ever-evolving cycles. She concludes the chapter "Sand-erlings" with a quote from Eric Fromm: "The whole life of the individual is nothing but the process of giving birth to himself; indeed, we should be fully born when we die" (232). At this point in her narrative, she returns to birds. In the next chapter, "Birds-of-Paradise," she finds herself pulling hairs out of her mother's brush, and she suddenly remembers the birds.

> I quietly open the glass doors, walk across the snow and spread the mesh of my mother's hair over the tips of young cottonwood trees—
>> For the birds—
>> For their nests—
>> In the spring. (233)

She has a flashback, a memory of a canoeing trip with her husband, Brooke, in Mexico, which she inserts into the telling of her journey. She remembers,

> Row upon row of flamingos are dancing with the current. It is a bal-let. The flamingos closest to shore step confidently, heads down as they filter small molluscs, crustaceans, and algae through their bills before the water is expelled through either side. These are not quiet birds.
>
> Behind the feeders, a corps de ballet tiptoes in line, flowing in the opposite direction like a feathered river. They too are nodding their heads, twittering, gliding with the black portion of their bills pointing upward. They move with remarkable syncopation. (236)

The dance that the birds enact before her eyes, in perfect rhythm, has cre-ated a memory that helps remind her of the patterns and rhythms that guide the universe. Earlier in *Refuge*, flamingos were "accidentals" associ-ated with abnormal change. Here Williams explains that their Latin name, *Phoenicopteridae*, derives "from the phoenix, which rose from its ashes to live again" (237). The flamingo, then, represents the unending cycle of life and death, and death giving birth to life.

Although gender issues have been a continuous aspect of Williams's journey to this point, they have been overshadowed by her involvement with her mother's cancer and the rise of the lake. Now, with a fully real-ized self, she most fully engages gender issues, ultimately seeking to provide more balance between men and women and to erase some of the gender inequalities that exist in her culture. In the chapter "Pintails, Mallards, and

Teals," with the lake level peaking at 4,211.85 feet for the second time, Williams rewrites Mormon theology to include the feminine. On the day of the General Conference when the Saints gather, she drives past "the cast-iron gates, heading west with the gulls" (240). Earlier in the text, the gulls offered Williams a strong sense of disorientation, allowing her to become dislocated from her cultural upbringing and listen to another voice, a forgotten language of interconnectedness. In the temple, they are singing "Abide with Me, 'Tis Eventide," and she reflects: "Abide: to wait for; to endure without yielding; to bear patiently; to accept without objection; to remain in a stable or fixed state; to continue in a place. 'Abide with me,' I have sung this song all my life" (240). Up until she embarked on this journey, Williams had remained fixed, abiding by the belief system of her culture. Having learned to accept change, she finds herself in a moment of transformation.

With the lake at its highest level, breaking the boundaries of human expectation, Williams leaves the place of her upbringing to encounter the primal wildness of Great Salt Lake. She explains, "Once out at the lake, I am free. Native. Wind and waves are like African drums driving the rhythm home. I am spun, supported, and possessed by the spirit who dwells here. Great Salt Lake is a spiritual magnet that will not let me go. Dogma doesn't hold me. Wildness does. A spiral of emotion" (240). The wind and the waves like African drums, symbolizing the origin, the home of humanity, beat their regular rhythms, freeing her of dogma, engaging her in wildness, connecting her to the spiritual through the physical, in a circular way of knowing and being. In his analysis of "soundscapes" in *Refuge*, Masami Yuki notes that Williams's memoir "interweaves the process of the narrator learning to listen to her dying mother and the birds at Great Salt Lake, both exemplifying wildness of life that will not be controlled by human intervention."[14] Yuki suggests that the sound environment depicted in this passage, with its repetition of sounds and specific words and phrases and its use of certain consonants, represents the lake "at its wildest. It is the wildness of the natural environment that helps make the narrator 'free' to reclaim her wild self by starting to question the social, cultural, and religious conventions of the society she belongs to."[15] Williams concludes: "Wind and waves. Wind and waves" (240), allowing the rhythms of the universe to enter her language. Shortly after this experience, the General Conference of Saints is adjourned.

Having freed herself from dogma, having embodied the primal wildness of a forgotten knowledge, Williams can rewrite Mormon theology to include the feminine. She explains that in the belief system of her culture, "the Holy Trinity is comprised of God the Father, Jesus Christ the Son, and the Holy Ghost. We call this the Godhead" (240). She continues:

> We are far too conciliatory. If we as Mormon women believe in God the Father and in his son, Jesus Christ, it is only logical that a Mother-in-Heaven balances the sacred triangle. I believe the Holy Ghost is female, although she has remained hidden, invisible, deprived of a body, she is the spirit that seeps into our hearts and directs us to the well. The "still, small voice" I was taught to listen to as a child was "the gift of the Holy Ghost." Today I choose to recognize this presence as holy intuition, the gift of the Mother. My prayers no longer bear the "proper" masculine salutation. I include both Father and Mother in Heaven. If we could introduce the Motherbody as a spiritual counterpoint to the Godhead, perhaps our inspiration and devotion would no longer be directed to the stars, but our worship could return to the Earth. (241)

In revising Mormon theology, Williams asserts a balance in gender, a coming together of the masculine with the feminine to create a new whole. Significantly, the feminine, which has been erased and silenced, is the voice of the spirit, the quiet inner voice of intuition, which offers the forgotten knowledge of interconnectedness, of our dependence on Earth, as opposed to the voice of intellect. She concludes: "My physical mother is gone. My spiritual mother remains. I am a woman rewriting my genealogy" (241). Such a balanced view of the Godhead within Mormon theology, although it provides a place for the feminine, seems to merely reinscribe women within the dualisms of patriarchal culture. Here the feminine becomes invisible, the intuition, and is connected to Earth.

Yet Williams's revision of Mormon theology does more than this, for it opens the door for establishing a voice that will ultimately undermine the binary oppositions of a dualistic worldview. Indeed, Williams suggests that her growth and transformation, which take her beyond this limited mindset, are mirrored in the men of her family. Williams sees a rattlesnake, its head and tail chopped off by a trophy hunter. When she walks on the shore of the lake, she sees several birds that have been randomly shot and left to die. Yet the journey through Williams's mother's death has changed not only her. She explains:

My father no longer hunts. Neither do my brothers.

"I can no longer participate in the killing," Dad said. "When I see the deer, I see Diane."

Hank put his gun down years ago. So did Dan. Steve carries his rifle into the hills, but he has not shot a deer since 1983.

"I see the buck in my scope but I can't find a good enough reason to pull the trigger."

For the men in my family, their grief has become their compassion. (251)

The change in the men's attitude toward animals, and by extension the landscape, represents a wider shift in the belief system guiding her culture from one of control and domination to one of care and compassion. While the governor proudly declares, after the completion of the West Desert Pumping Project, "We've harnessed the lake! . . . We are finally in control" (247), Williams and her family, men included, see the whole project as ridiculous. She concludes: "I realize months afterward that my grief is much larger than I could ever have imagined. The headless snake without its rattles, the slaughtered birds, even the pumped lake and the flooded desert, become extensions of my family. Grief dares us to love once more" (252). Here Williams embraces the meaningless death of animals and the futile attempts of humans to control the lake. As she has explained earlier, she recognizes that refuge cannot be an escape; rather, refuge must be a way of being that embraces the present, a love that accepts life and death, joy and despair. She successfully broadens her understanding of community to embrace the psychologically difficult components of our relationship with the land.

And with abnormal change. At least abnormal change that derives from natural causes. The last several chapters of *Refuge* demonstrate Williams's final understanding of the difference between natural abnormal changes, such as the rise of Great Salt Lake to unprecedented levels, and human-caused abnormal changes, such as cancer. This differentiation ultimately provides the foundation for a voice that speaks the land, that becomes a co-responding to the stillness of the land. At the beginning of "Pintails, Mallards, and Teals," Williams comments that "the birds have abandoned the lake" (239). Yet in the very next chapter, after she has offered a new vision of gender balance within her culture, she finds the birds. In "Bitterns," she exclaims: "I found the birds! Malheur National Wildlife Refuge in southeastern

Oregon . . . has adopted and absorbed the flocks of Great Salt Lake. Not all of them, of course. But many. Especially the colony-nesters" (253). Like the ancient Fremont people, the birds are able to flow with the natural changes of the landscape. She lists the birds that she sees and says, "It is like coming home" (253). Similarly, in "Great Blue Heron," Williams finds that the heron "has weathered the changes well. Throughout the high water and now its retreat, the true blue heron has stayed home" (266). Earlier, the great blue heron was described as one of the most sensitive of the colony-nesters that would most readily leave a disturbed area. The fact that the heron made it through this disturbance suggests that this abnormal change could be embraced, that through flexibility and adaptability this change can be accommodated within the larger patterns of the universe.

Williams reflects on the significance of the heron's steadfastness in the face of this change. She refers to the gnostics and what they have taught her: "For what is inside of you is what is outside of you and the one who fashions you on the outside is the one who shaped the inside of you. And what you see outside of you, you see inside of you, it is visible and it is your garment" (267). She fully grasps the unity of the internal and the external, the way in which the external landscape shapes and reflects our internal landscape and the way in which the internal shapes and reflects the external in an act of expropriative appropriating. She continues: "Refuge is not a place outside myself. Like the lone heron who walks the shores of Great Salt Lake, I am adapting as the world is adapting" (267). The birds' response to the abnormal rise of Great Salt Lake demonstrates their ability to accept and embrace natural changes in the landscape. Unlike humans who need to control the rise of the lake, the birds manifest an easy confluence with the changing shoreline and thus offer Williams a glimpse of an alternative worldview, one that challenges the technological and scientific worldview separating subject and object, men and women, culture and nature.

The different relationships to the landscape, which ultimately assist Williams in discerning the difference between natural and human-caused abnormal changes, can be seen in the two major artworks described in *Refuge*. The first, called "Metaphor" and described early in the book, is "the work of a European architect who saw the West Desert as 'a large white canvas with nothing on it.' This was his attempt 'to put something out there to break the monotony'" (127). The art work resembles a phallic symbol, an eighty-three-foot tower topped with enormous spheres. The work reflects our technological horizon of disclosure, our attitude that the landscape is an empty place to be written upon. Williams describes it: "With the light of morning, it cast a shadow across the salt flats like a mushroom cloud" (127), comparing the work to the explosion of an atomic bomb and foreshadowing the conclusion of *Refuge*. Charles Mitchell concludes that "Metaphor" "represents an evasion of intimate knowledge, a refusal to pay attention to place, a choice to impose an interpretation on that land rather than allowing the land to speak for itself."[16] As such, the work provides a counterpoint to the lesson Williams has learned from birds, the dynamic interrelationship of our connection to the land, the way the external and the internal, the physical and the spiritual become one. "Metaphor" imposes meaning on the land, silencing it, indeed erasing it.

The second artwork, called "Sun Tunnels" and described at the end of *Refuge*, represents the very interconnectedness to the land that "Metaphor" denies. Four tunnels, each eighteen feet long and configured in an X, are "aligned with the angles of the rising and the setting of the sun on the days of the solstices around June 21 and December 21. On those days the sun is centered through the tunnels, and is nearly centered for about ten days before and after the solstices" (267). Holes in the roofs of the tunnels cast "a changing pattern of pointed ellipses and circles of light on the bottom half of each tunnel" (268). The artwork neatly summarizes the wisdom that Williams has gained through telling her story. In her journey, she has reflected on many changing patterns, the feeding and mating rituals of birds, the ancient lifestyle of the Fremont people. Through this reflection she has come to accept the rise of Great Salt Lake as part of the larger order and meaning of the universe, an abnormal change that might be embraced. Williams then connects the significance of the artwork to the establishment of voice. "In Nancy Holt's 'Sun Tunnels,' the Great Basin landscape is framed within circles and we remember the shape of our planet, the shape of our eyes, our mouth in song and in prayer. These tunnels breathe as the ellipses expand and contract with the fickle light" (269). The Western, linear view of time has been abandoned for a more primal, circular view, which sees the rise and fall of the lake not as a problem to be controlled but rather as a change to be embraced as part of a larger cycle. She concludes: "The tunnels give import to my voice" (269).

In the epigraph of the book, Mary Oliver's poem "Wild Geese," and later in the book when her mother refers to the geese as her favorite bird,

Williams introduces the metaphor of migration, of the long journey to return home. The journey, which becomes the telling of her story in *Refuge*,
provides Williams with a new way of knowing, an understanding of an ancient and forgotten knowledge of interconnectedness and interrelationship, of the unity of dualisms—the inner and the outer, the spiritual and
the physical, heaven and Earth. In the penultimate chapter of *Refuge*, titled
"Screech Owls," Williams returns to this metaphor. Mimi, just before she
dies, tells Williams that she thinks she is going to see an owl; in response,
Williams asks her to send a sign when she dies. Shortly after Mimi dies, Williams sees two screech owls: "'*Dance. Dance. Dance,*' I hear Mimi say" (272).
Williams then inserts a poem from Rainer Maria Rilke:

> *Ah, not to be cut off,*
> *not through the slightest partition*
> *shut out from the law of the stars.*
> *The inner—what is it?*
> *if not intensified sky,*
> *hurled through with birds and deep*
> *with the winds of homecoming.* (272)

Through Mimi and birds, Williams has learned "the law of the stars" and
has come to live a life that connects the inner and the outer worlds. In remembering this lost knowledge and creating this new way of being, Williams has come home.

Her relationship with birds and with her grandmother has provided her
with a foundation for this journey and for this telling of her story. Beginning
with the childhood trip with the Audubon group recounted early in *Refuge*
up to this point in the memoir, Mimi, like birds, has allowed her to establish
her identity: "Mimi and I shared a clandestine vision of things. I could afford
to dream because she could interpret the story. We spoke through the short-
hand of symbols: an egg, an owl. And most of what we shared was secret,
much like the migration of birds" (273). With Mimi's death, Williams no
longer has someone to secretly share her story with. She concludes: "If I am
to survive, I must let my secrets out like white doves held captive too long. I
am a woman with wings" (273). Although the rise of Great Salt Lake and the
advance of her mother's cancer have been central features in the narrative,
ultimately *Refuge* is about Williams's journey, her return to home and self
and, consequently, voice. At this point in the text, the pumps to the West

Desert Pumping Project are turned off: "Great Salt Lake is on its own. The flood is over. . . . The Bear River Migratory Bird Refuge is able to breathe once again at lake level 4206.00'" (273).

Yet Williams still must contend with her mother's death. In the final chapter of *Refuge*, "Avocets and Stilts," Williams describes a canoeing trip on Half-Moon Bay in Great Salt Lake with her husband. As they rock "up and down, up and down" in the waves, she comments: "The past seven years are with me. Mother and Mimi are present. The relationships continue— something I did not anticipate" (275). Williams inserts in the middle of the description of this trip a memory of her journey to Mexico to participate in the Day of the Dead, an important ceremony honoring the difficult and painful aspects of life and thus one that helps her deal with the otherness inherent in a rich and complex understanding of community. She says: "I needed a ritual, a celebration to move me from death to life" (276). She visits a church where she joins others in remembering their dead: "A wave of emotion crested in me and broke. I wept silently for all I had lost. I reentered my own landscape of grief with perfect recall" (277). The participants share the stories of their dead, stories not unlike her own: "The voices of my Dead came back to me" (278). Later in the evening, she joins the ceremony, wearing an owl mask and dancing in the street. Williams's participation in the Day of the Dead reinforces her understanding of the close interrelationship between life and death and thus provides a foundation for what William Jordan calls an *"ecological* engagement with the world," one that embraces the challenging aspects of our relation with the other.[17] This ceremony, as an act of restoring Williams to herself by moving her through her grief, allows her to move beyond the worldview handed her by Western civilization and to engage an alternate worldview, one symbolized by the owl mask. Williams returns from Mexico with petals from a marigold, her mother's favorite flower, and sprinkles them on Great Salt Lake during her canoeing trip with Brooke. Although the lake has receded and the birds have returned to the Bear River Migratory Bird Refuge as part of a larger pattern, Williams's mother is gone, dead from cancer. Williams has come to see the abnormal change of the rise of the lake as natural, one that could be embraced in the flow of humans' relationship with the natural world. Yet her mother's death, although it has taught her about the ongoing flow of life and death, continues to haunt her and indeed ultimately provides her with the foundation for her voice.

Just as the human response to the rise of Great Salt Lake, an abnormal change that could be embraced, failed to acknowledge the naturalness of this change, humans have failed to accept and voice the unnatural nature of cancer. Early on in *Refuge*, Williams engages the language of cancer, which uses metaphors of war, and then asks: "How can we rethink cancer?" (43). She notes that whatever response we choose, surgery, radiation, chemotherapy, "we view the tumor as foreign, something outside ourselves. It is, however, our own creation" (44). Significantly, a similar response with similar metaphors is used in conjunction with the rising lake, a response that Williams ultimately comes to understand is unwarranted. She also, however, ultimately rejects her own early attempts to accept and embrace cancer because she learns that its cause is human and hence avoidable. In the epilogue to the book, "The Clan of the One-Breasted Women," Williams recounts to her father a recurring dream of a "flash of light in the night in the desert" (282). Her father explains that this vision was real, that she did see this flash of light, an atomic bomb set off in the desert in the middle of the night: "We pulled over and suddenly, rising from the desert floor, we saw it, clearly, this golden-stemmed cloud, the mushroom. The sky seemed to vibrate with an eerie pink glow. Within a few minutes, a light ash was raining on the car" (283). She concludes: "It was at this moment that I realized the deceit I had been living under" (283).

Williams's journey through the telling of the intertwined tales of the rising lake and her mother's cancer, a telling that allowed Williams to establish an identity based on a forgotten way of being, culminates in this moment and gives birth to her voice. She provides historical background on the testing of nuclear weapons in Utah, noting that the testing was halted after lawsuits were filed and won, a decision that was then overturned by the appeals court: "In January 1988, the Supreme Court refused to review the Appeals Court decision. To our court system it does not matter whether the United States government was irresponsible, whether it lied to its citizens, or even that citizens died from the fallout of nuclear testing. What matters is that our government is immune: 'The King can do no wrong'" (285). Williams connects the political landscape to her own cultural landscape: "In Mormon culture, authority is respected, obedience is revered, and independent thinking is not. I was taught as a young girl not to 'make waves' or 'rock the boat'" (285). Her mother tells her she should let things go, letting it suffice that she knows how she feels. The unwillingness to question political or religious authority, a silencing of voices, has led to an outrage committed on the land and on women's bodies: "I belong to a Clan of One-Breasted Women. My mother, my grandmothers, and six aunts have all had mastectomies. Seven are dead. The two who survive have just completed rounds of chemotherapy and radiation" (281). Cancer, then, is not something to be embraced or accommodated; it is not an abnormal change that is a part of the larger patterns of the universe. It is wholly human-caused and avoidable. The deceit, then, originates from a worldview that separates man from woman, culture from nature, and that silences, ravages, or ignores one side of the equation.

In this concluding chapter, Williams again acknowledges her complicity in the limited worldview that lies at the foundation of her culture. She acknowledges that for many years she has remained silent, accepting obediently the dictates of the patriarchal system that sees the desert, like women's bodies, as an empty canvas to be inscribed:

> For many years, I have done just that—listened, observed, and quietly formed my own opinions, in a culture that rarely asks questions because it has all the answers. But one by one, I have watched the women in my family die common, heroic deaths. We sat in waiting rooms hoping for good news, but always receiving the bad. I cared for them, bathed their scarred bodies, and kept their secrets. . . . In the end, I witnessed their last peaceful breaths, becoming a midwife to the rebirth of their souls.
>
> The price of obedience has become too high.
>
> The fear and inability to question authority that ultimately killed rural communities in Utah during atmospheric testing of atomic weapons is the same fear I saw in my mother's body. Sheep. Dead sheep. The evidence is buried. (285–86)

In this passage, in writing this final chapter of her journey, Williams has come home to herself and her voice. By listening to birds, she has come to understand a cyclical way of being, one in tune with the larger patterns of the landscape. She has also come to view the seeming abnormal rise of the lake as a change that could be embraced. Yet her journey has also taught her that the cancer that has claimed the lives of the women in her family is not to be embraced, a recognition demanding that she speak out. In doing so, Williams's own interior world—her emotions, her intuition, her spirit—become one with her exterior world, the world of her writing, her living, her being. She rises above the dualisms of her culture, indeed transcends the technological horizon of disclosure that has limited her identity and sense of self throughout her journey.

Because women have not only been silenced but also had their bodies, like the land, used to further a patriarchal and oppressive agenda, Williams recognizes that she must work toward reestablishing the place of women in the political, religious, and cultural landscape. Her revision of Mormon theology to incorporate the Mother body, the voice of intuition, is one step in this direction, though I would suggest that it operates from within the system oppressing her. Such an inclusiveness does not obviate the male perspective but rather supplements it, providing balance. Her recognition of the absence of the feminine leads to her vision in her epilogue: "One night, I dreamed women from all over the world circled a blazing fire in the desert. They spoke of change, how they hold the moon in their bellies and wax and wane with its phases. They mocked the presumption of even-tempered beings and made promises that they would never fear the witch inside themselves. The women danced wildly as sparks broke away from the flames and entered the night sky as stars" (287). Williams's vision of women uniting around a common fire is founded on the need for change but also on the concept of change as pattern—the waxing and waning of the moon—a pattern that connects women to the larger patterns of the universe. The dancing provides the foundation for reclaiming the land and themselves: "The women danced and drummed and sang for weeks, preparing themselves for what was to come. They would reclaim the desert for the sake of their children, for the sake of the land" (287). Just as Williams's journey through the telling of her tale has led to the establishment of her identity, the dancing and drumming leads to the empowerment of women.

Significantly, Williams then connects the journey toward identity with the political, noting that the desecration of the land under the dominant patriarchal order has led to infertility and lifelessness. She notes: "The women couldn't bear it any longer. They were mothers. They had suffered labor pains but always under the promise of birth. The red hot pains beneath the desert promised death only, as each bomb became a stillborn. A contract had been made and broken between *human beings* and *the land*. A new contract was being drawn by the women, who understood the fate of the earth as their own" (288, emphasis added). The new order that Williams asserts here, though it is conceived by women, is a remembering of an old contract founded on the intimate and fragile interrelationship between *humans* and the land. Significantly, the new contract necessarily derives from the voice of the oppressed, for they are the ones who have most fully experienced the destitution of our times, the ravaging of the land and of women's bodies. Yet the contract does not reinscribe dualistic thinking, like Williams's earlier revision of Mormon theology, for it is a *remembering* of an ancient contract between *all human beings* and the land. Specifically, her vision reacts to the testing of nuclear weapons: "The women closed their eyes. The time had come to protest with the heart, that to deny one's genealogy with the earth was to commit treason against one's soul" (288). The journey toward identity, then, necessarily results in the need to protest, to express the horror and treason of a human culture that disregards the land and, more importantly, to give voice to a new way of thinking and being.

*Refuge* concludes with a description of the women's act of civil disobedience, embodying their protest and manifesting their voice through action. Significantly, Williams demonstrates in this final action an awareness of the difference between the abnormal change of the rising lake, a change that could be embraced, and the abnormal change of cancer derived from exposure to nuclear fallout. More importantly, she associates this final act of discernment with birds. The women, wearing "long streamers of silver plastic around their arms to blow in the breeze," enter the town of Mercury, a "town that forbids pregnant women and children to enter because of radiation risks" (288). She continues: "The women moved through the streets as winged messengers, twirling around each other in slow motion" (288). Recalling Janisse Ray's silence at the end of *Ecology of a Cracker Childhood*, the women here, as winged messengers, do not speak but merely dance through the town, witnesses of the desecration of the land and of human bodies. Eventually, the women are arrested for trespassing on a military site. When Williams is searched, the officer finds "a pen and a pad of paper tucked inside [her] left boot" (290). When asked what they are, Williams responds, "Weapons," and smiles, insinuating the strength and confidence of the voice that she has established. The officials drive the women two hours to the nearest city but stop just short of the town. In the concluding passage of *Refuge*, Williams circles back to the image of migration that she initiates in her epigraph and prologue: "The officials thought it was a cruel joke to leave us stranded in the desert with no way to get home. What they didn't realize was that we were home, soul-centered and strong, women who recognized the sweet smell of sage as fuel for our spirits" (290). The long migration home, to self and voice, is complete in the telling of this final act of civil disobedience. Having taken up pen and paper, having established a voice founded on the wisdom of the landscape, Williams has returned home.

Beginning with early readings of *Refuge*, Williams has been criticized for propagating an essentialist, gendered view of the world, one founded on dualistic thinking: women versus men, nature versus culture, the spiritual versus the physical. Focusing on the final chapter, Cheryll Glotfelty concludes that the "book's final dream-vision is one of worldwide sisterhood," which comes at the expense of bridging the differences between the sexes.[18] Similarly, Elizabeth Dodd concludes that Williams desires to retain an "essentialist, gendered view; indeed, she finds it comforting and returns to similar tropes in later work."[19] Yet other readers have suggested that Williams is able to rise above this type of thinking. Karl Zuelke concludes that although Williams's work reveals essentialist thinking, it is used as "a deliberate strategy, a rhetorical stance arising from a specific situation"—what he calls a "constructed essentialism"; ultimately, Williams's essentialism is "a self-conscious rhetorical ploy with the political objective of reimagining the categories of 'woman' and 'nature' in order to subvert the dominant patriarchal culture's demeaning notions of them."[20] Finally, Cassandra Kircher concludes that Williams "problematizes both the female/nature and male/culture alliances," moving beyond dualistic thinking "to depict a circular notion of family [that] keeps the book from being essentialist."[21]

Such embattled and contradictory readings arise from a similar approach to *Refuge*, one that sees the book not as a journey that unfolds in the telling but rather as a linear, static, and unchanging whole. Katherine R. Chandler, in "Whale Song from the Desert," notes that in *Refuge* Williams "dramatizes the possibility of negotiating conflicting agendas by laying bare the means by which she navigates difficult terrain. Through her writing process, cultural dichotomies like those of objectivity and subjectivity, science and religion, body and spirit begin to disintegrate"; the reader experiences the book as a "dramatizing flux rather than rational, linearly reached conclusions."[22] Williams's journey in *Refuge*—one that unfolds through the telling of the tale, through the remembering of events—makes the point that we are all living unnatural lives, filled with materialism and hyperconsumption and nuclear weapons exploding in a flash at night aboveground. The question that Williams asks and explores in recounting the two intertwined narratives that become united in the narrative of the journey toward self and voice is how can we go home? That is, how can we return to ourselves? Cast in yet other terms, the questions are how do we dwell? and how might we dwell in more meaningful ways? Rather than providing a linear narrative that scientifically analyzes these issues, Williams reveals her own struggle with these central questions.[23] And in this struggle, Williams embodies, then engages, and ultimately refutes the cultural practices that have denied an identity and a voice to a large sector of reality—most notably women and the land. In situating Refuge within the genre of cancer literature, Tina Richardson concludes that the book "unravels the threads of cultural practice that form our social fabric to reveal the naturalized power structures that ensure social privilege through such determining factors as race, gender, and economic status."[24] Williams forces us to question our cultural conditioning, our culturally enforced ways of knowing and being, and ultimately to reject them. Our culture is patriarchal. It has led to the oppression of women and land and the denial of their voice. Refuge shows that we are all—including Williams herself—embedded and implicated in this power structure.

The great strength of the book, though, is that even as it takes us through all of this and shows the narrator's complicity (and thus implies our own), Refuge also offers an alternative way of knowing and being, one that the narrator comes to learn in remembering her journey and specifically in listening to birds. Masami Yuki, in "Narrating the Invisible Landscape," notes that "the birds symbolically criticize civilization, because, whereas people of modern culture have been isolated from the larger synergistic system of life, the birds manage to connect with the synergistic network by virtue of the wildlife refuge, even when it is on the verge of ecological disorder due to the encroaching water of the Great Salt Lake."[25] In listening to the birds, Williams models an alternative and engaged way of knowing, one founded not on calculative and scientific thinking but rather on emplacement, on being embedded in a particular context. Although Heidegger would dismiss a consideration of birds as beings capable of mentoring humans on our journey, his philosophy provides a foundation for considering "the human knower as pragmatically engaged in a world of meaningful concern," something paramount to feminist philosophers. According to Patricia Huntington, such an engagement entails "the intensification of one's inherence in existence." For Williams, this intensification means that she cannot escape but rather that she must enjoin the gendered and dualistic worldview of her culture; this is the abyss that must be plumbed in order to remember something deeper, to reconceptualize "human nature as care—custodian for what appears—rather than as the rational animal who lords over the earth."[26]

Like the paradoxical readings of *Refuge*, feminist readings of Heidegger's work have grappled with the seeming paradox of Heidegger's claim that Dasein is gender neutral even while recognizing our gendered standing in the world. Because we are thrown into the world in a particular time and place, "being incarnated into sexed bodies is a defining feature of worldly embodiment"; yet our sexuality can take on various meanings "because Dasein transcends gender difference," for it is, ultimately, the site of disclosure. Huntington suggests that this distinction between our embodiment and the gender neutrality of Dasein offers an avenue for transcending our particularity, our "finitude," in order to recover "an authentic relation to one's embodiment." She concludes that "the activity whereby one recovers explicit awareness of being the site of disclosure" is one that "counteracts fallenness into conventional modes of understanding the body and the sexes."[27] In *Refuge*, this activity might be Williams's participation in the Day of the Dead ceremony, a ritual that allows her to understand death as part of a wider journey, a circling of our bodies and our spirits, and thus to authentically engage mortality. The ceremony allows Williams to remember an ancient wisdom, that human beingness is the site of unconcealing, of revealing beings in their ownness. Thus, in *Refuge*, Williams is both embodied and emplaced as a woman in Mormon culture and, more broadly, in Western civilization, which offers a particular relation to the world around her, construing it as an object to be used, a blank canvas on which to make a mark. Yet, I would argue, she is also embodied and emplaced as a human being who learns to listen to and care for the land. That is, the journey in the book, which reveals Williams's complicity in a culture that entraps her, also creates a new possibility, a remembering that transcends her gender, a recovery of a *human* relation to our grand and mysterious Earth. In this moment of possibility, a moment that finally unfolds in the performative and ceremonial act of dancing through the sleeping town, Williams remembers that humans have the awesome responsibility to still their will, to let things be, and to witness.

Embedded in the technological worldview of our time, Williams reveals in *Refuge: An Unnatural History of Family and Place* the binary oppositions that frame our relation to the world and condition how we dwell, in turn creating a dualistic thinking that leads to the oppression of women and the degradation, the desacralization of the land. Yet Williams's relationship with birds offers her an alternative worldview, one based on reciprocity and the difficulties of our transactions with others. Learning from the birds, Williams recognizes the need to dwell differently, to change how we interact with the land, to become new beings who listen to the stillness of the land and allow the land to speak in a humble but powerful act of co-responding. But dwelling does not mean remaining passive and accepting the forces that frame our existence. Indeed, because of the double forgetting, the oblivion of Being, confronting us in the modern age, we must enact through ceremony new ways of thinking and being. Dwelling may mean protesting in such a way that land-language speaks, and we have the opportunity to glimpse an alternative worldview. Most importantly, dwelling becomes, in the end, a way of remembering an ancient knowledge, the sacred reason of Linda Hogan, that humans have a contract with the land that, when the contract is honored, opens the land and humans to a dance of reciprocity melding the interior and exterior landscapes, to the expropriative appropriating in Heidegger's terms or the reciprocal appropriation in N. Scott Momaday's words. Williams suggests that women are most able to remember this contract largely because they have most fully and most consciously experienced the abyss, the groundlessness of our contemporary culture, the oblivion of Being. Because of the patriarchal nature of our culture, they know, feel, and live the darkness and destitution of our time.

Heidegger suggests that only those who have entered the abyss and engaged the darkness can lead us out of destitution. For him, these are the writers and poets who can offer an honest assessment of our culture and the way in which we have come to accept scientific and calculative reason as the only access to truth or reality; such blindness has led to a double-order forgetting and the loss of our connection to something more primal, to Being. In *Refuge*, Williams demonstrates that it is women who have most fully experienced the destitution of our time, for women, like the land, have become the object of patriarchal culture's disdain. And thus it is women who remember. In a conversation about midway through *Refuge*, Williams's friend Wangari Waigwa-Stone explains: "I am Kikuyu. My people believe if you are close to the Earth, you are close to people" (137). She continues:

> What an African woman nurtures in the soil will eventually feed her family. Likewise, what she nurtures in her relations will ultimately nurture her community. It is a matter of living the circle.
>
> Because we have forgotten our kinship with the land, . . . our kinship with each other has become pale. We shy away from accountability and involvement. We choose to be occupied, which is quite different from being engaged. In America, time is money. In Kenya, time is relationship. We look at investments differently. (137)

Women, then, remember the human kinship with the land and honor the difficult and challenging aspects of our transactions with others. Women thus become the ones responsible for drawing the new contract, not one that reinscribes gender dualisms or attempts to overturn those dualisms, asserting women over men. Rather, the new contract is a remembered knowledge of the wisdom of elders like Wangari Waigwa-Stone, a remembering of the mysterious plenitude of Earth. The remembered ancient knowledge gleaned from birds returns Williams to herself and her home and offers the opportunity to remake her culture. In offering to tell her complicated and paradoxical journey to her audience through her pen and paper, which spill sand and feathers and smell of sage, Williams gives us a great and difficult gift.

# CHAPTER FIVE

# Healing the Severed Trust

## Linda Hogan's *Dwellings: A Spiritual History of the Living World* as Native Ceremony

In *The Sacred Hoop*, Paula Gunn Allen identifies two basic forms of Native American literature, the ceremony and the myth. According to Allen, "the ceremony is the ritual enactment of a specialized perception of a cosmic relationship, while the myth is a prose record of that relationship."[1] Both forms have the purpose of locating the individual within an interlocking and interconnected framework that includes the psychological, the social, the geographical, and the spiritual, all the way out to the cosmic. This holistic perception of the world—very different from the scientific, calculative way of thinking that separates and isolates things as resource-objects for our use—connects humans to the landscape and all the beings who grace the world around us. Ceremony plays a particular role in this way of thinking, for its purpose "is to integrate: to fuse the individual with his or her fellows, the community of people with that of the other kingdoms, and this larger communal group with the worlds beyond this one. A raising or expansion of individual consciousness naturally accompanies this process. The person sheds the isolated, individual personality and is restored to conscious harmony with the universe."[2] Allen states that because individuals from the West fail to think in this holistic way, in which all beings are interconnected, they very often struggle with an authentic understanding of the great power that exists in Native American literature. The structures and symbols of this literature "are designed to integrate the various orders of consciousness," not only within and among humans but also between humans and other entities who also participate in the ceremonial literature.[3] Most importantly, the literature itself is an "enactment of [this] specialized perception" of the cosmic interrelationship grounding our existence, not merely a record or description but an unfolding, a presencing of that way of thinking and thus, concomitantly, of the reciprocal appropriation, in Momaday's words, that pervades reality.

In her essay "First People," Linda Hogan mirrors Allen's depiction of Native American literature as embodying a cosmic interrelationship, describing the way in which ceremonies can heal the rift that has grown between the self and the world. She says: "The stories that are songs of agreement and safekeeping, and the ceremonies that are their intimate companions, tell us not only how to keep the world alive, they tell us how to put ourselves back together again. In the language of ceremony, a person is placed—bodily, socially, geographically, spiritually, and cosmologically—in the natural world extending all the way out into the universe. This placing includes the calling in of the animal presence from all directions." In this passage, Hogan connects storytelling with ceremony and notes that they both allow us to find our place in the intricate web of the natural world that sustains us and the cosmological order that grounds our existence. Moreover, stories and ceremonies are a happening, a lived event that places us within both the cultural and the natural worlds in such a way that we are restored to balance and the world is kept alive. She continues: "The ceremonial language and the images it evokes allow a human to see herself in relation to what's around, in, and outside of the seemingly singular human body. A ceremony enacts the recalled participation with nature. It reorients us, locates us in our human place, according to the natural laws of the world." Hogan emphasizes the way in which ceremony brings forth a once-forgotten way of being and thinking based on relationship and participatory experience. Rather than merely describing this remembered knowledge, ceremony draws forth an ancient mode of existence that recognizes an ecology of physical and spiritual being. After describing how Earth has been ravaged and poisoned, Hogan concludes: "We are hoping for, in need of, a ceremony that will heal this. In a changed world, we are in need of an ancient way being."[4]

The role of participatory interaction between humans and the landscape, including the plants and the animals, the hills and the valleys, the sky, the thunder, and the sun that grace our journey through life, is central to the renewal of this ancient way of being. In *Teaching Spirits*, Joseph Epes Brown explains that relationships between humans and the natural world follow a "circular pattern of reciprocity. In treating the world and all its beings in a sacred manner, one is in turn treated well by nature." Founded not on materialistic consumption or a quantitative and scientific mode of thinking but rather on "mutual respect," this participatory way of being "generates a profound metaphysics of nature. A sacred pact is forged among all beings of the world, who, instead of emphasizing their material differences, focus on their inherent commonality. The binding force in this pact is the sacred lore held by the people and supported and transmitted by legends, ceremonies, songs, and sense of humility."[5] Ceremonies and rituals, then, provide the foundation for remembering and enacting the ancient wisdom of Earth and elders, the specialized perception, indeed the sacred reason of Linda Hogan. Significantly, this ancient wisdom ultimately constitutes a "sacred pact," an agreement between humans and the world that we would ground our way of being in a mutual reciprocity, that our metaphysics, our way of knowing the world around us, would be founded not on separation and distinction but rather on unity and interdependence. Brown continues: "This relatedness not only ties together seemingly disparate beings such as water and rocks but also identifies humans with all of creation. For most Native American culture[s], the relatedness is rooted in the perception of a shared spiritual reality that transcends physical differences. Some believe this common essence is the life breath; others refer to it as the presence of the Great Spirit." Brown's conception of ceremony as the reenactment of an agreement between humans and the landscape recalls the contract that is being rewritten by women at the end of Williams's *Refuge*. Brown concludes: "The interrelationships between the nonhumans and the humans constitute a sacred reciprocity and, indeed, a sacred pact."[6]

Remembering this ancient way of being and healing the rift that has grown between humans and the land through ceremony is a central theme in Hogan's collection of essays titled *Dwellings: A Spiritual History of the Living World*. She states in her preface that the purpose of her essays is to "search out a world of different knowings, [to] enter a doorway into the mythical world, a reality known by [her] ancestors, one that takes the daily into dimensions both sacred and present" (12). In her analysis of this collection, Donelle Dreese observes: "Informed by her Native heritage that encourages reverence for, and reciprocity to, the natural world, Hogan's respect for the earth's terrestrial intelligence is clear in her insistence on a more balanced relationship between the spirit world and human world."[7] Similarly, Katherine Chandler remarks: "The essays in *Dwellings* demonstrate that if we focus our attention outward, become more intuitively perceptive, attend to our senses, then listen in ways not necessarily auditory, we *will* understand more about the natural world and its spirit."[8] Both Dreese and Chandler rightly note Hogan's primary concern with the need to reestablish a balance between the physical and the spiritual. Dreese concludes that *Dwellings* acts as "a guidebook on how to nurture a more spiritual connection with the world and its inhabitants."[9] Likewise, Chandler states that while the essays in *Dwellings* are not a "cohesive assemblage," they present Hogan's "values and beliefs," which are founded on "the integration of nature and spirit."[10] I would like to build on both of these readings by suggesting that Hogan's reference to bringing the mundane, the "daily," into "dimensions" that are both "sacred and present" makes this collection more than a guidebook or a random assemblage of essays. Indeed, recalling Heidegger's insistence that the saving grace will occur in the "here and now and little things," I would like to offer a reading of *Dwellings* that suggests the way in which this collection re/places us in such a way that we can remember our bodily and spiritual connection to the natural world and, in turn, can remember the sacred trust between humans and Earth.

In her collection of native oral tales, *Grandmothers of the Light: A Medicine Woman's Sourcebook*, Paula Gunn Allen notes that "stories connect us to the universe of medicine—of paranormal or sacred power. This universe of power referred to by the old people of some of the tribes as the Great Mystery is the universe that medicine people inhabit."[11] She explains that for Native Americans, myths "inform consciousness and direct awareness within as well as without, and they connect with deep levels of being, not because the figures they tell about are immaterial denizens of the shadowy world of the unconscious, but because the supernaturals live within the same environs that humans occupy, and interchanges with them are necessarily part of the fabric of human experience."[12] Emphasizing the role of storytelling as a restorative and healing process, Allen suggests an entwinement between our inner and our outer worlds, which in turn provides us with access to "deep levels of being," our rightful place in the much larger universe, one that includes both the physical and the spiritual as natural and necessary elements and indeed as twin components of reality. Similarly, Hogan notes in her preface to *Dwellings* that her writing "connects the small world of humans with the larger universe, containing us in the same way that native ceremonies do, showing us both our place and a way of seeing" (12). Hogan suggests here that her essays provide an ecological perspective that reveals the interrelationship of humans, plants, animals, and Earth itself along with the stars and the planets in the heavens, a perspective that opens our eyes and ears to the supernatural world surrounding us. But more than that, her essays, which she equates with ceremonies, enact this ecology of being and knowing.[13] *Dwellings* thus ultimately seeks to bring forth an ancient way of being founded on harmony and balance; the collection of essays as presented to the reader enacts a ceremony of healing, a healing of self (narrator and reader) and of Earth that restores reciprocity and relationship and that brings the sacred and the mythical into the real.

While Janisse Ray's *Ecology of a Cracker Childhood* and Terry Tempest Williams's *Refuge: An Unnatural History of Family and Place* demonstrate the authors' embeddedness within the technological horizon of disclosure that confines and constrains their existence, only to disrupt (in the case of Ray) or transcend (in the case of Williams) that worldview, Hogan, as a Chickasaw poet, novelist, and essayist, resides on the boundaries between this worldview and an ancient, remembered wisdom and is thus able to reveal to those of us in the Western world our own limitations as a part of this ceremony of healing. She opens her preface, explaining, "As an Indian woman I question our responsibilities to the caretaking of the future and to the other species who share our journeys. These writings have grown out of those questions, out of wondering what makes us human, out of a lifelong love for the living world and all its inhabitants. They have grown, too, out of my native understanding that there is a terrestrial intelligence that lies beyond our human knowing and grasping" (11). Hogan's recognition that our human attitude toward the world should be one of "caretaking," where we "spare and preserve" the world in Heidegger's terms, rather than one of "grasping," demonstrates the way in which she straddles two worlds and thus can offer a critique of our Western worldview. She notes: "It is clear that we have strayed from the treaties we once had with the land and with the animals. It is also clear, and heartening, that in our time there

are many—Indian and non-Indian alike—who want to restore and honor
these broken agreements" (11). Hogan's reference to the broken treaties between humans and the land recalls the end of Williams's *Refuge*, where the
women who have most fully experienced the destitution of our time work
to restore those treaties. Such a restoration, I have suggested, would allow
us to re/place ourselves, reconnecting us to the land and allowing us to become new beings.

Hogan's concern for restoring reciprocity between humans and the
land, as she outlines it in her preface, is grounded in her work with animals,
her love for Earth, and her "hunger to know what dwells beneath the surface of things" (11). She desires to discover the essence of the beings surrounding her, to understand and to presence those beings as more than
merely objects for our use. And in doing this, in offering a new horizon of
disclosure different from Enframing, Hogan will reveal to us "the different
histories of ways of thinking and being in the world" (12). She writes, she
says, "out of respect for the natural world, recognizing that humankind is
not separate from nature" (12). Like Ray's autobiography, which writes the
lost forests into existence, and Williams's journals that spill sand and sage,
Hogan's essays are *of* the land: "These are lessons learned from the land and
it is my hope that this work contributes to an expanded vision of the world.
*Dwellings* is both of and about this alive and conscious world. Its pages come
from forests, its words spring from the giving earth" (12). Hogan offers a
very different understanding of language than that which we hold in the
Western world. Words and Earth, pages and forests are one, and the act of
writing becomes an act of ecological restoration that in turn allows for a
healing of the self.[14] Such an act of writing expands our vision of the world,
allowing us to glimpse Earth in its mysterious plenitude and to be placed—
bodily and spiritually—on the land in a new way in which the internal and
the external landscapes unite and we become replaced, become new beings.

Hogan's deep care both for the act of writing and for the land—and the
way in which the two become united—suggests that we take care in reading this collection of essays. Central to the collection is the theme of healing
the trust between humans and the natural world, which has been severed,
a theme taken up explicitly in the fourth essay, titled "All My Relations,"
which describes Hogan's own process of healing, providing the reader
with an understanding of the rightful place of humans, of the participatory and reciprocal relation of humans to the natural world, and especially

to animals. The three essays leading up to "All My Relations," titled "The Feathers," "The Bats," and "The Caves," remind us of the sacredness of the universe in order to reconnect us to our origins. These essays open a path to a new way of being and thinking and thus prepare the reader for the healing process and the enactment of ceremony. The essays that follow after "All My Relations" first sharpen the reader's awareness of the disharmony in our lives, allowing us to see the world with new eyes, and then ultimately open up and bring to life the potential for harmony and interrelatedness. As Heidegger suggests, we must first fully experience the abyss, the oblivion of Being, the double-order forgetting wrought by our technological horizon of disclosure, before we can enact new ways of thinking and being and heal the chasm that has grown between humans and a more primal order, between humans and Being. While Chandler notes that "reading *Dwellings* can become a ceremonial act in itself," I want to build on Allen's statement that stories connect us to the healing powers of the universe and to my discussion in previous chapters about the role of storytelling in healing and restoration and suggest that the essays in the collection as arranged can indeed be read as a ceremony.[15] Linda Hogan's *Dwellings* thus takes the narrator and the reader on a journey toward healing and wholeness; read as an integrated and carefully fashioned whole, the collection becomes a ceremony that brings an ancient way of being and knowing into the present.

The first three essays of *Dwellings* chart a path that begins in the heavens and descends into Earth, providing a reverse of the emergence story. Traditional emergence tales, which provide a sense of connectedness to the landscape, ground a people in a particular place and allow for the merging of the interior and the exterior landscapes. Significantly, for many Native American cultures, emergence could only occur when interdependence is realized; that is, the people could emerge as a distinct culture only when a lived reciprocity existed between humans and the landscape. When this sense of interconnectedness is forgotten, a return to origins is necessary. Significantly, Hogan describes this journey in the first three essays partly to provide the reader with an awareness of the need to return to our origins in times of physical or spiritual illness. Yet her way of initiating and traversing this path does more than raise awareness; indeed, it enacts the very return it describes on the part of the narrator in such a way that the reader has the opportunity to participate in the return to origins. Beginning with "The Feathers," Hogan reminds us of the mystery inherent in the natural and the spiritual worlds and the way in which neglect of these worlds causes us to forget an ancient way of being and knowing. Concluding with "The Caves," Hogan unfolds her own healing as she immerses herself in the depths of Earth. As the reader engages this process of forgetting and remembering, we participate in the journey back to creation and origin.

"The Feathers" opens with a mystical story of a dream that participates in a different way of knowing than that of reason and logic. In the dream, the narrator finds herself in a temple, a "holy place"; when she looks up at the domed ceiling, she sees that it is "engraved with gold designs of leaves and branches" (16). She calls to others to look up, and in doing so, she wakens herself from the dream only to look out her open window and see a golden eagle flying toward her. When she goes outside, the eagle is gone, but a feather lies in the road, one that could not have possibly reached the ground in the time it took her to run outside. She says:

> I know there is a physics to this, a natural law about lightness and air. This event rubs the wrong way against logic. How do I explain the feather, the bird at my window, my own voice waking me, as if another person lived in me, wiser and more alert. I can only think there is another force at work, deeper than physics and what we know of wind, something that comes from a world where lightning and thunder, sun and rain clouds live. Nor can I say why it is so many of us have forgotten the mystery of nature and spirit, while for tens of thousands of years such things have happened and been spoken by our elders and our ancestors. (16–17)

For many Native Americans, sleep and dreaming provide access to another way of knowing, different from our calculating reason, a way of knowing that offers a deeper truth and connection to reality. Here the truth that is discovered in sleep, a wisdom of Earth and elders forgotten in our daily lives, is carried forward into the real world and brought into presence. Hogan then tells the story of the loss of her daughter's umbilical cord, which represents connection to mother, to life, to origins. She calls the umbilical cord "the most valuable thing in our home" (17). She talks to a friend who is Blackfeet and tells him of her loss: "It was a sign to me that I have neglected my spiritual life, which I often do when working and living and teaching in a world of different knowings" (18). Hogan here suggests that our loss of connection to origins, which in turn represents our loss of connection to the natural world and to the spiritual in the natural, derives from our Western "logic," our scientific and calculative way of thinking, which is part of our technological horizon of disclosure. Her Blackfeet friend tells her of a ceremony that might allow her to find the umbilical cord, insinuating the significant role of ceremonies in maintaining our spiritual lives. After enacting the ceremony outside at night, she returns to her home and finds the feather missing from its box. When she locates the feather on the ground, she sees it pointing toward the umbilical cord in a place where she had already searched.

Ultimately, the ceremony not only allows her to relocate the umbilical cord, a symbol of origins, but it also reconnects her to an ancient way of being and knowing, one that stands in stark contrast to her life at that time. She states:

> Perhaps there are events and things that work as a doorway into the mythical world, the world of first people, all the way back to the creation of the universe and the small quickenings of earth, the first stirrings of human beings at the beginning of time. Our elders believe this to be so, that it is possible to wind a way backward to the start of things, and in so doing find a form of sacred reason, different from ordinary reason, that is linked to forces of nature. In this kind of mind, like in the feather, is the power of sky and thunder and sun, and many have had alliances and partnerships with it, a way of thought older than measured time, less primitive than the rational present. (19)

Hogan offers the reader a window into a forgotten knowledge, a type of reason that operates in conjunction with the natural world, with "sky and thunder and sun." Such a way of knowing, which we can access through events such as ceremonies and objects such as feathers, is sacred and full of power. The more we understand of this mythical world, the closer we come to the "magical origins of creation" (19). Significantly, our access to "sacred reason" depends on a stilling of our minds and our will, a silencing of our human language and an opening of ourselves to an ancient wisdom and to mystery: "There is a still place, a gap between worlds, spoken by the tribal knowings of thousands of years. In it are silent flyings that stand aside from human struggles and the designs of our own makings. At times, when we are silent enough, still enough, we take a step into such mystery, the place of spirit, and mystery, we must remember, by its very nature does not wish to be known" (20). Hogan concludes the essay, returning to the power of the feather. She says: "There is something alive in a feather. The power of it is perhaps in its dream of sky, currents of air, and the silence of its creation. It knows the insides of clouds. It carries our needs and desires, the stories of our brokenness. It rises and falls down elemental space, one part of the elaborate world of life where fish swim against gravity, where eels turn silver as moon to breed" (20). The feather for Hogan, and the essay "The Feathers" for the reader, becomes part of a ceremony that returns the narrator and the reader from "brokenness" to renewed life, to a place in the elaborate web connecting the heavens and Earth.

Hogan follows "The Feathers" with an essay titled "The Bats" to prefigure the move into Earth that takes place in "The Caves." After noting the importance of silencing our human voice in order to access sacred reason, Hogan explains that bats, who exist between two worlds, have access to a language we cannot hear. Andrew Smith, in his reading of Hogan's *Mean Spirit*, explains that the "nature of bats—a unification of the seemingly irreconcilable physical differences of bird and animal in one creature—suggests a power to mediate, to exist in more than one world and to move in and out of oppositional space."[16] Hogan says:

> Bats hear their way through the world. They hear the sounds that exist at the edges of our lives. Leaping through blue twilight they cry out a thin language, then listen for its echo to return. It is a dusky world of songs a pitch above our own. For them, the world throws back a language, the empty space rising between hills speaks an open secret then lets the bats pass through, here or there, in the dark air. Everything answers, the corner of a house, the shaking leaves on a wind-blown tree, the solid voice of bricks. A fence post talks back. An insect is located. A wall sings out its presence. There are currents of air loud as ocean waves, a music of trees, stones, charred stovepipes. Even our noisy silences speak out in a dark dimension of sound that is undetected by our limited hearing in the loud, vibrant land in which we live. (25–26)

Bats have access to a language that humans cannot hear, and, as a result, the world is alive to them in ways that it isn't for humans. Hogan's contrast between humans, who cannot hear their own "noisy silences" much less the "loud, vibrant land," and bats, who hear "a world alive in its whispering songs, the currents of air loud as waves of an ocean, a place rich with the music of trees and stones" (26), reinforces the way in which sacred reason depends on stilling the human mind (and voice) in order to hear the wisdom of Earth and elders. Hogan here suggests that as a result of our way of being and knowing, we have lost contact with the mythical and sacred dimension of the world around us and thus have no access to the "dusky world of songs" that is the language of the bats.

As in the first essay, Hogan connects her topic to healing. She notes that bats are a "key element in the medicine bundles of some southern tribes" (26). Because they "live in the first circle of holiness," they become "intermediaries between our world and the next" (27), guides who help us traverse our own lostness and return us to peace: "Hearing the chants of life all around them, they are listeners who pass on the language and songs of many things to human beings who need wisdom, healing, and guidance through our lives, we who forget where we stand in the world. Bats know the world is constantly singing, know the world inside the turning and twisting of caves, places behind and beneath our own" (27). Central to the role of bats, who are able to pass between worlds, is their ability to remind humans "where we stand in the world," to allow us to be placed on the land in such a way that we can participate, once again, in land-language speaking. She concludes the essay with a series of questions:

> How can we get there from here, I wonder, to the center of the world, to the place where the universe carries down the song of night to our human lives. How can we listen or see to find our way by feel to the heart of every yes or no? How do we learn to trust ourselves enough to hear the chanting of earth? To know what's alive or absent around us, and penetrate the void behind our eyes, the old, slow pulse of things, until a wild flying wakes up in us, a new mercy climbs out and takes wing in the sky? (28)

Here Hogan connects descent into Earth with reestablishing our place in the universe and our ability to hear the lost voice of the land, with remembering how to dwell. Such a remembering is founded on a new way of being and thinking that relies more on intuition and participation than on logic and egocentrism.

The next essay, "The Caves," answers the questions posed at the end of

"The Bats" by completing the journey that begins in "The Feathers" with the eagle in the heavens and concludes with a descent into the "center of the world." This journey is a return to origins and thus reverses the traditional emergence story. Hogan describes caves as a place of transition between two worlds, between the real and the mythical; thus she completes the movement initiated in the "The Feathers" toward a new way of being and knowing, one founded on a spiritual or mythical plane. She notes that caves are "places of healing" (29) and connects them to origins: "They are a feminine world, a womb of earth, a germinal place of brooding. In many creation stories, caves are the places that bring forth life" (31). Hogan's emphasis on the feminine recalls Williams's insistence in *Refuge* that women will write the new contract with Earth because they have most fully experienced the oppression and desecration wrought by a patriarchal culture. Earlier in the essay, Hogan suggests that caves are the place where tribes went to resolve their conflicts because they were considered "a sanctuary outside the reign of human differences, law, and trouble" (30). In this way, Hogan, like Williams, suggests that the feminine provides a foundation for remembering an ancient knowledge that predates our isolation, separation, and difference, from one another and from the land.

The frame of the essay "The Caves" describes the narrator's descent into a cave with hot springs. She recounts a dream in which she entered a cave to search for her mothers: "the earth, my human mother, my own life as a woman" (32). She then enters the hot springs: "Submerged in the hot water of this cave, I know this story; my blood remembers it. There is a different way of knowing here and I see all around me the constellations of animals" (32). She notes that the depictions of animals covering the walls constitute "the fetal beginnings of life to come, of survival" (33). This descent, then, marks her journey back to origins, before the cutting of the umbilical cord between humans and the land. Other women join her in the hot springs, and she concludes the essay emphasizing the role of healing in her journey inward: "We are welcome here. I love this inner earth, its murmuring heartbeat, the language of what will consume us. Above is the beautiful earth that we have come from. Below is heat, stone, fire. I am within the healing of nature, held in earth's hand" (35). The narrator's descent into Earth, her proximity to the stone and fire that give birth to Earth, provides her with a connection to creation. As Leslie Marmon Silko says, "In the end we all originate from the depths of the earth. Perhaps this is how all beings share in the spirit of the Creator."[17]

The first three essays of *Dwellings*, then, enact a ceremony of healing for both the narrator and the reader. The narrator describes her own spiritual disharmony in the "The Feathers," offering a critique of our own way of thinking and being, while also initiating a journey toward healing and wholeness. "The Bats" acts as a transition essay, introducing the significant role of animals in ceremonies of healing, a fact that will become important toward the end of *Dwellings*, and preparing the reader for the final descent into Earth. "The Caves," the final essay leading up to "All My Relations," completes the journey from the outer world to the inner world, returning the narrator and the reader to origins. Although Hogan focuses on the importance of the feminine in the last essay, she does not reinscribe the dualisms of our culture, just as Williams ultimately transcends such thinking in *Refuge*. In "The Caves," Hogan describes her father's journey and how, toward the conclusion of his life, he had "returned to the inner world of his own self, as strong men do in their passage through life," to a place where he knows that there is "something deeper than [the] human" in his experiences, "something of the world of myth" (34). The final image of the essay, depicting the narrator cradled in Earth's hand with fire and stone, the originary sources of Earth itself, beneath it, reconnects the narrator and reader with the primal forces of the universe, forces that predate our separation of the world into binary oppositions, which allows us to treat the world and other people as objects for our use.

The fourth essay in *Dwellings*, titled "All My Relations," builds on the work completed in the first three essays, which prepare the reader and the narrator for ceremony and then enact a healing, a restoration to origins. "All My Relations" opens in the narrator's home with a communal meal being prepared as is customary in a Native American household. The narrator is asked if she still reads books, and she says that she does, explaining, "Reading is not 'traditional' and education has long been suspect in communities that were broken, in part, by that system, but we laugh at my confession because a television set plays in the next room" (36–37). In this opening passage, Hogan sets up a disjunction between her current way of being, which involves formal education and books and television, and a more traditional way of being that builds community and depends on participation.

The narrator then introduces a guest who has come to enact a healing ceremony. She continues to draw a distinction between these two ways of being by describing the guest: "A girl takes him a plate of food. He eats. He is a man I have respected for many years, for his commitment to the people, for his intelligence, for his spiritual and political involvement in concerns vital to Indian people and nations. Next to him sits a girl eating potato chips, and from this room we hear the sounds of the freeway" (37). While the guest eats the traditional Native American food, the young girl eats potato chips as the sound of the modern world invades the home. The eruption of a Western way of being within the traditional home sets up a stark contrast between two different ways of being and thinking, similar to the juxtaposition of the laws of physics with the mythical appearance of the feather in the first essay.

The narrator then brings the guest tobacco and explains why she needs him. Significantly, in this passage, Hogan again connects storytelling with ceremony, suggesting that her own writing allows the reader to participate in healing. She says: "I know this telling is the first part of the ceremony, my part in it. It is story, really, that finds its way into language, and story is at the very crux of healing, at the heart of every ceremony and ritual in the older America" (37). She continues, connecting stories to the wisdom of elders: "The ceremony itself includes not just our own prayers and stories of what brought us to it, but also includes the unspoken records of history, the mythic past, and all the other lives connected to ours, our families, nations, and all other creatures" (37). For Hogan, the telling of the story of her illness through language begins the process of healing and is the first stage in enacting the ceremony. The telling not only reveals the history of the teller but also reconnects the teller and the audience to the deep past, to the wisdom of elders, and to the natural and spiritual worlds, thus initiating the process of reestablishing an ecology of physical and spiritual being, one founded on interrelationship and interdependence. The role of the guest is to assist the narrator in crossing "over the boundaries of what we think, in daily and ordinary terms, is real and present" (38). The next day, as they drive to the ceremonial site, passing by "billboards and little towns and gas stations," an "eagle flies overhead," which they all agree is a "good sign" (38). Ultimately, the journey that the narrator has begun will allow her to recognize and participate in "that which is around us daily but too often unacknowledged, a larger life than our own" (38). Hogan's journey at this point recalls

Heidegger's insistence that the saving power will occur through recognition
of the destitution of our times, through entering the abyss, and through
recognition of the sacred in the "here and now and little things." When the
narrator and the guest, who is now referred to as "the leader," stop at a con-
venience store to buy gas and soda, the guest "drums and is silent. He is going into the drum, going into the center" (38).

When they arrive at the ceremonial site, they begin to place rugs over
the skeletal structure of the sweat lodge, and they fasten prayer ties filled
with tobacco to the frame. When they are ready for the ceremony, everyone
moves inside, and the hot lava stones, which "remind [them] of earth's red
and fiery core, and of the spark inside all life" (39), have water poured over
them, filling the lodge with steam. The description of the stones in this passage recalls the conclusion of the "The Caves" with its reference to fire and
stone deep inside Earth. Hogan then explains the importance of ceremony:

> In a sweat lodge ceremony, the entire world is brought inside the en-
> closure. The soft odor of smoking cedar accompanies this arrival.
> It is all called in. The animals come from the warm and sunny dis-
> tances. Water from dark lakes is there. Wind. Young, lithe willow
> branches bent overhead remember their lives rooted in ground, the
> sun their leaves took in. They remember that minerals and water
> rose up their trunks, and birds nested in their leaves, and that plan-
> ets turned above their brief, slender lives. The thunderclouds travel
> in from far regions of earth. Wind arrives from the four directions. It
> has moved through caves and breathed through our bodies. It is the
> same air elk have inhaled, air that passed through the lungs of a griz-
> zly bear. The sky is there, with all the stars whose lights we see long
> after the stars themselves have gone back to nothing. It is a place
> grown intense and holy. It is a place of immense community and of
> humbled solitude; we sit together in our aloneness and speak, one at
> a time, our deepest language of need, hope, loss, and survival. We
> remember that all things are connected. (39–40)

The ceremony reconnects all the elements of the natural world—animals,
water, wind, thunderclouds, sky, stars—and opens a space for remembering the right place of individual lives that are dependent on other lives: the
willow that remembers the sun and minerals and water that gave it life, the
birds and planets that participated in its growth, or the wind that has moved

through caves and the bodies of elk and grizzly and human. In ceremony, all
other lives and all aspects of the natural world reconnect in a community of
reciprocity and interrelatedness that is described as a sudden confluence of
interiority and exteriority. David Abram suggests that before the scientific
revolution, we perceived the world as a vast interior enfolding humans as
participants in a matrix that melded the interior and exterior landscapes.[18]
The sweat lodge ceremony returns us to this place, where we do not recognize our differentiation, before emergence. Everything joins together as
one at the same time that each individual remembers her or his rightful and
humble place in the larger order so that our individuation does not lead to
isolation or separation.

Hogan continues, in another long passage, explaining the way in which
ceremony brings forth a new way of being and thinking that is necessary for
healing:

> Remembering this [that all things are connected] is the purpose of
> the ceremony. It is part of a healing and restoration. It is the mend-
> ing of a broken connection between us and the rest. The partic-
> ipants in a ceremony say the words "All my relations" before and
> after we pray; those words create a relationship with other people,
> with animals, with the land. To have health it is necessary to keep all
> these relations in mind. The intention of a ceremony is to put a per-
> son back together by restructuring the human mind. This reorgani-
> zation is accomplished by a kind of inner map, a geography of the
> human spirit and the rest of the world. We make whole our broken-
> off pieces of self and world. Within ourselves, we bring together the
> fragments of our lives in a sacred act of renewal, and we reestablish
> our connections with others. The ceremony is a point of return. It
> takes us toward the place of balance, our place in the community of
> all things. It is an event that sets us back upright. (40)

Again, the healing ceremony is centrally about remembering a broken contract between humans and the land. In order for humans to be restored to
a state of health, to overcome the destitution of our time, we must remember that the foundation of our lives is in relationship with the other rather
than in the act of objectifying the other. To remember this is to be restored
to our essence, to have our minds restructured such that we experience the
world no longer through binary oppositions but rather through reciprocity

and interdependence and such that the world becomes a happening, an event for us. Ceremony reestablishes an ecology of the physical and spiritual through the restoration within the individual of an ancient way of being in the world. Hogan continues: "But it is not a finished thing. The real ceremony begins where the formal one ends, when we take up a new way, our minds and hearts filled with the vision of earth that holds us within it, in compassionate relationship to and with our world" (40–41). Hogan thus concludes that care and compassion are at the heart of this ancient knowledge, one that restores us to our rightful place.

The first three essays of *Dwellings* introduce the key image of "home" and "dwelling" in their movement from the narrator's built home in "The Feathers" to her earthen home in "The Caves." This movement is part of the journey from the physical to the spiritual, the rational to the mythical, and thus from illness to health. "All My Relations" emphasizes this same movement yet at the same time restructures the image of home. The narrator says: "We speak. We sing. We swallow water and breathe smoke. By the end of the ceremony, it is as if skin contains land and birds. The places within us have become filled. As inside the enclosure of the lodge, the animals and ancestors move into the human body, into skin and blood. The land merges with us. The stones come to dwell inside the person" (41). The human body becomes the dwelling place of animals and ancestors, of the land, of the lava stones that represent the source of creation. The two landscapes, then, that of our interior and that of our exterior, merge and become one. As we are placed differently on the land and remember our entwinement with the other, we become replaced; that is, when we remember an ancient wisdom of interdependence, we become new beings who learn to dwell, recognizing that just as we are in the world, the world is in us. Hogan continues: "Gold rolling hills take up residence, their tall grasses blowing. The red light of canyons is there. The black skies of night that wheel above our heads come to live inside the skull. We who easily grow apart from the world are returned to the great store of life all around us, and there is the deepest sense of being at home here in this intimate kinship. There is no real aloneness. There is solitude and the nurturing silence that is relationship with ourselves, but even then we are part of something larger" (41). The ceremony that reignites our spirits through restoring to us an ancient way of being ultimately brings us home to ourselves and to the larger community of life that sustains us.

In connecting the enactment of ceremony to the image of dwelling, the title image of the collection as a whole, Hogan suggests even more clearly the role of the essays in the book as part of a process that elicits a new way of being and thinking that reminds us of the intimate interrelatedness of all things and restores us to our rightful place in the universe. The ceremony revealed in "All My Relations" provides more than simply an intellectual understanding of this new way of being; rather, it restructures and rearranges our very bodies, our very being. Annie Booth and Harvey Jacobs have remarked that "rituals such as those used for healing are not designed to ward off illness or directly cure the ill person. Rather, they are designed to remind the ill person of a frame of mind which is in proper relationship with the rest of the world, a frame of mind which is essential to the maintenance of good health."[19] Through the telling of the stories collected in *Dwellings* and through the reading of these stories, narrator and reader are realigned and restored to our home, to our rightful place in the larger cosmos, and we remember how to dwell, how to unite the fourfold of Earth and sky, divinities and mortals into a onefold. And in so doing, we become the beings who provide the clearing for the presencing of things in their own right.

As the narrator notes at the end of "All My Relations," the formal ceremony "is not a finished thing" but rather the beginning, where "we take up a new way, our minds and hearts filled with the vision of earth that holds us within it, in compassionate relationship to and with our world" (40–41). The remaining essays in *Dwellings* build on the formal ceremony enacted in "All My Relations" to firmly establish this new way of being and thinking. As in the first three essays, those that follow "All My Relations" describe an arc that moves from awareness of the disharmony and imbalance in our lives, the destitution of our time, to engaging Earth and the cosmos in a reciprocal and participatory relation, one that recognizes the difficult and complex transactions with the other and manifests the spiritual in the real. Similar to the beginning of "All My Relations," where the narrator must tell the story of her illness as the first part of the healing ceremony, the essays immediately following "All My Relations," including "What Holds the Water, What Holds the Light," "A Different Yield," and "Deify the Wolf," provide a critique of our culture, our way of being and knowing, and call for a new way based on listening. The telling that occurs in these essays is the first step in reconnecting the narrator and the audience with the wisdom of the ancient world. Significantly, the last essay highlights the important role of animals, who provide humans with guidance in this process of remembering, like the bats in the opening triad of essays and the birds in Williams's *Refuge*.

Hogan opens the essay "What Holds the Water, What Holds the Light" with a description of a walk she takes with a friend after a rain. The two stop "to drink fresh rain collected in a hollow bowl that had been worn into stone over slow centuries" (42). She then comments on the generosity of Earth and the relationship between humans and the world around them: "Drinking the water, I thought how earth and sky are generous with their gifts, and how good it is to receive them. Most of us are taught, somehow, about giving and accepting human gifts, but not about opening ourselves and our bodies to welcome the sun, the land, the visions of sky and dreaming, not about standing in the rain ecstatic with what is offered" (43). Hogan here asserts that the proper relation between humans and the world around them is one of appreciation and thankfulness, a recognition that Earth is a gift that we should receive with enthusiasm and ecstasy. Such a recognition is the beginning of a restorative and healing process, for we must learn to acknowledge that what we have been given may not be deserved, that it may and often does exceed what we can repay. As William Jordan observes in *The Sunflower Forest*, recognizing that our interaction with the world around is an "exchange of gifts" is central to a participatory and engaged interaction with that world.[20] Jordan suggests that the exchange of gifts is "intrinsically ritualistic . . . an intimate encounter with the shame of difference and of dependence, one of many experiences that dramatize the distance between souls."[21] The consideration of the world around us as a gift, then, places us differently on the land such that we become aware of the otherness of the other and open ourselves to our entwinement with that otherness.

Yet Hogan suggests that our way of being in the present time ignores the need for reciprocal participation. Hogan describes several incidents in which humans desecrated the land and natives to the land, including Cortés' burning of Iztapalapa with its incredible aviaries and looters' desecration of the Spiro burial mounds in Oklahoma. She then comments: "It seems, looking back, that these invasions amounted to a hatred of life itself, of fertility and generation. The conquerors and looters refused to participate in a reciprocal and balanced exchange with life. They were unable to receive the best gifts of land, not gold or pearls or ownership, but a welcome acceptance of what is offered. They did not understand that the earth is generous and that encounters with the land might have been sustaining, or that

their meetings with other humans could have led to an enriched confluence of ways" (44). She concludes this long passage with her critique of our
culture: "These actions, all of them, must be what Bushman people mean
when they say a person is far-hearted. This far-hearted kind of thinking is
one we are especially prone to now, with our lives moving so quickly ahead,
and it is one that sees life, other lives, as containers for our own uses and not
as containers in a greater, holier sense" (45). According to Hogan, the far-
heartedness of our culture, the inability to participate in an ecology of being that recognizes interdependence and interrelatedness, has separated us
from the holy and the sacred. Rather than engaging the world around us
with humility, with the recognition that all lives participate equally in the sacred, we perceive the world and others as means to an end, as the "standing-
reserve" with its consideration of all beings as resource objects for our use.

After offering this critique, Hogan emphasizes the role of language, of
storytelling and ceremony, in the creation of our way of being and thinking.
In a long passage that begins to suggest a pathway out of our ailing state,
Hogan again connects storytelling with ceremony:

> As one of our Indian elders has said, there are laws beyond our hu-
> man laws, and ways above ours. We have no words for this in our
> language, or even for our experience of being there. Ours is a lan-
> guage of commerce and trade, of laws that can be bent in order that
> treaties might be broken, land wounded beyond healing. It is a lan-
> guage that is limited, emotionally and spiritually, as if it can't accom-
> modate such magical strength and power. The ears of this language
> do not often hear the songs of the white egrets, the rain falling into
> stone bowls. So we make our own songs to contain these things,
> make ceremonies and poems, searching for a new way to speak, to
> say we want a new way to live in the world, to say that wilderness
> and water, blue herons and orange newts are invaluable not just to
> us, but in themselves, in the workings of the natural world that rules
> us whether we acknowledge it or not. (45–46)

The language of our contemporary culture is founded on ownership, domination, and control, and as such, it fails to capture the true magical nature
of language. Significantly, this language is not reciprocal or participatory, for
it lacks ears to connect with the audience. In Okanagan terms, our speaking
is not land-language speaking but is rather human-willed domination of the

other. Such a speaking does not give voice to Earth, for it does not participate in the stillness of the land, and the end result is a sundering of the contract between humans and the land. In response, Hogan asserts the need to
create a new language founded on emotion and the spirit that offers a new
way of living in the world, one that acknowledges the greater force of nature that holds us. Such a language, Hogan insists, has magical power that
unfolds the true nature of reality and our place in the natural world.

The essay concludes with a return to the opening frame, which describes a Mexican water jar that friends had filled for her during her stay
with them. She describes the jar as connecting worlds, just as the bats in the
second essay brought together Earth and the heavens, the physical and the
spiritual. She says that the water jar

> was not only a bridge between the elements of earth, air, water, and
> fire but was also a bridge between people, a reservoir of love and
> friendship, the kind of care we need to offer back every day to the
> world as we begin to learn the land and its creatures, to know the
> world is the container for our lives, sometimes wild and untouched,
> sometimes moved by a caretaker's hands. Until we learn this, and
> learn our place at the bountiful table, how to be a guest here, this
> land will not support us, will not be hospitable, will turn on us.
>
> That water jar was a reminder of how water and earth love each
> other the way they do, meeting at night, at the shore, being friends
> together, dissolving in each other, in the give and take that is where
> grace comes from. (46)

Significantly, Hogan again insists that a reciprocity exists between humans
and the land, that we must recognize the way in which the land holds us and
cares for us and through this recognition we will come to care for the land.
Yet our way of being is one that denies us access to the true gifts of the land,
to a meeting of humans and animals and plants that would allow for reciprocity and humble participation. We have become closed to the gifts offered us because of our desire to loot and possess and destroy. Hogan suggests an alternative way of being, founded on care and the give-and-take of
water and shore that leads to grace.

While "A Different Yield" continues to offer a critique of our culture
and thus makes the reader aware of the lack of harmony and balance in
our lives, this next essay more fully unfolds an alternative way of being and

knowing, one founded on listening. Hogan opens the essay with a personal
story: "A woman once described a friend of hers as being such a keen listener that even the trees leaned toward her, as if they were speaking their
innermost secrets into her listening ears. Over the years I've envisioned that
woman's silence, a hearing full and open enough that the world told her its
stories. The green leaves turned toward her, whispering tales of soft breezes
and the murmurs of leaf against leaf" (47). A resounding contrast is set up
between the woman as listener and the despoilers of the land described in
"What Holds the Water, What Holds the Light," whose limited language
does not hear the voice of Earth. Through a willingness to stay her own
voice, the listener creates a space where the world's stories can be told—
where things can presence in their ownness. Hogan describes the work of
Barbara McClintock, who received the Nobel Prize for her work on corn;
Hogan notes that "her method was to listen to what corn had to say, to
translate what the plants spoke into a human tongue" (48). She also describes the work of artists such as Everald Brown and Paul Klee who "return to the origins of things and their meanings, to the secret places where
original law fosters all evolution, to the organic center of all movement in
time and space, which is the mind or heart of creation" (50). Finally, Hogan
observes: "In American Indian traditions, healers are often called interpret-
ers because they are the ones who are able to hear the world and pass its
wisdom along. They are the ones who return to the heart of creation" (50).
Jennifer Love concludes that the "ability to hear and communicate nature's
sounds is for Hogan one way to heal the Western-inscribed alienation between humans and nonhuman nature."[22] But more than that, scientists like
McClintock, artists like Brown and Klee, and Native American healers communicate an ancient wisdom of Earth and elders that returns us to our origins, to our place in the grand order of the universe.

  As a result of their willingness to listen with humility and patience,
these scientists and artists have access to a language that originates from
Earth and heals the rift that occurred when humans relegated truth or reality to what occurs inside our minds, which also led to a separation between
land and language. Hogan describes a "mythic time" when "there was no
abyss between the word and the thing it named," a time that ended when
humans "acquired consciousness" of themselves and "broke away from the
natural world" only to make themselves "another world inside" (51–52). The
end result is that "this broken connection appears not only in language and

myth but it also appears in our philosophies of life. There is a separation that has taken place between us and nature. Something has broken deep in the core of ourselves" (52). How we relate to the world—through objectifying it and thus, ultimately, willingly destroying it—leads to our own fragmentation. She concludes: "In a time of such destruction, our lives depend on this listening. It may be that the earth speaks its symptoms to us" (52). A language exists around us, waiting to be heard, speaking to us of the ailment of Earth. Hogan tells us that the "voices of the world infuse our every act, as much as does our own ancestral DNA. They give us back ourselves, point a direction for salvation. Sometimes they even shake us down to the bedrock of our own human lives" (52–53). The problem, of course, is that we have forgotten how to listen to these voices.

Like Heidegger, Hogan is very interested in the role of language in our relation to Earth. She describes language experiments conducted on chimpanzees in the 1970s, which, she concludes, were significant less for what they taught us about the animals and more for what they revealed "about human beings and our relationships with other creatures" (53). While the scientists debated the nature of the chimpanzees' language and intelligence evinced in these experiments, she suggests that their arguments obscured "the real issue, that of how we treat other living beings" (53). She continues: "The questions raised throughout this project were primarily questions about ourselves, our own morality, our way of being in the world, and our responsibility for the caretaking of the earth" (54). What Hogan insists here is that our actions in the world should allow us to reflect on how we are placed on Earth. These experiments reveal an emplacement that objectifies the other, that separates humanity from the rest of the living world. Upon reflection, we should come to recognize that our placedness, which allows us to hover above Earth, as it were, as rulers and lords of Earth and all its creatures, does not honor our responsibility either to those other creatures or to ourselves, for when we refuse to act with care we become fragmented, isolated, and diminished. She notes that these experiments are a kind of "intellectual emergency" and then expands our understanding of emergency: "For this is not merely a crisis of the mind, but it is a potential act of emergence, of liberation for not only the animals of earth, but for our own selves, a freedom that could very well free us of stifling perceptions that have bound us tight and denied us the parts of ourselves that were not objective or otherwise scientifically respectable" (54). Having returned us to our origins in earlier essays, Hogan now prepares us for a new emergence, one that will be founded not on the logic of reason but rather on the logic of intuition and emotion, on sacred reason. More importantly, recalling the necessary understanding of interdependence and reciprocity in the act of emerging in Native American cultures, this new emergence will structure our way of knowing and being in the world.

Hogan first suggests that the significance in the language experiments lies in what it tells us about ourselves; she then returns to the role of language itself and "its power" (57). She notes that language "is the most highly regarded human ability"; it "determines social and class order" and helps us know "what lies beneath the surface of one another" (57). She acknowledges that communication goes deeper than "our somewhat limited human spoken languages," as we often communicate "via gesture, stance, facial expression, scent," a way of communicating that "is more honest, more comprehensible, than the words we utter" (57). Indeed, she suggests, the inner core of our beings gives rise to a "speechlessness" that we try to express through poetry, painting, and music (57). She then concludes, most importantly, that "there is even more a deep-moving underground language in us. Its currents pass between us and the rest of nature. It is the inner language that Barbara McClintock tapped for her research" (57). Significantly, Hogan moves through the noise that humans make in their speech acts into their silence, into the place where we communicate our emotions and intuitions, the alternative logic of sacred reason. From there she goes deeper, suggesting that humans have access to yet another language, the inner language of the natural world, the voice of Earth. Yet by moving through and away from our own speech acts into silence, she implies that this language of Earth is a matter of, to use Heidegger's term, co-responding, of humans listening to the stillness of the land and allowing land-language to speak in Okanagan terms. When we open ourselves to the external landscape through an attitude of care and an awareness of the interdependence of humans with the land, we learn to dwell, and in dwelling our internal landscape is refashioned and we are re/placed.

Hogan follows up this point about language by reminding us that we have become guided by "distorted values" and "abstract concepts" that in turn create a loss of clarity about how we should act in the world (58). And the end result is, as Hogan has noted, an objectification of the world that causes a separation between humans and the land and all the life that it

holds. She then returns to the role of language: "What we really are searching for is a language that heals this relationship, one that takes the side of
the amazing and fragile life on our life-giving earth. A language that knows
the corn, and the one that corn knows, a language that takes hold of the
mystery of what's around us and offers it back to us, full of awe and wonder. It is a language of creation, of divine fire, a language that goes beyond
the strict borders of scientific inquiry and right into the heart of the mystery itself" (59).

The voice of Earth, according to Hogan, in contrast to that of commerce and trade, heals our relationship with the natural world. It is a voice
originating from the creative forces of the universe, the "divine fire" at the
"heart of the mystery itself." When we still our minds and quiet our voices,
we open ourselves to this other voice, to another language that returns us
to ourselves, that places us on Earth in such a way that we remember how
to dwell. She explains the relation between this language and humans: "We
are looking for a tongue that speaks with reverence for life, searching for
an ecology of mind. Without it, we have no home, have no place of our
own within the creation. It is not only the vocabulary of science we desire.
We want a language of that different yield. A yield rich as the harvests of
earth, a yield that returns us to our own sacredness, to a self-love and respect that will carry out to others" (60). The language of Earth restructures
our way of thinking, opening to us the intricate interrelatedness and interdependence of all things and thereby showing us our "home." We become
re/placed, remembering that the right attitude of humans within creation
is one of reverence, of self-love, of a respect that participates in the recognition of the sacredness of all creation. She concludes this essay: "Do you
remember the friend that the leaves talked to? We need to be that friend.
Listen. The ears of the corn are singing. They are telling their stories and
singing their songs" (62).

Hogan suggests that the remedy to our way of being and thinking is
to recognize the unhealthy relation we have with creation and to learn to
listen to Earth. More specifically, Hogan, like Williams in *Refuge*, suggests
that animals can act as guides in our journey toward wholeness. In "Deify
the Wolf," the next essay in the collection, she notes that "anyone who has
heard the howl of wolves breaking through a northern night will tell you
that a part of them still remembers the language of that old song. It stirs inside the body, taking us down from our world of logic, down to the deeper

lost regions of ourselves into a memory so ancient we have lost the name for it" (64). The language of wolves allows us access to an ancient wisdom that we can no longer speak, to a place apart from reason and logic that resides deep within. She explains why she has come to this place with several others in search of wolves: "[We want to hear] them wail the song our ancestors knew the words to. We are looking for the clue to a mystery, a relative inside our own blood, an animal so equal to us that it reflects back what we hate and love about ourselves" (65). The wolves, then, offer a pathway back to the wisdom of our elders, to mystery, and to a more complete understanding of our own natures. When the visitors encounter a dead wolf, several of them take pictures with the wolf in various disrespectful poses. Hogan concludes: "I've worked with death and I respect it, so it is hard to understand these human beings, let alone come close to knowing the inner terrain of the wolf. I believe people fear their own deaths, so they must belittle it. There are lessons to be learned in our behavior" (73). As in Terry Tempest Williams's *Refuge*, our unwillingness to engage mortality becomes an impediment to our ability to connect authentically with the other. Yet we must learn to accept our own finite lives as one element in the fourfold if we are to dwell and thus to inhabit a place where the fourfold becomes a onefold. Because Hogan has worked with and come to respect death, she speaks from this place of honoring our limitations.

The essay "Deify the Wolf" concludes with another reflection on language, on the need to quiet the human voice in order to listen to the other and the way in which this listening and co-responding is akin to a ceremony. She says: "We are walking the road near the dump. We are quiet. I'm thinking of how the elaborate ritual of one wolf greeting another is called a ceremony. It's ceremony we want a share of. We are walking here to speak with the wolves. That's what we want. We want to reach out to them, to tell them we are here. We want them to answer, acknowledge us, maybe even to like us. We think they will see our souls" (75). The next several paragraphs depict the voice of the universe that continually offers itself to humans; the sky that shimmers; the northern lights that dance like ghosts; the trees, lakes, and islands that are magic; the deep rock beneath that tugs at us. She then returns to the wolves: "We walk up the road. None of us speak. Then there is the howl. It is soft and long. Even the loose skin of the trees holds still. Everything listens. There is another slow, rising howl. It is a man. It's a man speaking. In a language he only pretends to know, he calls out to the wolves" (76). Rather than remain silent, rather than listen and open himself to the voice of Earth, the man rushes in to fill the silence in an act of pretense. She continues: "We wait. We are waiting for the wolves to answer. We want a healing, I think, a cure for the anguish, a remedy that will heal the wound between us and the world that contains our broken histories. If we could only hear them, the stars themselves are howling, but there is just the man's voice, crying out, lonely" (76). We can't hear the stars or the sky or the rocks because of our own insistent voices that we cling to as a result of our isolation and our loneliness. The divide that we have created, that we so desperately want and need to heal, perpetuates itself in our technological and scientific approach to Earth, in our relegation of all beings to the status of mere objects for our use.

The next several essays, including "Creations," "Stories of Water," and "The Kill Hole," follow a similar pattern of first critiquing our way of being and knowing and then offering an alternative, one that enacts an "ecology of mind." "Creations" describes in elaborate detail the Mayan creation story, emphasizing the role of language and storytelling. After recounting the origin story, Hogan explains that "inside people who grow out of any land there is an understanding of it, a remembering all the way back to origins, to when the gods first shaped humans out of clay, back to when animals could speak with people, to when the sky and water were without form and all was shaped by such words as *Let there be*" (80). She continues: "In nearly all creation accounts, as with the Maya, life was called into being through language, thought, dreaming, or singing, acts of interior consciousness" (80–81). The confluence of the interior and the exterior in the act of creation provides the foundation for our deep remembering in the current time, a remembering that will return us to our origins, to a place where "it was all sacred" (81). The role of the first humans, who were made of mud, is "to offer prayer, tell stories, and remember the passage of time" (81). But these beings did not endure, so in the next creation, humans were "lovingly carved of wood" (81). In time, these people "forgot to give praise to the gods and to nurture the land. They were hollow and without compassion. They transformed the world to fit their own needs. They did not honor the sacred forms of life on earth, and they began to destroy the land, to create their own dead future out of human arrogance and greed. Because of this, the world turned against them," and they perished (81). In the third and final incarnation, the people are made of corn, the same substance as the gods. They are "care-taking, life-giving people" who see what gods see (82). "In order to make them more human, less godlike, some of this vision was taken away so there might be mystery, and the mystery of creation and of death inspired deep respect and awe for all of creation" (82). Each of the three phases of human creation "speaks against human estrangement from land" (82), reminding us that our limitations should inspire awe and wonder at the world around us and lead us to an attitude of care and compassion. Rather than using the land for our own selfish needs and taking an arrogant attitude toward the land, we should remember that we are of the land and the land is of us.

Hogan then turns from recounting the Mayan origin story to connecting that story to our own plight in this destitute time. She states: "Emptiness and estrangement are deep wounds, strongly felt in the present time. We have been split from what we could nurture, what could fill us. And we have been wounded by a dominating culture that has feared and hated the natural world, has not listened to the voice of the land, has not believed in the inner worlds of human dreaming and intuition, all things that have guided indigenous people since time stood up in the east and walked this world into existence, split from the connection between self and land" (82). She notes that while we are alienated from the forces that could sustain us, we have a deep memory of this connectedness. She explains that like the "wooden people" in the Mayan creation story,

> many of us in this time have lost the inner substance of our lives and have forgotten to give praise and remember the sacredness of all life. But in spite of this forgetting, there is still a part of us that is deep and intimate with the world. We remember it by feel. We experience it as a murmur in the night, a longing and restlessness we can't name, a yearning that tugs at us. For it is only recently, in earth time, that the severing of the connections between people and land have taken place. Something in our human blood is still searching for it, still listening, still remembering. (83)

Our biological and evolutionary history has formed a deep connection between us and the natural world, and only recently has this intimacy been severed. Yet we remember this ancient connection and even experience it in those moments when we silence the voice of commerce and hypermaterialism and listen quietly to the other. We long, she explains, "to be whole and connected with the earth" and with "our ancestors," whom we remember "deep in our bodily cells" (83). She continues: "We desire to see the world intact, to step outside our emptiness and remember the strong currents that pass between humans and the rest of nature, currents that are the felt voice of land, heard in the cells of the body" (84).

Hogan explains that her journey into the Mayan culture is an attempt to reconnect with her own origins and thus to heal the rift between humans and the land. She notes the indigenous belief in circular time, in time turning back on itself in order to offer renewal and redemption. If we are to foster this return to our beginnings, Hogan suggests that "we need new stories, new terms and conditions that are relevant to the love of land, a new narrative that would imagine another way, to learn the infinite mystery and movement at work in the world" (94). I would suggest that this collection, like Ray's *Ecology of a Cracker Childhood* and Williams's *Refuge*, offers such a story that assists us in remembering to "give praise and nurture creation" (94). She concludes: "We come from the land, sky, from love and the body. From matter and creation. We are, life is, an equation we cannot form or shape, a mystery we can't trace in spite of our attempts to follow it back to its origin" (95–96). Hogan's repeated emphasis on the paramount importance of mystery reminds us that we can't know everything, that despite the advances in our sciences we can't ever know the ultimate origins of the universe from whence everything comes: "We do not know the secrets of stars. We do not know the true history of water. We do not know ourselves. We have forgotten that this land and every life-form is a piece of god, a divine community, with the same forces of creation in plants as in people. All the lives around us are lives of gods" (96). Yet without true reverence for the surrounding world, "there is an absence of holiness, of any God" (96). In Heidegger's terms, the divine has fled the world, and even worse, we have completely lost the trace of the holy.

The concept of circularity, of constant renewal and rebirthing, is then emphasized in the next essay, "Stories of Water." Hogan notes that the sea is a "primal magnet" that allows us to encounter "mystery and wilderness, a pull toward healing, toward a baptism in the enormous world of life" (104). She describes the journey of water itself as one of "circular infinity, of a planet birthing itself" (106). But this journey is being interrupted especially through the deforestation of the rainforests, "the place our air is born" (107). She continues: "We are only dreamers in such abundance as could feed our hungry world. Its soil is the living tissue of our earth. It is living membrane, these rain forests carried across the globe in the shape of toothpicks and fatted cattle that will feed sharp-toothed world-eaters who have never known such richness, such fertility" (107). She concludes: "The journey of water is round, and its loss, too, moves in a circle, following us around the world as we lose something of such immense value that we do not yet even know its name" (107–8). Hogan's emphasis on circularity offers the foundation for a new way of thinking, one counter to the linear and analytical worldview that we inhabit now. In remembering the interconnectedness of all things, we remember our origins and find our place, once again, amid mystery and holiness.

The essay concludes lyrically, embodying the circular nature of the universe by chanting the cycles of water into being. Hogan tells us: "Outside it is thawing. The creek is breaking apart. Water seeps out of the rock canyon above me. It has been around the world. It has lived beneath the lights of fireflies in bayous at night when mist laid itself about cypress trunks. It has held sea turtles in its rocking arms. It has been the Nile River, which at this moment is the smallest it has been in all recorded history. It has come from the rain forest that gave birth to our air. It brings with it the stories of where it's been" (108). Rhetorically, this passage, with its constant reference to water as a thing that presences amid fireflies, sea turtles, and the rain forest, acts as a kind of ceremony, a story of both origins and the journey of this life-giving element. She continues: "It reminds us that we are water people. Our salt bodies, like the great round of ocean, are pulled and held by the moon. We are creatures that belong here. This world is in our blood and bones, and our blood and bones are the earth" (108). Hogan shifts here from the "it" of the water to our "salt bodies" to the "world" that our bodies come from, enacting the very circularity that she discusses. She concludes the essay with the water breaking forth and flowing: "Out from bare rock the water flows, from times before our time. The clouds flying overhead are rivers. Thunder breaks open, and those rivers fall, like a sprinkling of baptismal water, giving itself back, everything a round river, in a circle, alive and moving" (108). The ceremony that reminds us that we are of the land and the land is of us heals the wound separating us and allows the landscape to return to its natural and healthy state, to its radiant and holy divinity.

Finally, "The Kill Hole" returns to the significance of animals in offering us guidance in finding our rightful place in the world. Early in the essay, she describes the discovery of Ishi, "the last Yana Indian," in 1911 (110). After his discovery, Ishi lived "in a museum as a living exhibit" only to die, four years later, from tuberculosis (110–11). Hogan tells us that the story of Ishi "illuminates the world of civilization and its flaws. It tells us what kind of people we are, with our double natures. It speaks of loss and of emptiness that will never again be filled, of whole cultures disappeared, of species made extinct, all of these losses falling as if through a hole, like a spirit leaving earth's broken clay" (111). The story of Ishi speaks of our loss of the wisdom of elders, a central component in our ability to remember something deeper, back to our origins. She concludes that this story gives "us reason to ask what is our rightful place within the circle of life, we beautiful ones who are as adept at creation as we are at destruction?" (111). She then describes the language experiments that were conducted with apes and created "a dialogue that bridged the species barrier" (111). This dialogue opened our awareness to the emotional lives of apes and precipitated "an identity crisis equal to that in Galileo's time when the fabric of belief was split wide open to reveal that Earth was not the center of the universe. This event bespeaks our responsibility to treat with care and tenderness all the other lives that share our small world" (112). Hogan points out that rather than narrow the gap that we have created with other beings, these experiments led some to proffer new distinctions that would allow us to maintain our distance.

Hogan reminds us, again, that we are a part of the natural world surrounding us, not distinct, not separate. She says: "We are of the animal world. We are part of the cycles of growth and decay. Even having tried so hard to see ourselves apart, and so often without a love for even our own biology, we are in relationship with the rest of the planet, and that connectedness tells us we must reconsider the way we see ourselves and the rest of nature" (114–15). She continues: "A change is required of us, a healing of the betrayed trust between humans and earth. Caretaking is the utmost spiritual and physical responsibility of our time, and perhaps that stewardship is finally our place in the web of life, our work, the solution to the mystery of what we are. There are already so many holes in the universe that will never again be filled, and each of them forces us to question why we permitted such loss, such tearing away at the fabric of life, and how we will live with our planet in the future" (115). Hogan asserts that the foundation of our new way of being and thinking must rest on the concept of caretaking, an idea that she has advanced in interviews: "If you believe that the earth, and all living things, and all the stones are sacred, your responsibility really is to protect those things. I do believe that's our duty, to be custodians of the planet."[23] By becoming good stewards of Earth—of plants and animals and rocks—we can find our rightful place, our home, and learn to dwell, to participate in the mystery of creation. Caretaking allows us to be placed differently and in so doing to be replaced, to become new beings whose work it is to repair the holes we have created, an act of ecological restoration. She concludes the essay: "A mending is taking place, a life emerging like the thread out of the labyrinth, the thread leading out of a Navajo rug's pattern of loss. The old woman in the sky is looking down on us, keeping watch" (116).

Significantly, the next essay, "Dwellings," the title essay of the collection, is paired with the one that follows it, "The Voyagers," to expand again the meaning of the image of home. Hogan often uses the image of the home as a way of critiquing and renewing our way of thinking and being in the world.[24] "Dwellings" opens with a description of an exposed hillside where bees have built their home in the raw earth. Through their collective memory, the bees know how to do their work of building a home and finding pollen. The narrator notes: "Sitting in the hot sun, watching the small bees fly in and out around the hill, hearing the summer birds, the light breeze, I felt right in the world. I belonged there. I thought of my own dwelling places, those real and those imagined" (118–19). Home and dwelling become attached to an authentic way of being in the world, one connecting us to our landscape and our rightful place in the world. Hogan describes a wide variety of dwellings, all in harmony with Earth, before describing one, a cave where a man brings his bride, that the couple alters in such a way that they violate the inner workings of Earth. Hogan concludes: "In other days and places, people paid more attention to the strong-headed will of earth. Once homes were built of wood that had been felled from a single region in a forest. That way, it was thought, the house would hold together more harmoniously, and the family of walls would not fall or lend themselves to the unhappiness or arguments of the inhabitants" (120). Here Hogan captures the essence of dwelling, to be of a place in such a way that Earth is honored, and in that honoring harmony is created not only between humans and the natural world but also among humans.

In a long passage, Hogan describes finding two fetal mice that are being attacked by ants. Not wanting to see them in such pain, she rinses them off in a bucket of water, "trading one life for another" (122). She concludes: "Death and life feed each other. I know that" (122). Here Hogan acknowledges the way in which mortality lies at the heart of dwelling, how an acceptance of death is necessary for the fourfold to unite in a onefold, for culture and nature to become balanced. Hogan emphasizes this point when she describes a corn dance at Zia Pueblo. After the dance, the old pottery is shattered and left on the ground "to be smoothed back to earth" (123). But the tourists who are visiting pick up the pottery shards because they do not understand the importance of this ritual. Hogan explains: "The pieces of earth that were formed into bowls, even on their way home to dust, provide the new people a lifeline to an unknown land, help them remember that they live in the old nest of earth" (123). The pottery becomes a kind of umbilical cord, assisting in remembering a forgotten wisdom, that Earth cradles and nurtures us. She concludes the essay describing an abandoned bird's nest that includes a blue thread from one of her skirts and a black hair from her daughter: "I didn't know what kind of nest it was, or who had lived there. It didn't matter. I thought of the remnants of our lives carried up the hill that way and turned into shelter. That night, resting inside the walls of our home, the world outside weighed so heavily against the thin wood of the house. The sloped roof was the only thing between us and the universe. Everything outside of our wooden boundaries seemed so large. Filled with night's citizens, it all came alive. The world opened in the thickets of the dark" (124). Her reminiscence on the nest leads her to reflect on her own home and the wider home of the universe. Yet, as Melanie Bleck has observed, the concept of home does not include containment or separation for Hogan.[25] Although the narrator feels the dark universe pressing down on her home for a moment, the universe ultimately comes alive and opens itself to her. After remembering all the dwellings she has seen, she remarks: "The whole world was a nest on its humble tilt, in the maze of the universe, holding us" (124). This passage reminds the reader of the passage at the end of "The Caves" where the narrator and reader were held "in earth's hand" (35) and brings full circle the journey from sky in "The Feathers" into Earth and back into the heavens. Here we are reminded that if we dwell, if we remain connected to the forces that animate the universe, we will be protected and cared for.

"The Voyagers" concludes this journey as the barrier between house and universe is erased, allowing us to understand our rightful place in creation. The essay includes a reflection on our limitations as humans, our finitude and smallness.

> To dream of the universe is to know that we are small and brief as insects, born in a flash of rain and gone a moment later. We are delicate and our world is fragile. It was the transgression of Galileo to tell us that we were not the center of the universe, and now, even in our own time, the news of our small being here is treacherous enough that early in the space program, the photographs of Earth were classified as secret documents by the government. It was thought, and rightfully so, that the image of our small blue Earth would forever change how we see ourselves in context with the world we inhabit. (126–27)

Our lives are brief, a fact that should lead to a sense of humility and an attitude of care, yet in the Western world we do what we can to ignore this fact.

Seeing our blue planet from space offered an opportunity to change that, to remind us of our place in the wider and grander universe. Hogan quotes Steven Meyers, a photographer, who explains that "when we saw the deep blue and swirling white turbulence of our Earth reflected back to us, . . . we also saw 'the visual evidence of creative and destructive forces moving around its surface, we saw for the first time the deep blackness of that which surrounds it, we sensed directly, and probably for the first time, our incredibly profound isolation, and the special fact of our being here'" (127). Throughout *Dwellings*, Hogan has demonstrated the way in which birth and death, creation and destruction are part and parcel of our status as humans and our relation to the world. To accept mortality means to accept a circular notion of time rather than a linear notion and to accept divinity and the sacred as immanent rather than transcendent. She then describes the launching of the *Voyager* spacecrafts in the 1970s with messages from Earth that capture what we care about most as opposed to what we encounter on a daily basis. The contrast between what occurs in our daily lives and what was included on the spacecraft highlights our disconnection from an ancient harmony: "The broken link between us and the rest of our world grows too large, and the material of nightmares grows deeper while the promises for peace and equality are empty, are merely dreams without reality" (130). Our inability to honestly engage the content of our daily lives, to become aware of the double-order forgetting and the destitution of our times, in Heidegger's terms, means that we will continue down a path that fails to heal.

Hogan then steps back to reflect on a possible reason for the *Voyager* time capsule: our need to find another world before we destroy Earth, our home. She concludes: "We have come so far away from wisdom, a wisdom that is the heritage of all people, an old kind of knowing that respects a community of land, animals, plants, and other people as equal to ourselves. Where we know the meaning of relationship" (133). Yet despite the problems with the *Voyager* records, with what was included and what was left out, Hogan suggests that

> this innocent reaching out is a form of ceremony, as if the Voyager were a sacred space, a ritual enclosure that contains our dreaming the way a cathedral holds the bones of saints.
>
> The people of earth are reaching out. We are having a collective vision. Like young women and men on a vision quest, we seek a way to live out the peace of the vision we have sent to the world of stars. We want to live as if there is no other place, as if we will always be here. We want to live with devotion to the world of waters and the universe of life that dwells above our thin roofs. (134)

Expressing our need and indeed our desire to recapture peace and tranquility, "The Voyagers," like the other essays in *Dwellings* up to this point, enacts an important part in the journey toward healing and wholeness. As a ceremony, these essays formulate and make present a new way of being and thinking founded on a compassionate relation with Earth. Yet this essay, like "Dwellings" before it, takes this journey a step further, reminding the reader that just as Earth embraces us, the universe embraces Earth. The frame of the essay describes a night that the narrator spends "lying on the moist spring earth beside my mother" with "such black immensity" above her (125). She concludes the essay with a reflection on that night and her relation to her mother: "Her body I came from, but our common ancestor is the earth, and the ancestor of earth is space. That night we were small, my mother and I, and we were innocent. We were children of the universe. In the gas and dust of life, we are voyagers. Wait. Stop here a moment. Have you eaten? Come in. Eat" (134). In this way, Hogan returns to the ultimate origins, to the origins of the universe, our ancestor and elder. She invites the ancestor in for a moment to join them in a meal, demonstrating our need to remember that a greater wisdom exists beyond the little and innocent minds of humans, a wisdom that we must invite into our lives.

While these last two essays journey the narrator and the reader into the heavens, in the next three essays Hogan returns to the significant role of animals in our quest for healing and wholeness. In her essay "First People," Hogan describes what contemporary science has revealed to us about the intelligence of animals, an intelligence that reaches into the "the mystical and the miraculous." She concludes that all this research

> speaks about intelligences beyond ours, and as we learn this world, we are coming to realize how mighty and wise is the intelligence all around us, even beneath us. What we are now learning about animals returns us to a world so powerfully beyond our contemporary imaginations that we have almost missed it, even though such things have been contained in ancient stories, informed by animals themselves in a world of dynamic interchanges. We have been in the midst of the holy and amazing all along, the sacred, the lives and journeys of animals. There are ways of knowing and being in the world that have not been available to our own human intelligence, that have only recently entered our own perceptual maps, territories, and records. And together all the different intelligences equal a whole. This, I think, is the telling thing.[26]

Hogan emphasizes the role of animals in containing and offering a deeper wisdom than the knowledge and experience of the Western world. Dreese notes that Hogan's references to snakes and bats "strives to break down the human/nature dichotomy and heal the alienation between humans and the natural world."[27] Hogan describes the native belief that "the animals are our elders, our ancestors, our sisters. In many reaches of this Earth, they were the first people created";[28] thus animal stories become another way of returning us to our origins, the place of healing.

Significantly, Hogan concludes *Dwellings* with a series of essays emphasizing the importance of animals in our journey toward healing. "The Snake People," "Porcupine," and "Waking Up the Rake" complete the enactment of ceremony and bring into presence a new way of being founded on an ancient knowledge that the world around us is "holy and amazing," that we live in the midst of the "sacred." In the first essay, "The Snake People,"

Hogan describes the many encounters that she has had with snakes, which have created in her a love for them. She recounts a dream of a woman who merges with a snake and dances; after a short time, the music that the snake woman is dancing to stops, and she removes the snake from her being and places "it on a wall where it hung alive and beautiful, waiting for another ceremonial dance" (138). The snake woman then says "'All the people have pieces of its skin. If they save the pieces, it will remain alive. If everyone owns it, it will be preserved'" (138). Hogan then concludes: "At first I thought this dream was about Indian tradition, how if each person retains part of a history, an entire culture and lifeway remains intact and alive, one thing living through the other, as the snake and woman in the dream. But since that time, I've expanded my vision. Now, it seems that what needs to be saved, even in its broken pieces, is earth itself, the tradition of life, the beautiful blue-green world that lives in the coiling snake of the Milky Way" (138–39). Hogan's expanded vision reminds us of the previous essay, "The Voyagers," which describes Earth as nestled in the universe. Her vision insists that each of us holds within our care a piece of Earth and that saving Earth is a responsibility of all humans.

Hogan then counters the traditional Western view of snakes as "the dark god of our underworld, burdened with human sin" (140) with the indigenous view of snakes as "a being of holy inner earth," "the symbol of healing and wholeness" (140). She concludes that in more recent history, the snake has been connected to our overreaching knowledge, "our search and desire for the dangerous revelations of life's mystery. In only a short duration of time in earth's history, the power of that search, the drive toward knowledge, has brought ruin to our Eden. Knowledge without wisdom, compassion, or understanding has damned us as we have been stirring about in the origins of life, breaking apart the miniature worlds of atoms just to see where that breaking will take us" (141). Our way of thinking in the twentieth and twenty-first centuries, which has separated subject and object, creating a distance between the knower and the known such that we have lost our sense of care and compassion, has brought on the destitution of our times. Toward the end of the essay, she muses: "Perhaps Snake dwells at the zero of ourselves, takes us full circle in a return to the oldest knowledge, which says that the earth is alive. Our bodies, if not our minds, know that zero, that core, the constellation of life at our human beginnings, that same shape of the galaxy" (142). The snake, which returns us to our origins, allows access to an awareness of the aliveness of Earth and locates us in our rightful place. Dreese interprets the "spiraling circles" of the snakes as a representation of "the circular life philosophy of continuity, reciprocation, and holistic living."[29]

The following essay, "Porcupine," describes the narrator's honoring of the life and death of this creature and the way in which its death allows the porcupine and the narrator to participate in the circularity of the universe. She opens the essay describing the porcupine that she has seen lumbering on the edge of a dirt road for many years. One evening, she discovers the porcupine dead, "her inner light replaced by the light of sky" (145). She then states: "As for me, I have a choice between honoring that dark life I've seen so many years moving in the junipers, or of walking away and going on with my own human busyness. There is always that choice for humans" (145). She decides, of course, to honor it, reminding us that mortality is a necessary component in our own lives and in our transaction with the other. The next day, she discovers maggots eating the porcupine, maggots that then turn into beetles and fly away "in their first changing of life" (146). The porcupine, then, in its death, participates in the ongoing cycle of life: "In that crossing over, that swallowing, the battle of life with life, the porcupine lives on. It lives on in the buzzing of flies and the ants with their organized lives. In its transformation, life continues. My life too, which stopped only for a small moment in history, in the great turning over of the world" (146). This concluding passage insists that even in death, even in the eventual mortality of all beings, life surges forward, a transformation, indeed a mystery. And when we honor this fact, when we pause and pay attention to the "here and now and little things," the old lumbering porcupine, the fat white maggots, we participate in the grand revolving of Earth as it spins through the universe. In taking care and in acting with compassion, we find that we awake to a world filled with the divine and thus participate in the sacred.

The third animal essay, "Waking Up the Rake," brings the ceremonial journey into fruition as it most fully enacts the new way of being and thinking that is at the heart of *Dwellings*. In the essay, Hogan describes her work at the Birds of Prey Rehabilitation Foundation, where she regularly encounters death. Her experience of the turning over of life broadens her view of the world: "Over time, the narrow human perspective from which we view things expands. A deer carcass begins to look beautiful and rich in its torn redness, the muscle and bone exposed in the shape life took on for a while as it walked through meadows and drank at creeks" (149). By engaging the cycle of life and death and acknowledging and honoring mortality, we come to see the beauty in the bodies that act as a way of passing their energy on from the meadows and creeks to rich muscle to what next eats the carcass. She calls her work at the rehabilitation center an "apprenticeship, and the birds are the teachers" who ask us "to be still and slow and to move in time with their rhythms, not our own," who "require the full presence of a human" (150). Before entering into the presence of the birds, she must ready herself: "There is a silence needed here before a person enters the bordered world the birds inhabit, so we stop and compose ourselves before entering their doors, and we listen to the musical calls of the eagles, the sound of wings in air, the way their feet with sharp black claws, many larger than our own hands, grab hold of a perch. Then we know we are ready to enter, and they are ready for us" (150). The silence that Hogan embodies recalls Heidegger's insistence that humans must hear the stillness of the land for their voice to become a co-responding, to allow land-language to speak in Okanagan terms. She continues: "The most difficult task the birds demand is that we learn to be equal to them, to feel our way into an intelligence that is different from our own" (150). Such a state is difficult to achieve because "they know that we are apart from them, that as humans we have somehow fallen from our animal grace, and because of that we maintain a distance from them, though it is not always a distance of heart" (150). Having fallen from our true state as animals who dwell on Earth, we have become separated from all that gives life. She concludes: "We are the embodiment of a paradox; we are the wounders and we are the healers" (151). Such a description parallels William Jordan's depiction of ecological restoration, the way in which the act of restoring the land allows us to accept our role as the destroyers, with all the shame that comes with this role, and as the healers who offer a gift that in no way compensates for what we have taken. Yet if we offer this gift in a ceremonial act that brings attention and awareness to our paradoxical role, we find healing not just for the land but for ourselves.

Hogan captures this sense of our humble participation in a larger order as she continues to unfold the nature of her work at the rehabilitation center. She quotes Fritjof Capra, who writes: "'Doing work that has to be done over and over again helps us recognize the natural cycles of growth and decay, of birth and death, and thus become aware of the dynamic order of the universe'" (151). Our ready and continuous participation in the work of the hands and the heart, work that engages the difficult and therefore rich elements of our transaction with the other, places us differently on the land, for we come to see that a grand order guides all things. Hogan continues: "And it is true, in whatever we do, in the brushing of hair, the cleaning of cages, we begin to see the larger order of things. In this place, there is a constant coming to terms with both the sacred place life occupies, and with death" (151). Our emplacement, the connection we establish to the places we inhabit, allows us to understand and to honor the sacred nature of all things. She concludes, in a long passage: "I'm filled with awe at the very presence of life, not just the birds, but a horse contained in its living fur, a dog alive and running. What a marvel it is, the fine shape life takes in all of us. It is equally marvelous that life is quickly turned back to earth-colored ants and the soft white maggots that are time's best and closest companions. To sit with the eagles and their flutelike songs, listening to the longer flute of wind sweep through the lush grasslands, is to begin to know the natural laws that exist apart from our own written ones" (151). When we honor life, and when that honoring accepts the transitions and transformation of life even through death, we become filled with awe, we hear a larger voice than our own, the wind sweeping through the grasslands, and we then know that something grander exists than our own small lives, natural laws that connect all things in a dance of reciprocity, an act of reciprocal appropriation in the words of Momaday or expropriative appropriating in the words of Heidegger. One of these laws, Hogan observes, "which we carry deep inside us, is intuition" (151)—the alternative logic of the heart, different from the calculating reason that has caused a double-order forgetting and blinded us to the divinity and the sacredness in all things.

One of Hogan's primary responsibilities at the rehabilitation center is to rake the birds' cages. In the act of raking, Hogan finds and brings into being a new presence, a new manifestation of self that heals both self and Earth. She explains that

> The word *rake* means to gather or heap up, to smooth the broken ground. That's what this work is, all of it, the smoothing over of broken ground, the healing of the severed trust we humans hold with earth. We gather it back together again with great care, take

the broken pieces and fragments and return them to the sky. It is work at the borderland between species, at the boundary between injury and healing.

There is an art to raking, a very fine art, one with rhythm in it, and life. On the days I do it well, the rake wakes up. Wood that came from dark dense forests seems to return to life. That water that rose up through the rings of that wood, the minerals of earth mined upward by the burrowing tree roots, all come alive. My own fragile hand touches the wood, a hand full of my own life, including that which rose each morning early to watch the sun return from the other side of the planet. Over time, these hands will smooth the rake's wooden handle down to a sheen. (153)

The ceremony of healing moves toward completion as the broken pieces of our lives and of Earth are gathered together in a quiet act of reverence. In this ceremonial act, the mystery of the universe, the creative life force that dwells inside and unites every plant and animal and mineral, is revealed, and the mythical becomes the real. The wooden handle of the rake that is worn to a sheen represents more than the labor of the hands; it becomes the work of the spirit.

In describing the sacred tobacco pipe ceremony of the Plains Indian, Joseph Epes Brown notes that effective rituals, perhaps like that described in "Waking Up the Rake" and indeed enacted in the writing and reading of *Dwellings*, involve three cumulative states. The first, purification, is a necessary precursor to any type of healing because ceremony is an attempt to reconnect with the sacred, and only the pure can reunite with the sacred power. The second, expansion, allows the individual to move toward wholeness, for only a fully realized individual can connect with "absolute perfection and holiness." In this stage, the individual ceases "to be a part, an imperfect fragment," recognizing instead "what one really is so as to expand to include the Universe within oneself." In the final stage, "one's identity is grounded in a union with all that is."[30] This three-step process, as in other Native American ceremonies, provides the foundation for the creation of "a new identity," one in which the individual lives through mutual reciprocity and thus heals the "severed trust we humans hold with earth." The act of raking begins in humility and recognition of the brokenness of our way of being in the world, of our "far-hearted" nature, which then allows for an awareness of the interconnectedness of all things—of the forest, water, and minerals that eventually gave birth to the rake, the forest, water, and minerals that are then held by the hand—and thus for an expansion of the small self into the much grander universe. And in this purification and expansion a new being is born, one that remembers and lives the sacred trust between humans and all our relatives.

Ultimately, Hogan demonstrates in "Waking Up the Rake" that ceremony, in healing the rift between humans and Earth, re/places us within the sacred and the divine. As we reconnect with the ancient wisdom of our elders, we learn what is essential and what is real. Hogan continues:

> Raking. It is a labor round and complete, smooth and new as an egg, and the rounding seasons of the world revolving in time and space. All things, even our own heartbeats and sweat, are in it, part of it. And that work, that watching the turning over of life, becomes a road into what is essential. Work is the country of hands, and the way they want to live there in the dailiness of it, the repetition that is time's language of prayer, a common tongue. Everything is there, in that language, in the humblest of labor. The rake wakes up and the healing is in it. The shadows of leaves that once fell beneath the tree the handle came from are in that labor, and the rabbits that passed this way, on the altar of our work. And when the rake wakes up, all earth's gods are reborn, and they dance and sing in the dusty air around us. (153–54)

Raking, then, becomes a ceremonial act, one that participates in the circular nature of time, the revolving of seasons, and returns us to our origins, our essence. In this ceremonial act, this work of the hands and the heart, we are all called to consider how our own work, our active involvement in the world, our placement, participates in ceremony. We are called to question whether our placedness is one that co-responds, that embodies stillness and opens us to the voices of the eagles and the owls and the cycles of life and death, to the language of prayer. The ceremony that is raking and that is the act of reading this collection of essays comes to an end as the mythical world, the world of spirit, comes alive, and we partake in the dancing and singing that honors and keeps alive Earth. The journey of the narrator and the reader through story, through the telling of the illness that has befallen us and the remembering of an ancient wisdom of Earth and elders that sustains us, comes to a close as the divine that had fled our world rein-habits Earth.

Almost.

As Hogan notes at the end of "All My Relations" and suggests even here with her emphasis on the circular nature of all things, the close of the cer-emony is only the beginning of the journey. While the essay "Waking Up the Rake" concludes the ceremony that occurs in the telling and the read-ing of *Dwellings*, one final essay reminds us of the ongoing nature of cer-emony, of healing, and of the need to honor and keep alive our precious Earth. The final essay, "Walking," most fully reveals the new way of being and knowing brought to life in ceremony. Hogan opens the essay with a de-scription of the magical and mysterious growth of a lone sunflower on a hillside and the community of ants and bees and grasshoppers that were a part of its growth. She notes: "It was as if this plant with its host of lives was a society, one in which moment by moment, depending on light and moisture, there was great and diverse change" (156). She continues: "In this one plant, in one summer season, a drama of need and survival took place. Hungers were filled. Insects coupled. There was escape, exhaustion, and death. Lives touched down a moment and were gone" (156–57). After having explored the furthest reaches of the universe in previous essays and reawak-ened the sleeping gods in the world around, Hogan concentrates on a sin-gle sunflower and discovers in it the same beauty and mystery she found in the cradling of Earth in the dusky Milky Way. She then concludes: "I was an outsider. I only watched. I never learned the sunflower's golden language or the tongues of its citizens. I had a small understanding, nothing more than a shallow observation of the flower, insects, and birds. But they knew what to do, how to live. An old voice from somewhere, gene or cell, told the plant how to evade the pull of gravity and find its way upward, how to open. It was instinct, intuition, necessity. A certain knowing directed the seed-bearing birds on paths to ancestral homelands they had never seen. They believed it. They followed" (157). As she describes here with the sunflower and the birds, Hogan has assisted readers throughout *Dwellings* in finding our place in a much grander order that operates through instinct and intu-ition, a "certain knowing" that exists in contradistinction to the reason and logic driving us in the Western world.

Awareness of this other way of knowing and being in the world is cen-tral to ceremony and healing. Hogan provides several other examples of this inner voice that pervades the world. She describes the once-in-a-century flowering of a certain type of bamboo, all on the same day, all over Earth. She describes the beat she hears emanating from a redwood forest and the booming voice of an ocean storm. The narrator's ability to hear these voices and witness the ecology of plants and animals reveal her new state at the end of the healing journey that is *Dwellings*, one where she recognizes and participates in the interdependence and interrelatedness of all beings. She quotes John Hay, who says, "There are occasions when you can hear the mysterious language of the Earth, in water, or coming through the trees, emanating from the mosses, seeping through the undercurrents of the soil, but you have to be willing to wait and receive" (157). Hogan's insistence on the need to still ourselves and to open ourselves to the gift of Earth recalls Heidegger's reminder that all modes of disclosure, including even Enframing, our technological worldview, are a granting, a way of presencing beings that comes to us as a gift from Being. When we can remember this, that Enframing is one mode among many, we remember the mysterious plenitude of Earth, and we become the ones who presence others in their ownness rather than as objects for our use. Hogan notes that she occasionally participates in this mysterious language, for an "underground current stirred a kind of knowing inside [her], a kinship and longing, a dream barely remembered that disappeared back to the body" (158).

She concludes this essay in silence, walking in honor of all those who came before her and all that surrounds her. She says, "Tonight I walk. I am watching the sky. I think of the people who came before me and how they knew the placement of stars in the sky, watched the moving sun long and hard enough to witness how a certain angle of light touched a stone only once a year. Without written records, they knew the gods of every night, the small, fine details of the world around them and of immensity above them" (158). Her journey in the night recognizes the wisdom of her elders, their willingness and ability to witness the mystery of the world, their deep knowledge of the divinity existing all around us. She concludes the essay: "It's winter and there is smoke from the fires. The square, lighted windows of houses are fogging over. It is a world of elemental attention, of all things working together, listening to what speaks in the blood. Whichever road I follow, I walk in the land of many gods, and they love and eat one another. Walking, I am listening to a deeper way. Suddenly all my ancestors are behind me. Be still, they say. Watch and listen. You are the result of the love of thousands" (158–59). In this last passage of the book, Hogan most fully describes the new way of being brought forth in ceremony. Through listening to what is elemental, through an awareness of the deep interrelatedness of all things, narrator and reader participate in the sacred, indeed participate in the fullness of creation extending behind us and before us. Through listening, through a humble silence that recalls the end of Ray's *Ecology of a Cracker Childhood* and Williams's *Refuge*, Hogan opens herself to the ancient wisdom of her elders, to a sacred reason that reminds us all to be still, to witness the world around us in its mysterious plenitude, to listen to a deeper voice than our own, and to remember that love is the origin of all things, life and death and the cycles of the seasons and the slow revolving of Earth cradled in this grand and glorious universe.

# CHAPTER SIX

# Walking in the Land of Many Gods

## Remembering the Mysterious Plenitude of Earth

In the essay "Landscape and Narrative," Barry Lopez suggests the way in which storytelling acts as a kind of ceremony that heals the rift between our inner and outer worlds. He defines "two landscapes—one outside the self, the other within. The external landscape is the one we see—not only the line and color of the land and its shading at different times of the day, but also its plants and animals in season, its weather, its geology, the record of its climate and evolution." Yet Lopez's interest is in describing a less tangible aspect of this external landscape. After delineating the physical attributes of "a dry arroyo in the Sonoran Desert," he concludes: "These are all elements of the land, and what makes the landscape comprehensible are the relationships between them. One learns a landscape finally not by knowing the name or identity of everything in it, but by perceiving the relationships in it—like that between the sparrow and the twig." Lopez continues: "The second landscape I think of is an interior one, a kind of projection within a person of a part of the exterior landscape." Like the external landscape, the internal depends on connections between the elements of that landscape: "The speculations, intuitions, and formal ideas we refer to as 'mind' are a set of relationships in the interior landscape with purpose and order; some of these are obvious, many impenetrably subtle." But even more significantly, Lopez describes the intimate connection between the two landscapes:

> The shape and character of these relationships in a person's think-
> ing [in the internal landscape] . . . are deeply influenced by where
> on this earth one goes, what one touches, the patterns one observes
> in nature—the intricate history of one's life in the land, even a life
> in the city, where wind, the chirp of birds, the line of a falling leaf,
> are known. These thoughts are arranged, further, according to the
> thread of one's moral, intellectual, and spiritual development. The
> interior landscape responds to the character and subtlety of an exte-
> rior landscape; the shape of the individual mind is affected by land
> as it is by genes.[1]

For Lopez, then, the external landscape, the various relationships that connect all the different elements of the physical world along with less tangible elements like the soft light of an autumn sunset, influences our internal
world, the shape of our mind.

After defining the nature of these two landscapes and the nature of the
external landscape's influence on the internal landscape, Lopez connects his
discussion to stories, healing, and ceremony. He notes: "With certain stories
certain individuals may experience a deeper, more profound sense of well-
being. This . . . phenomenon, in my understanding, rests at the heart of storytelling as an elevated experience among aboriginal peoples. It results from
bringing two landscapes together." The healing effected by certain stories
results from an authentic rendering of the external landscape—a deep listening that comes from opening ourselves to the land—which in turn influences the internal order of the listener. That is, when the storyteller quiets
the human voice, allowing the land to presence in its ownness and thus to
speak through its own voice, the storyteller and the listener or reader become, as Hogan says, put "back together by restructuring the human mind"
(40). Lopez explains that this reordering occurs because "the exterior landscape is organized according to principles or laws or tendencies beyond human control. It is understood to contain an integrity that is beyond human
analysis and unimpeachable. Insofar as the storyteller depicts various subtle
and obvious relationships in the exterior landscape accurately in his story,
and insofar as he orders them along traditional lines of meaning to create
the narrative, the narrative will 'ring true.' The listener who 'takes the story

to heart' will feel a pervasive sense of congruence within himself and also with the world."[2]

Stories, then, when they accurately depict the mysterious and subtle interconnectedness of the world around us, when they reveal the unity of what Heidegger calls the fourfold, the intertwining of Earth and sky, divinities and mortals, have the potential to restore us to balance and harmony both within ourselves and with the world around us. Stories work through an alternative logic, not through calculating reason or scientific analysis but rather through our emotions, intuitions, and imagination. In this way, stories help us understand how we are placed in the world, and more importantly, they assist us in placing ourselves differently on the land, that is, in allowing us to become replaced, to become new beings.

Lopez notes that a similar congruence between the internal and the external landscapes occurs in Navajo ritual, which reveals the "sacred order" of the land and allows the Navajo "to achieve a balanced state of mental health." He describes one ritual in particular, "Beautyway," which is intended to "recreate in the individual" the "order of the exterior universe, that irreducible, holy complexity that manifests itself as all things changing through time." He then adds: "I believe story functions in a similar way. A story draws on relationships in the exterior landscape and projects them onto the interior landscape. The purpose of storytelling is to achieve harmony between the two landscapes, to use all the elements of story—syntax, mood, figures of speech—in a harmonious way to reproduce the harmony of the land in the individual's interior. Inherent in story is the power to reorder a state of psychological confusion through contact with the pervasive truth of those relationships we call 'the land.'"[3] Lopez asserts that story is significant because of the way in which it enacts a restoration of our inner world by authentically rendering the ecology of the physical world. In this way, the ecology of the physical and the spiritual become one, and the reader or listener is healed. Lopez concludes his essay with a reflection on the relationship between this process of healing and the body of literature that we call our own: "Our national literatures should be important to us insofar as they sustain us with illumination and heal us. They can always do that so long as they are written with respect for both the source and the reader, and with an understanding of why the human heart and the land have been brought together so regularly in human history."[4]

I have suggested that Janisse Ray's *Ecology of a Cracker Childhood*, Terry

Tempest Williams's *Refuge: An Unnatural History of Family and Place*, and Linda Hogan's *Dwellings: A Spiritual History of the Living World* enact the very healing and restoration that Lopez describes in his essay, for both the writer and the reader. Ray's *Ecology* unfolds the way in which our culture manifests the world as objects for our use and abuse, and ultimately for our discarding. The land becomes clear-cuts, pine plantations, and junkyards; it is ignored when it is convenient to ignore and used when it is convenient to be used. Yet Ray disrupts the story of the desecration of the land by inserting and thus remembering the story of the lost forests, the longleaf pine ecosystem that once spread across the southeastern United States. In remembering the story of the land and reinscribing it in her autobiography, she disrupts the story of her life, mending her childhood. Williams's *Refuge* similarly reveals the technological horizon of disclosure that constrains us, that allows us to see Great Salt Lake, like women's bodies, as objects to be dominated and controlled. To do nothing, to be still and to listen to the land, to move with its fluctuations and its changing contours like the ancient people, the Fremont, is not an option. Like Ray, Williams captures her own embeddedness in this worldview as she struggles to accept her mother's impending death and, more broadly, the changes that occur as a part of the flowing of energy that circulates through the universe. Ultimately, Williams's ability to discern change—even unusual change—that is natural from change that is man caused, unnecessary, and unnatural provides her with the foundation for a voice and a new way of being, one that she has learned from listening to the birds. Hogan's *Dwellings* also explores our separation from the natural world, the way in which we have become "far-hearted," forgetting our embeddedness in the landscape, forgetting especially that Earth is a gift that we should receive with care and compassion. Yet Hogan's work moves through the noise of our own ways into a place of silence and listening, enacting a healing ceremony through storytelling. In quieting the human mind and will and honoring the deep wisdom of eagles, Hogan shows us a pathway back to sacred reason, where we remember all our relations.

This is the restoration of balance and harmony in the individual that Lopez describes. Yet this is only one part of the story, for the interaction between the internal and the external landscapes not only maintains the health of the human mind; this confluence is also integral to the health of the land. That is, to maintain balance and harmony in the external landscape and to keep the land healthy, humans must have what the Western

Apache call wisdom, a right mind that causes the individual to act appropriately in the world. Such appropriate action, which originates from wisdom, from sacred reason, is an ethical imperative, for it is the foundation for the regeneration and restoration of the land. Significantly, such a conception of our responsibility toward the landscape can be found in our evolutionary past. Mircea Eliade explains that for primitive peoples sacred history, the intimate connectedness to the mysterious rhythms of the cosmos, was captured in their myths and ceremonies, which reactualize the sacred events of that history. He observes: "The myths preserve and transmit the paradigms, the exemplary models, for all the responsible activities in which men engage. By virtue of these paradigmatic models revealed to men in mythical times, the Cosmos and society are periodically regenerated."[5] Stanley Diamond explains that, unlike modern Western society, primitive societies were built not on dualisms but rather on antinomies: "The sacred is an immediate aspect of [primitive] man's experience. Good and evil, creation and destruction—the dual image of the deity as expressed in the trickster—are fused in the network of actions that define primitive society." And these actions are very carefully monitored because of their impact on the community of humans and nonhumans: "Every step of the way, the person is held to account for those actions that seriously threaten the balance of society and nature." In the West, we no longer understand the reciprocal relation of humans and the land or the deep power and responsibility of our words and actions. Having separated the self from the external world and relegated the mind to an isolated interior, we have forgotten that the technological horizon of disclosure that we inhabit today is only one mode of granting and that this way of revealing beings, and more importantly the double-order forgetting that comes with it, shapes, and in this case greatly diminishes, reality. Diamond notes that "even while creating their myths and ceremonials, their meanings and their insights, primitive people are aware of the reality that they mold."[6] For our hunter-gatherer forebears, then, the human-land relationship was not unidirectional as described in Lopez's account but rather multidirectional, whereby both the human and the land were influenced in a dance of reciprocity, of gift and receipt, a dance that depended on generosity but also on care and compassion.

Within Native American cultures, the concept of reciprocity depends on recognizing the way in which humans—like all the animate and inanimate beings surrounding us—participate in the ongoing act of creation.

Paula Gunn Allen, in contrasting a Christian worldview with that of Native cultures, identifies an acknowledgment of the "essential harmony of all things" within Native American beliefs. She explains: "Christians believe that God is separate from humanity and does as he wishes without the creative assistance of any of his creatures, while the non-Christian tribal person assumes a place in creation that is dynamic, creative, and responsive. Further, tribal people allow all animals, vegetables, and minerals (the entire biota, in short) the same or even greater privileges than humans. The Indian participates in destiny on all levels, including that of creation."[7] The concept of an ongoing and collaborative creation, quite contrary to ideas in the West, suggests a very different type of relationship between humans and the world around us: "The American Indian sees all creatures as relatives (and in tribal systems relationship is central), as offspring of the Great Mystery, as cocreators, as children of our mother, and as necessary parts of an ordered, balanced, and living whole."[8] The expansion of biota to include the living nature of what we in the West consider inanimate (things such as minerals) so that the term encapsulates the entire world, vibrant and alive, and the recognition of all things within this living world as sisters and brothers, aunts and uncles, grandmothers and grandfathers reorders our thinking, placing us anew on the land in such a way that we find ourselves dwelling among divinities. Allen concludes that the ability for all beings "to share in the process of ongoing creation makes all things sacred."[9]

Stories and ceremonies, then, not only "tell us how to put ourselves back together again," as Linda Hogan reminds us in "First People," they also, just as significantly, tell us "how to keep the world alive."[10] Such a conception of our relationship with the natural world is common among Native American cultures. Vine Deloria Jr. notes that beneath the physical world is an ineffable spiritual energy that many Native cultures simply call the "Great Mystery." Not only do all animate beings participate in this spirit world but so too does the inanimate, "so that the mountains, rivers, waterfalls, even the continents and the earth itself have intelligence, knowledge, and the ability to communicate ideas. The physical world is so filled with life and personality that humans appear as one minor species without much significance and badly in need of the assistance from other forms of life."[11] As a result of the divinity pervading our world, the mysterious plenitude of Earth, humans have a moral obligation to behave in certain ways, including participating in particular ceremonies, that keep Earth alive. Deloria explains that

the "Higher Powers" have revealed themselves to humans in specific loca-
tions, which have become sacred: "People have been commanded to perform ceremonies at these holy places so that the earth and all its forms of
life might survive and prosper." Tribal peoples feel a "moral responsibility"
to "perform certain ceremonies at specific times and places in order that
the sun may continue to shine, the earth prosper, and the stars remain in
the heavens." These ceremonies are an expression of gratitude, completing and renewing "the entire and complete cycle of life, ultimately including the whole cosmos present in its specific realizations, so that in the last
analysis one might describe ceremonials as the cosmos becoming thank-
fully aware of itself."[12] Such an attitude of appreciation, one arising out of
a strong sense of humility, generosity, care, and compassion, changes our
relationship with the landscape and in so doing keeps the land alive. That
is, when we open ourselves to the external landscape, learning to recognize
and appreciate the myriad interrelationships that exist within it and that sustain it, we become new beings, placed differently on the land, and in such an
emplacement the land prospers.

To return to stories. We must remember that for Heidegger, Being constitutes our horizon of disclosure and the beings that presence through that
horizon along with all the other possible horizons existing beyond our limited and constrained understanding. Earth, as part of this intertwining, is a
mysterious plenitude, and when we quiet our human voices and open ourselves to the land so that we learn to co-respond, to allow land-language to
speak, then we honor Earth and let it reveal itself in all its majesty. I have
suggested that the co-responding resulting from writing and reading of
*Dwellings* gives voice to Earth, indeed melds the interior and the exterior
landscapes. We remember, through the healing ceremony, all our relations,
and in so doing the land becomes once again sacred. The gods that had fled
repopulate the land, and we walk among divinity. As Hogan says, "When
the rake wakes up, all earth's gods are reborn, and they dance and sing in
the dusty air around us" (154). The conclusion of *Dwellings* suggests an extension of Lopez's unidirectional movement of the exterior landscape into
the interior, a movement that reorganizes our minds so that we return to a
state of harmony and balance. In remembering sacred reason, in "listening
to a deeper way" with "all [our] ancestors behind [us]," attaining once again
a mind of sky and thunder and sun, not only is the human mind healed
but *so too is the land*, and we once again "walk in the land of many gods"

(159). N. Scott Momaday notes: "The native American ethic with respect to the physical world is a matter of reciprocal appropriation: appropriations in which man invests himself in the landscape, and at the same time incorporates the landscape into his own most fundamental experience. That suggests a dichotomy, or a paradox, and I think it is a paradox."[13] This is the act of expropriative appropriating described by Heidegger or the act of emergence, which depends on mutual interdependence as defined by Silko. This two-way flow of landscapes, the human into the land and the land back into the human, marks the paradoxical reciprocity that Momaday discerns at the heart of a Native American land ethic. The landscapes appropriate each other in a kind of mirror-play, in which they give and receive in a dance of mutuality and interdependence.

Ideally, the interplay between the two landscapes that gives rise to our way of being in the world occurs on an ongoing basis, continually reminding us of an ancient wisdom of Earth and elders. But when we sever ourselves from the land, when the rift grows too large as it has in our own destitute time with its double-order forgetting and oblivion of Being, we need ceremonies and stories to heal us, to place us once again on the land so that we remember the myriad influences of plants and animals, sky and sun, rocks and valleys and trees and the flow and exchange of energy that is life turning over life. And in this replacement, we become new beings who embody our animal selves, listening to the hum of creation and honoring everything surrounding us. William Jordan suggests that ecological restoration, if done attentively, offers such a ceremony, a ritual that reconnects us with the creative and the destructive forces of the universe. So, too, do stories, as Lopez, Momaday, and many others have demonstrated. Building on Heidegger's later philosophy, I have suggested that works of environmental literature, and particularly women's environmental literature, offer us an understanding of how we are placed in the world—the destitution of our times, the totalized horizon of disclosure that has severed us from our own essence as the ones who offer a space for the presencing of beings—and of how we might replace ourselves. We have come to accept a Cartesian separation of subject and object, a dualistic framework for interacting with the world, as natural, as truth, *as the way things are*, forgetting that this worldview is a granting like any other, *one mode* of disclosing reality.

But a mode, unfortunately, without care and compassion. The literary works explored here not only describe our destitute state and offer a vision of healing. More than that, they enact the very healing they describe. Ray's act of (re)writing the story of the lost forests and her own lost self creates a new set of values that, in turn, creates a new person who works to preserve and replant the longleaf pine ecosystem. Williams attains a voice that allows her to protest the unnatural history of her place, both in her silent act of civil disobedience and in her writing of *Refuge*. Hogan calls forth the divinity of the landscape, which becomes repopulated with the many gods who surround us on a daily basis yet remain invisible to our cauterized eyes. Words have power. Longleaf and wiregrass, sand and sage, wolves and sunflower emerge from stories that spring from a love for our Earth gently rolling through the universe. Each of these works demonstrates the author's bodily engagement with place, a listening so deep and so profound that their interior and exterior landscapes become one and their stories become a corresponding, become the voice of Earth. Ray sings the wind through the longleaf pines. She chants the gopher tortoise and the flatwoods salamander into being. Williams gives birth to her mother's life through witnessing and compassionately unfolding her death. Her journals spill desert sand onto our laps as the smell of sage rises from the leaves of her book. Hogan heals us through a ceremony that moves outside the realm of our scientific and calculative thinking, floating eagle feathers and their flutelike songs into our lives. Her stories originate from forests so that her words arise from the generous Earth. In each of these works, we come to understand not only how we are placed in this world but, more importantly, how we might be replaced, and in this new emplacement we chant the world into being, remembering and keeping alive the mysterious plenitude of Earth.

# NOTES

CHAPTER ONE. INTRODUCTION

1. Wilson, *Biophilia*. See especially his prologue, where he describes his own originary experience before defining biophilia as "the innate tendency to focus on life and lifelike processes"; he continues: "To explore and affiliate with life is a deep and complicated process in mental development. To an extent still undervalued in philosophy and religion, our existence depends on this propensity, our spirit is woven from it, hope rises on its currents" (1).

2. Heidegger, "Question Concerning Technology," 19, 25, 23.

3. Aho, *Heidegger's Neglect of the Body*, 128.

4. Heidegger, "Question Concerning Technology," 28.

5. Young, "Fourfold," 375.

6. Heidegger, "Building Dwelling Thinking," 148–49.

7. Young, "Fourfold," 374.

8. Aho, *Heidegger's Neglect of the Body*, 139.

9. Jordan, *Sunflower Forest*, 22, emphasis in original.

10. Ibid., 14.

11. Ibid., 176.

12. Aho, *Heidegger's Neglect of the Body*, 128.

13. Ibid., 132.

14. Ibid., 140.

15. Young, *Heidegger's Later Philosophy*, 57.

16. Ibid., 58.

17. I would refer here to my opening reference to Wilson; see his first chapter, "Bernhardsdorp," in *Biophilia*, 3–22. See also Berry, *Great Work*, where he describes the way in which a childhood experience interacting with a particular meadow has provided a foundation for his worldview: "Whatever preserves and enhances this meadow in the natural cycles of its transformation is good; whatever opposes this meadow or negates it is not good. My life orientation is that simple. It is also that pervasive. It applies in economics and political orientation as well as in education and religion" (13).

CHAPTER TWO. REMEMBERING DEEP SPACE AND DEEP TIME

1. Charles Guignon provides a substantive discussion of Heidegger's early thinking and the turn in his thinking that begins in a 1930 essay, "On the Essence of Truth." See

Guignon, introduction, 1–26. I am greatly indebted to Guignon's work in this cursory overview.

2. Lovitt, introduction, xiii.

3. See Young, *Heidegger's Later Philosophy*, 7–8; I am greatly indebted to Young's discussion of Heidegger's later philosophy. See also Lovitt, introduction, xxxiv.

4. Heidegger, "Question Concerning Technology," 19.

5. Lovitt, introduction, xxviii–xxix.

6. Ibid., xxxiv. See also Guignon, who notes, "The history of metaphysics is therefore a history of forgetfulness or 'withdrawal,' in which entities obtrude as actually existing and as having essential properties, while being—that which first makes it possible for anything to show up in its *existentia* and *essentia*—remains concealed" (introduction, 17).

7. Young, *Heidegger's Later Philosophy*, 8–9. See also Guignon, introduction, 15.

8. Young, *Heidegger's Later Philosophy*, 9.

9. Ibid., 10–16.

10. Ibid., 12.

11. Ibid., 12–13.

12. Ibid., 13.

13. Heidegger, "What Are Poets For?," 90.

14. Heidegger, "Thing," 177.

15. Momaday, "Native American Attitudes," 80.

16. Heidegger, "Thing," 179.

17. Heidegger, "Language," 196.

18. Ibid., 197.

19. Ibid., 199.

20. Ibid., 206.

21. Ibid., 207.

22. Guignon, introduction, 18.

23. Ibid., 19.

24. Ibid., 20.

25. Ibid., 23.

26. As several critics have noted, an important concern is that much of Heidegger's thinking is intertwined with the rise of the Nazis in Germany in the 1930s and 1940s, a fact that has been explored in several important works, most notably Michael Zimmerman's *Heidegger's Confrontation with Modernity*. Zimmerman concludes that Heidegger's conception of metaphysics was colored by his historical circumstances, that indeed his philosophy was developed partly in response to the cultural milieu in which he was writing. Zimmerman devotes an entire half of his book to tracing this connection.

Charles Guignon provides an overview of Heidegger's relationship to the Nazis, explaining Heidegger's attraction to the conservative strain in this movement, one that depended on the recovery of the essence of the common people and that sought to chart a third way between capitalism and Marxism. Guignon claims that Heidegger began pulling back from the Nazis by 1936 (see introduction, 26–36).

Greg Garrard, in "Heidegger Nazism Ecocriticism," claims that Heidegger's relationship to Nazi ideology existed through 1945, when he ended his affiliation with the National Socialist party. Garrard both describes Heidegger's support of the Nazis and their racial policies and debunks the Nazi connection to any meaningful environmentalism.

Garrard then critiques two works of ecocriticism for their reliance on Heidegger's ideas, Robert Pogue Harrison's *Forests: The Shadow of Civilization* and Jonathan Bate's *The Song of the Earth*, attempting to "show that what is distinctive in Heidegger's work after *Being and Time* (1927) is wrong, and what is persuasive is not distinctive" (251).

Garrard's primary critique is that Heidegger's philosophy of Being is nonsense, a mere grammatical error that mistakes the question of being, which doesn't truly exist, for some important philosophical question (260). At the heart of Garrard's criticism is the fallacy that lies behind what Dorothea Frede calls "substance ontology"—which is the very aspect of Western philosophy that Heidegger responds to in his early philosophy. Heidegger would agree with Garrard that just because we might say that "unicorns are" (this is Garrard's example, borrowed from Richard Pott), it does not mean that they physically exist. Rather, Heidegger would be interested in the sociolinguistic practices behind such a statement that would allow (or not allow) unicorns to show up for us (as mythical creatures, perhaps, or as a primary character in a children's story, say, or maybe even, for a unicorn hunter, as a potential physical being).

I would suggest that these considerations—of our horizon of disclosure and how this horizon conditions our interaction with the world around us—is of paramount importance in this time and is very useful in environmental history, environmental philosophy, and environmental literature. The role of Nazism in Heidegger's philosophy cannot be overlooked and should provide a cautionary note to any use of his thinking, though I agree with Zimmerman that it does not invalidate that work.

See Zimmerman, *Heidegger's Confrontation with Modernity*; Guignon, introduction; Garrard, "Heidegger Nazism Ecocriticism," 255–59; and Frede, "Question of Being," 42–45.

27. For Heidegger and Eastern thought, see Zimmerman, "Heidegger, Buddhism, and Deep Ecology," 304–12.

28. Ibid., 294.

29. Ibid., 300.

30. Frede, "Question of Being," 65–66.

31. Rigby, "Earth, World, Text," 433.

32. Leakey, *Origin of Humankind*, 123. I am indebted to Leakey's book and to the work of Steve Olson, in *Mapping Human History*, for background on the development of humans. On Heidegger's rejection of Darwinism, see Zimmerman, "Heidegger, Buddhism, and Deep Ecology," 319.

33. Olson, *Mapping Human History*, 86.

34. Abram, *Becoming Animal*, 170–71.

35. A note about my reference to our planet. I greatly appreciate David Abram's distinction between his use of the terms "the earth," "earth," and "Earth" (and even, sometimes, "Eairth") in order to fully capture the sense of awe and wonder that we should hold regarding our planet (see "Note to the Reader" in the beginning of *Becoming Animal*). However, within this project, rather than using the rather common phrase "the Earth" or "the earth," I will refer to our planet as a planet—without the definitive article "the." We do not say "the Saturn" or "the Mars" when referring to other planets, and with good reason for it makes little sense. I would like to acknowledge Steven Rockefeller's work with the Earth Charter in bringing this forward (see Rockefeller, "Crafting Principles for the Earth Charter," 3–23). Having said that, I must again acknowledge my

deep appreciation for David Abram's efforts to ignite wonder in his readers. We need more awe and wonder in our world and other philosophers and poets who lead the way back to the land of many gods.

36. A word about my use of "place" and "re/place" (and all their configurations, including especially "placed" and "emplacement"). As noted, my understanding of our relationship to the external world depends on an entwinement between the inner and outer landscapes. This suggests that the act of being "placed" is one that has a reciprocating effect: we interact with the land on which we live, and it interacts with us. When we become "placed" in such a way that we dwell—opening ourselves to the stillness of the land in an act of what Heidegger calls "co-responding"—we become "re/placed"; that is, our interrelationship with the land, our "emplacement," changes and, in turn, we become new beings. Thus, by using the slash I want to emphasize both that we are "placed" differently on the land when we learn to dwell and unite the fourfold as a one-fold and that our being, our identity or "self," is replaced and we become new beings.

37. See Shepard, *Coming Home to the Pleistocene*. Shepard notes, at the end of his introduction, that "when we grasp fully that the best expressions of our humanity were not invented by civilization but by cultures that preceded it, that the natural world is not only a set of constraints but of contexts within which we can more fully realize our dreams, we will be on the way to a long overdue reconciliation between opposites that are of our own making. The tools we have invented for communicating our ideas and carrying information have actually impaired our memories. We must begin by remembering beyond history" (5–6).

38. In his book *In Search of Nature*, E. O. Wilson offers an interesting critique of the humanities and the social sciences that is relevant to my own desire to extend Heidegger's thinking. Wilson argues that the "social sciences and humanities have been blinkered by a steadfastly nondimensional and nontheoretical view of mankind" (99). First, he explains, these disciplines "focus on one point, the human species, without reference to the space of all possible species natures in which it is embedded. To be anthropocentric is to remain unaware of the limits of human nature, the significance of biological processes underlying human behavior, and the deeper meaning of long-term genetic evolution. That larger perspective can be gained only by moving back from the species, step by step, and taking a deliberately more distanced view" (99–100). For Wilson, writing in the mid-1990s, the humanities and the social sciences have a very limited perspective on their subject matter, one that focuses exclusively on the human without considering the wider landscape in which the human is embedded. The second point that Wilson makes in his critique is that these disciplines are founded on a severely limited understanding of time. Because of the great length of time involved in the evolution of multiple genes that allow for complex patterns of behavior, perhaps hundreds or even thousands of generations, Wilson posits that "we do not expect to find that human nature has been altered greatly during historical times, or that people in industrial societies differ basically from those in preliterate, hunter-gatherer societies" (103). Yet the humanities and the social sciences to a great extent have failed to embrace this notion of deep time, constraining their view to the historical past, the last ten thousand years or so. Wilson concludes: "Thus social theory could profit by extending its reach just beyond the historical period dominated by cultural evolution to the near prehistoric period during which more nearly balanced combinations of genetic and cultural change occurred" (104). Wilson argues that the study of literature and other humanities and social science

disciplines might embrace a deep view of space, one that moves outward to engage other species and the relationship between humans and the natural world, one biocentric in nature, and a deep view of time, one that moves backward to embrace the prehistoric period, backward through the rise of agriculture and into our hunter-gatherer roots. Such a view takes us beyond Heidegger's thinking and more closely parallels Hogan's sense of sacred reason. Wilson, *In Search of Nature*, 99–104.

39. Descartes, *Philosophical Writings of Descartes*, 1:127.

40. Grosz, *Volatile Bodies*, 7. I am also indebted to the discussions about Descartes's dualistic thinking in Peter Markie's essay "The Cogito and Its Importance" and John Cottingham's essay "Cartesian Dualism: Theology, Metaphysics, and Science," as well as Marleen Rozemond's *Descartes's Dualism*, which provides a historical context for understanding Descartes's dualistic thinking.

41. See, for example, Baker and Morris, *Descartes' Dualism*; S. B. Smith, "Exemplary Life"; Nadler, "Descartes' Dualism?"; and Hagberg, *Describing Ourselves* (2–3). Rozemond counters these arguments by offering a historical context that grounds Descartes's thinking in the intellectual milieu of the time (see especially *Descartes's Dualism*, chaps. 5 and 6).

42. Hagberg, *Describing Ourselves*, 3.

43. Oelschlaeger, *Idea of Wilderness*, 85–89. See also Abram, *Spell of the Sensuous*, 31–37.

44. Descartes, *Philosophical Writings of Descartes*, 1:142–43.

45. For a counterargument, see Wee, "Cartesian Environmental Ethics," who claims that "Descartes is not a dominion theorist [one who advances the belief that humans should dominate Earth]. There are also good grounds for arguing that he grants animals (and plants) moral standing. More importantly, Descartes considers it a human good to subordinate one's own interests to that of the universe as a whole, and to act for the good of the larger universe of which one is a part. He can be seen as a forerunner of the ecocentric world view" (276). Steven B. Smith also suggests that focusing on the dualistic philosophy that seems to emanate from Descartes's writing is a misreading because Descartes is more concerned, in his *Discourse on Method*, with moral and ethical questions (what should I do?) than with epistemological questions (what can I know?) ("Exemplary Life," 573). Although I find the disagreements about how Descartes should be read fascinating, they do not play into my own discussion; whether dualistic thought issues from Descartes or not, I am concerned with the trajectory of this thought, which pervades Western civilization and is attributed, rightly or wrongly, to Descartes.

46. Merchant, *Death of Nature*, xvi.

47. Ibid., 128–29.

48. Ibid., 192.

49. Ibid., 193.

50. Walsh, "Paying for Nature."

51. Costanza et al., "Value," 259.

52. Ibid., 255.

53. Walsh, "Paying for Nature."

54. The authors of the *Nature* article discuss the issue of valuation of ecosystem services, including moral and economic arguments for and against such a valuation; they conclude that "although ecosystem valuation is certainly difficult and fraught with uncertainties, one choice we do not have is whether or not to do it. Rather, the decisions we make as a society about ecosystems imply valuations (although not necessarily expressed

in monetary terms). We can choose to make these valuations explicit or not; we can do them with an explicit acknowledgement of the huge uncertainties involved or not; but as long as we are forced to make choices, we are going through the process of valuation" (Costanza et al., "Value," 255).

55. Shepard, *Coming Home to the Pleistocene*, 7–8.

56. Shepard, *Nature and Madness*, 7.

57. Shepard, *Coming Home to the Pleistocene*, 39.

58. Shepard, *Nature and Madness*, 9.

59. Ibid.

60. Ibid., 34.

61. Shepard, *Coming Home to the Pleistocene*, 39.

62. Shepard, *Nature and Madness*, 11.

63. Shepard, *Coming Home to the Pleistocene*, 39.

64. Ibid., 40.

65. Ibid., 45.

66. Diamond, *In Search of the Primitive*, 138.

67. Ibid., 141.

68. Abram, "Air Aware," 18.

69. Ibid., 24.

70. Ibid., 25.

71. Silko, "Interior and Exterior Landscapes," 5–6.

72. I use the term "landscape" throughout this work in the way that Silko uses it here and that Shepard would define it—and counter to the way in which our Western worldview conceives of it. The landscape is not an external object, nor is it a human-created conception; landscape is, rather, a confluence between our inner and outer worlds, mediated by our bodily experience and determined by interrelationships. Such a view is similarly advanced in Barry Lopez's essay "Landscape and Narrative," where he considers the close connection between "two landscapes—one outside the self, the other within" (64). He defines the essence of these landscapes as residing not in the elements of the landscape (for the external landscape, that which we see, the plants and animals, weather and geology, light and shadow of the land; for the internal landscape, the ideas and intuitions that course through our minds) but rather in the relationship between the elements. Ultimately, he is interested in the influence of the external landscape on the internal and the relationship of this influence to storytelling, which I will return to in my concluding chapter. For a rich exploration of the melding of our internal and external worlds, mediated by our body, see Abram, *Becoming Animal*.

73. Silko, "Interior and Exterior Landscapes," 8.

74. Ibid., 14–15.

75. Ibid., 15–16.

76. Basso, *Wisdom Sits in Places*, 32.

77. Basso cites Vine Deloria Jr., a Standing Rock Sioux, who observes that "most American Indian tribes embrace 'spatial conceptions of history' in which places and their names—and all that these may symbolize—are accorded central importance." See Basso, *Wisdom Sits in Places*, 34.

78. Basso, *Wisdom Sits in Places*, 34.

79. Ibid., 58–59.

80. Jordan, *Sunflower Forest*, 46.

81. Ibid., 50.

82. Basso, *Wisdom Sits in Places*, 146.

83. Armstrong, "Land Speaking," 175–76.

84. Ibid., 176.

85. Ibid.

86. Ibid., 178–79.

87. Perhaps the best recent history of the study of literature and the environment is included in Glen Love's *Practical Ecocriticism*, in the introduction and the first chapter. For good overviews of the literature and environment movement, see Heise, "Hitchhiker's Guide to Ecocriticism"; Fromm, "Ecocriticism's Big Bang"; and Fromm, "New Darwinism in the Humanities."

Several collections of scholarship have been compiled in response to the growing field of literature and the environment; see Glotfelty and Fromm, *Ecocriticism Reader*; Branch et al., *Reading the Earth*; a special edition of *New Literary History* (30, no. 3 [Summer 1999]); Tallmadge and Harrington, *Reading under the Sign of Nature*; Mazel, *Century of Early Ecocriticism*.

88. Glotfelty, introduction, in *Ecocriticism Reader*, xvi.

89. Ibid., xix.

90. Oelschlaeger, *Idea of Wilderness*, x. Oelschlaeger states that "Reason is ordinarily understood to eventuate in thoughts: a product of human cognition in social context. My position is different. I refer elliptically to Heidegger's observation that human beings never come to thoughts; thoughts happen—out of historical and linguistic inevitability—to us. To allow thought to be bounded by social context is not to think philosophically. And yet to be human is to be linguistically and historically enframed. Consequently, philosophical discourse must at some point affirm the presence of what can never be revealed through words" (ix).

Heidegger's primary influence on Oelschlaeger is on his consideration of language. In his analysis of *Walden*, Oelschlaeger notes how "Thoreau achieved insight into the imprisoning subtleties and liberating potentialities of language from a mid-nineteenth-century vantage point—there was no rich tradition of hermeneutics to draw upon—realizing through his own persistent efforts that *humankind is language* and that conventional language enframes the human project"; according to Oelschlaeger, Thoreau works to recover "words that speak granitic truth" (156–157).

91. Oelschlaeger, Idea of Wilderness, 134–71.

92. Ibid., 170–71.

93. For Muir, see Oelschlaeger, *Idea of Wilderness*, 200–201; for Leopold, 205–6.

94. Ibid., 280.

95. Ibid., 351–52.

96. Ibid., 349.

97. Meeker, *Comedy of Survival*, 38–39.

98. G. A. Love, *Practical Ecocriticism*, 41–57.

99. Ibid., 57.

100. Ibid., 70.

101. Buell, *Environmental Imagination*, 2.

102. Ibid., 22.

103. Elder, *Imagining the Earth*, 1.

104. Heidegger, *Fundamental Concepts of Metaphysics*, 177.

105. Ibid., 237, 248.

106. Ibid., 259.

107. For Heidegger's understanding of the "inanimate" world, see *Fundamental Concepts of Metaphysics*, 177.

108. Hogan, "First People," 15.

109. Jordan, *Sunflower Forest*, 35.

110. Hogan, "First People," 14.

## CHAPTER THREE. RESTOR(Y)ING THE SELF

1. Jordan, *Sunflower Forest*, 11.

2. Ibid., 22.

3. Ibid., 12.

4. Ibid., 151.

5. Ibid., 176.

6. Momaday, "Native Voice in American Literature," 15–16.

7. Autobiographical theory has exploded over the last thirty years with a wide array of perspectives on the act of telling the story of a life. Several theorists in particular have influenced my thinking in this chapter, including especially those who move beyond the traditional assumptions of classical autobiography, which accepted a Cartesian sense of the self as separated from the world, an interior self that gains its selfhood through removing itself from the world in order to think. As Janet Varner Gunn notes in her work *Autobiography*: "At the center of these assumptions about autobiography is the hidden or ghostly self which is absolute, ineffable, and timeless" (8). Such a consideration of self not only separates subject and object, but it also ignores bodily experience and our integration with the world around us.

Two early works that provided a foundation for the shift to current autobiographical theory should be mentioned. The first, Georges Gusdorf's "Conditions and Limits of Autobiography," originally published in 1956, recognizes the way in which the autobiographical act is a creative act; that is, the autobiographer in the process of exploring his or her past in a present moment necessarily (re-)creates the past and in so doing creates a new identity in the present. The second, James Olney's *Metaphors of Self*, suggests that metaphor, as a means of making order or meaning out of the world, provides a rich foundation for considering the autobiographical act, which is centrally about making connections between disparate events, feelings, and perspectives so that they cohere into a whole.

Other works that have stressed the role of language have also influenced my project. Gunn, in *Autobiography*, focuses on two moments of reading that occur within the autobiography, the first by the autobiographer who is reading his or her life and the second by the reader of the autobiography itself; she focuses on the way in which these acts of reading occur within inhabited worlds where the self becomes displayed through language. Paul John Eakin, in *Fictions in Autobiography*, considers the rhythms of identity formation that occur in the lived experience, which are then replicated in the act of writing about that experience, especially as these two experiences relate to the acquisition of language. In a more recent work, *How Our Lives Become Stories*, Eakin considers the relation between the subject or self of autobiography and the role of language and storytelling; in this work, Eakin includes a rich summary of theories of the nature of the self and self-experience in his first chapter, including the role of culture in identity formation and the role of the body.

8. Eakin, *Fictions in Autobiography*, 3.

9. Maxwell, *So Long, See You Tomorrow*, 27.

10. Jordan notes in *The Sunflower Forest* that "the hard logic of ecology—the principle that everything interacts with (and therefore influences) everything else—makes the conclusion unavoidable: preservation in the strict sense is impossible" (14). For the perpetually changing self, see Eakin, who connects the continual transformation of the self to the experience of the body: "When we look at life history from the perspective of neural Darwinism, it is fair to say that we are all becoming different persons all the time, we are not what we were; self and memory are emergent, in process, constantly evolving, and both are grounded in the body and the body image" (*How Our Lives Become Stories*, 20). For a more recent discussion that connects the body to a prelinguistic conception of the self, see Eakin, *Living Autobiographically*, 60–86.

11. Eakin, *Fictions in Autobiography*, 5.

12. For a discussion of the relation between self and memory in autobiographical theory, see Eakin, *How Our Lives Become Stories*, 18–21.

13. Gunn notes in *Autobiography* that in the act of writing the self, "what is made present is not merely a past that is past. What is presenced is a reality, always new, to which the past has contributed but which stands, as it were, in front of the autobiographer. To lay claim to one's life . . . is to understand that reality as something to which one is continually trying to catch up but which one can never outstrip" (17).

14. Barnes, "On Place," 17.

15. Sturrock, "New Model Autobiographer," 197.

16. Barnes, "On Place," 17.

17. Watson, "Economics of a Cracker Landscape," 497.

18. Ibid., 507.

19. Robertson, "Junkyard Tales," 168.

20. Ibid., 174.

21. Kindell, Smith, and Reynolds, review of *Ecology*, 98.

22. Very little scholarship has been completed on Ray's works, perhaps because of the unorthodox form of books such as *Ecology* and the sequel *Wild Card Quilt*. Reviewers have largely missed the intimate interconnection between the chapters on family history and the chapters on natural history. Susan Williams comments in her review of *Wild Card Quilt*: "As in *Ecology of a Cracker Childhood*, chapters about the forest alternate with chapters about her life. I wish I could say that these sections, clearly so close to Ray's heart, were the best part of the book. But I often found myself skipping them, wanting to get back to her memories of the junkyard and day-to-day life reclaiming the farm" ("Home, Difficult Home"). Similarly, Jan Grover notes: "If there's a structural problem to *Ecology*, it's that Ray separates the history of her family and the ecological history of the place they inhabit so emphatically"; she continues, the natural history chapters "suffer by contrast, for they're too short to be very complex, and they're so bent on offering information that they can feel a bit like a thin filling surrounded by sumptuous bread" ("Real Places," 10). For two reviews that engage and appreciate the complexity of

*Ecology,* see Godine, review of *Clear Springs: A Memoir,* by Bobbie Ann Mason and *Ecology of a Cracker Childhood,* by Janisse Ray; and Corcoran and Wohlpart, review of *Ecology of a Cracker Childhood.*

23. For a discussion of the relation between the subject/self and the body in autobiographical theory, see Eakin, *How Our Lives Become Stories,* 10–42.

24. Heidegger describes our current horizon of disclosure, Enframing, as both the "supreme danger" and the "saving power." The question becomes, then, how do we as humans, who do not control Being but rather are thrown into its draft, assist in the remembering of what we have (doubly) forgotten? Heidegger answers: "Here and now and in little things, that we may foster the saving power in its increase. This includes holding always before our eyes the extreme danger" (*Question Concerning Technology,* 33). By paying attention in this moment to the beings that are near to us, no matter how seemingly insignificant, and by doing so with care and compassion, we remember our role as the clearing of Being.

25. Neil Evernden in *The Natural Alien* provides an interesting gloss on the relation of humans to technology that characterizes humans as exotics. Because of an interesting flexibility in our nature, humans have the ability "to believe in an abstract reality which pits us against, or more correctly separates us from, the earth that houses all organic worlds" (103). He notes that the version of reality that we have adopted, which is Cartesian and scientific, has created a new way of acting in the world, one where we can no longer grasp context and meaning in the same way that other beings, such as animals, can. Evernden calls such beings who have become disassociated from the context and meaning of their environment "exotics" and suggests that a central reason for our own displacement as humans is technology. As a result of this shift in our way of thinking and acting in the world, humans have moved into a state of confusion that only becomes more amplified as we search for solutions to our uncertain state by using more technology.

26. Eakin, *Fictions in Autobiography,* 226.

27. Interestingly, Ray uses language similar to Eakin's in describing the urge to tell the story of her childhood. In *Wild Card Quilt,* the sequel to *Ecology,* Ray states: "What is it in us that wants to return to the dream of childhood, to reenact it or fix it?" (33).

28. Jordan, *Sunflower Forest,* 28–30.

29. Ibid., 35.

30. Ibid., 39.

31. Ibid., 78.

32. Deming, review of *Wild Card Quilt,* 74.

33. Jordan, *Sunflower Forest,* 85.

34. Ibid., 85.

35. Gunn, *Autobiography,* 16.

36. Ibid., 18.

37. Jordan, *Sunflower Forest,* 171.

38. Gunn, *Autobiography,* 18. See also Olney, *Metaphors of Self,* 32–25; and Gusdorf, "Conditions and Limits of Autobiography," 44 and 47.

39. Ray, *Wild Card Quilt,* xi.

40. Ibid., 132.

41. Ibid., 137.

42. In his review of Ray's work titled "The New Naturalists," Thomas Crowe includes Ray among a group of activist writers who "are, through their work and deeds, inspiring, organizing, and participating in nonviolent 'actions' and activities that provide alternatives to community apathy and destruction of the natural habitat" (10). Ray transforms herself in this act into the adult autobiographer with a certain set of values that allows her to become an activist with an intimate connection to the natural world.

43. Ray, *Wild Card Quilt*, 302.

44. Ibid., 304.

CHAPTER FOUR. THE LONG MIGRATION HOME

1. Jordan, *Sunflower Forest*, 42.

2. Ibid., 44.

3. Mitchell, "Reclaiming the Sacred Landscape," 169.

4. Glotfelty, "Flooding the Boundaries of Form," 161.

5. Farr, "American Ecobiography," 94.

6. Glotfelty, "Flooding the Boundaries of Form," 165.

7. Ibid.

8. Zuelke, "Ecopolitical Space of *Refuge*," 241–42.

9. Kircher, "Rethinking Dichotomies," 169.

10. Mitchell, "Reclaiming the Sacred Landscape," 169.

11. Riley, "Finding One's Place," 587.

12. Jordan, *Sunflower Forest*, 83.

13. Ibid., 85.

14. Yuki, "Sound Ground to Stand On," 82.

15. Ibid., 87.

16. Mitchell, "Reclaiming the Sacred Landscape," 173.

17. Jordan, *Sunflower Forest*, 42.

18. Glotfelty, "Flooding the Boundaries of Form," 166.

19. Dodd, "Beyond the Blithe Air," 4.

20. Zuelke, "Ecopolitical Space of *Refuge*," 242.

21. Kircher, "Rethinking Dichotomies," 161.

22. Chandler, "Whale Song from the Desert," 656. The disparity in readings of *Refuge* can be found in the contrast between this perspective and that of several other critics. Although Cassandra Kircher recognizes the role of circles in *Refuge*, she concludes that Williams's circular expansion of the notion of family is romanticized and ignores her own embeddedness in a materialistic culture ("Rethinking Dichotomies," 168); yet Williams's experiences in the middle of the text are not the sum of its whole. Williams certainly acknowledges the contradictory nature of the life she leads by depicting scenes in which she shops with her dying mother or discusses the family business. Such an acknowledgment, I would suggest, creates a healthy tension, making the narrator's journey fraught with the fragile nature of what it means to be human, making it real, palpable, useful—making it, ultimately, an unnatural history. Similarly, Sarah McFarland demonstrates the way in which Williams comes to understand the sacred interrelatedness of all beings through her contact with wild birds, yet also the way in which she ignores the environmental justice issues surrounding the raising, killing, and eating of domestic birds (McFarland, "Invisible Birds," 45). Yet MacFarland's criticism of Williams's

privileging of wild birds over domestic birds again misses Williams's own recognition of the way in which she is embedded in—even implicated in—her own cultural practices. Finally, Karla Armbruster, while acknowledging Williams's seeming reinscription of dualistic thinking, claims that the poststructuralist nature of *Refuge* allows Williams to depict identity as relational and shifting and thus to rise above those cultural practices enframing her: "Eventually she [Williams] comes to accept that her identity must constantly shift and change as the places and people she is connected to shift, change, and even die" ("Rewriting a Genealogy with the Earth," 215).

The contested nature of these readings suggests the complexity of *Refuge* and the way in which narrative layers fold one over the other to produce a contradictory, paradoxical, and yet somehow coherent and unified text.

23. Jeannette Riley, in "The Eco-Narrative and the Enthymeme," suggests that *Refuge*, as an eco-narrative, models "ecofeminist principles of interdependence, the importance of relationships, and the value of nature" such that the reader necessarily becomes a participant in the creation of the meaning of the text (82). Through the use of a particular rhetorical strategy, the enthymeme, Williams creates a space where "readers enter into the text itself and find themselves listening, or assenting to the discussion of issues taking place" (84).

24. Richardson, "Corporeal Testimony," 230.

25. Yuki, "Narrating the Invisible Landscape," 84.

26. Huntington, "Introduction I," 27.

27. Ibid., 28.

CHAPTER FIVE. HEALING THE SEVERED TRUST

1. Allen, *Sacred Hoop*, 61.

2. Ibid., 62.

3. Ibid., 63.

4. Hogan, "First People," 14–15.

5. Brown, *Teaching Spirits*, 85.

6. Ibid., 87.

7. Dreese, "Terrestrial and Aquatic Intelligence," 6–7.

8. Chandler, "'How Do We Learn?,'" 32.

9. Dreese, "Terrestrial and Aquatic Intelligence," 7.

10. Chandler, "'How Do We Learn?,'" 19.

11. Allen, *Grandmothers of the Light*, 3.

12. Ibid., 7.

13. Melanie Bleck, in her analysis of Hogan's novels titled "Linda Hogan's Tribal Imperative," states that "Hogan offers her books as a new type of ceremony to heal the 'lost or stolen souls.' . . . Her works act as a continuation of the oral traditions and songs that remain a crucial part of many tribal societies, but with one notable exception, that they are written rather than spoken" (36). In an interview published in the *Missouri Review*, Hogan describes her poetry, fiction, and essays as "a descent into something older, deeper and more powerful than our everyday being or reality" (Hogan, interview, 132).

14. Chandler, in "'How Do We Learn?,'" states that in *Dwellings*, Hogan "is searching for the 'ecology of mind' that allows the merging of rationality, intuition, and faith. . . . All are needed to access a terrestrial spirituality" (29). To do so, Hogan uses a

"land language," which Chandler notes is "not a language the land speaks"; rather, "a land language demonstrates genuine respect for the land, assumes our interconnectedness with organizing ecosystems, acknowledges our role in relation to other life-forms" (29). I will build on this notion through the Okanagan and Heideggerean concepts of land-language as a co-responding of humans to the primal call of Being; as such, this language is a form of the land speaking.

15. Chandler, "'How Do We Learn?,'" 27.

16. A. Smith, "Hearing Bats and Following Berdache," 181.

17. Silko, "Interior and Exterior Landscapes," 5.

18. Abram, "Air Aware," 24.

19. Booth and Jacobs, "Ties That Bind," 39.

20. Jordan, *Sunflower Forest*, 51.

21. Ibid., 137.

22. J. Love, "Rhetorics of Truth Telling," 82.

23. Hogan, "Interview with Laura Coltelli," 79.

24. Castor, "Making the Familiar Strange," 138.

25. Bleck, "Linda Hogan's Tribal Imperative," 30–31.

26. Hogan, "First People," 16.

27. Dreese, "Terrestrial and Aquatic Intelligence," 9.

28. Hogan, "First People," 8.

29. Dreese, "Terrestrial and Aquatic Intelligence," 8.

30. Brown, *Teaching Spirits*, 111–12.

## CHAPTER SIX. WALKING IN THE LAND OF MANY GODS

1. Lopez, "Landscape and Narrative," 64–65.

2. Ibid., 66.

3. Ibid., 67–68.

4. Ibid., 71.

5. Eliade, *Myth of the Eternal Return*, xxviii.

6. Diamond, *In Search of the Primitive*, 290–91.

7. Allen, *Sacred Hoop*, 56–57.

8. Ibid., 59.

9. Ibid., 57.

10. Hogan, "First People," 14.

11. Deloria, *God Is Red*, 151.

12. Ibid., 279–80.

13. Momaday, "Native American Attitudes," 80.

# BIBLIOGRAPHY

Abram, David. "The Air Aware: Mind and Mood on a Breathing Planet." *Orion* (September–October 2009): 16–25.

———. *Becoming Animal: An Earthly Cosmology*. New York: Pantheon Books, 2010.

———. *The Spell of the Sensuous: Perception and Language in a More-than-Human World*. New York: Vintage, 1996.

Aho, Kevin. *Heidegger's Neglect of the Body*. Albany: State University of New York Press, 2009.

Allen, Paula Gunn. *Grandmothers of the Light: A Medicine Woman's Sourcebook*. Boston: Beacon Press, 1991.

———. *The Sacred Hoop: Recovering the Feminine in American Indian Traditions*. Boston: Beacon Press, 1986.

Armbruster, Karla. "Rewriting a Genealogy with the Earth: Women and Nature in the Works of Terry Tempest Williams." *Southwestern American Literature* 21 (1995): 209–20.

Armstrong, Jeannette C. "Land Speaking." In *Speaking for the Generations: Native Writers on Writing*, edited by Simon J. Ortiz, 174–94. Tucson: University of Arizona Press, 1998.

Baker, Gordon, and Katherine J. Morris. *Descartes' Dualism*. New York: Routledge, 1996.

Barnes, Kim. "On Place." In *Landscapes with Figures: The Nonfiction of Place*, edited by Robert Root, 14–21. Lincoln: University of Nebraska Press, 2007.

Basso, Keith H. *Wisdom Sits in Places: Landscape and Language among the Western Apache*. Albuquerque: University of New Mexico Press, 1996.

Bate, Jonathan. *The Song of the Earth*. Cambridge, Mass.: Harvard University Press, 2000.

Berry, Thomas. *The Great Work: Our Way into the Future*. New York: Bell Tower, 1999.

Bleck, Melani. "Linda Hogan's Tribal Imperative: Collapsing Space through 'Living' Tribal Traditions and Nature." *Studies in American Indian Literatures*, 2nd ser., 11, no. 4 (Winter 1999): 23–45.

Booth, Annie L., and Harvey M. Jacobs. "Ties That Bind: Native American Beliefs as a Foundation for Environmental Consciousness." *Environmental Ethics* 12 (Spring 1990): 27–43.

Branch, Michael P., Rochelle Johnson, Daniel Patterson, and Scott Slovic, eds. *Reading the Earth: New Directions in the Study of Literature and the Environment*. Moscow: University of Idaho Press, 1998.

Brown, Joseph Epes, with Emily Cousins. *Teaching Spirits: Understanding Native American Religious Traditions.* New York: Oxford University Press, 2001.

Buell, Lawrence. *The Environmental Imagination: Thoreau, Nature Writing, and the Formation of American Culture.* Cambridge, Mass.: Belknap Press of the Harvard University Press, 1995.

Castor, Laura. "Making the Familiar Strange: Representing the House in Sarah Orne Jewett's 'The Landscape Chamber' and Linda Hogan's 'Friends and Fortunes.'" In *The Art of Brevity: Excursions in Short Fiction Theory and Analysis,* edited by Per Winther, Jakob Lothe, and Hans H. Skei, 138–50. Columbia: University of South Carolina Press, 2004.

Chandler, Katherine R. "'How Do We Learn to Trust Ourselves Enough to Hear the Chanting of Earth?' Hogan's Terrestrial Spirituality." In *From the Center of Tradition: Critical Perspectives on Linda Hogan,* edited by Barbara J. Cook, 17–33. Boulder: University Press of Colorado, 2003.

———. "Whale Song from the Desert: Refuge without Resolution and Community without Homogeneity in Terry Tempest Williams's *Refuge.*" *Women's Studies* 34 (2005): 655–70.

Corcoran, Peter Blaze, and A. James Wohlpart. Review of *Ecology of a Cracker Childhood. Encounter* 14, no. 4 (Winter 2001): 56–57.

Costanza, Robert, Ralph d'Arge, Rudolf de Groot, Stephen Farber, Monica Grasso, Bruce Hannon, Karin Limburg, Shahid Naeem, Robert V. O'Neill, Jose Paruelo, Robert G. Raskin, Paul Sutton, and Marjan van den Belt. "The Value of the World's Ecosystem Services and Natural Capital." *Nature* 387 (May 15, 1997): 253–60.

Cottingham, John. "Cartesian Dualism: Theology, Metaphysics, and Science." In *The Cambridge Companion to Descartes,* edited by John Cottingham, 236–57. Cambridge: Cambridge University Press, 1992.

Crowe, Thomas Rain. "The New Naturalists." *Virginia Libraries* 50, no. 1 (January–March 2004): 8–12.

Deloria, Vine, Jr. *God Is Red: A Native View of Religion.* 3rd ed. Golden, Colorado: Fulcrum, 2003.

Deming, Alison Hawthorne. Review of *Wild Card Quilt: Taking a Chance on Home,* by Janisse Ray. *Orion* 22, no. 6 (November–December 2003): 74.

Descartes, René. *The Philosophical Writings of Descartes.* Translated by John Cottingham, Robert Stoothoff, and Dugald Murdoch. 3 vols. Cambridge: Cambridge University Press, 1985.

Diamond, Stanley. *In Search of the Primitive: A Critique of Civilization.* New Brunswick, N.J.: Transaction, 1974.

Dodd, Elizabeth. "Beyond the Blithe Air: Williams's Postnuclear Transcendentalism." In *Surveying the Literary Landscapes of Terry Tempest Williams: New Critical Essays,* edited by Katherine R. Chandler and Melissa A. Goldthwaite, 3–13. Salt Lake City: University of Utah Press, 2003.

Dreese, Donnelle N. "The Terrestrial and Aquatic Intelligence of Linda Hogan." *Studies in American Indian Literatures,* 2nd ser., 11, no. 4 (Winter 1999): 6–22.

Eakin, Paul John. *Fictions in Autobiography: Studies in the Art of Self-Invention.* Princeton, N.J.: Princeton University Press, 1985.

———. *How Our Lives Become Stories: Making Selves.* Ithaca, N.Y.: Cornell University Press, 1999.

————. *Living Autobiographically: How We Create Identity in Narrative.* Ithaca, N.Y.: Cornell University Press, 2008.

Elder, John. *Imagining the Earth: Poetry and the Vision of Nature.* 2nd ed. Athens: University of Georgia Press, 1996.

Eliade, Mircea. *The Myth of the Eternal Return: Cosmos and History.* Translated by Willard R. Trask. Princeton, N.J.: Princeton University Press, 1954.

Evernden, Neil. *The Natural Alien: Humankind and the Environment.* 2nd ed. Toronto: University of Toronto Press, 1993.

Farr, Cecilia Konchar. "American Ecobiography." In *Literature of Nature: An International Sourcebook,* edited by Patrick D. Murphy, 94–97. Chicago: Fitzroy Dearborn, 1998.

Frede, Dorothea. "The Question of Being: Heidegger's Project." In *The Cambridge Companion to Martin Heidegger,* edited by Charles Guignon, 2nd ed., 42–69. New York: Cambridge University Press, 2006.

Fromm, Harold. "Ecocriticism's Big Bang: A Review of *Practical Ecocriticism: Literature, Biology, and the Environment,* by Glen A. Love." *Logos: A Journal of Modern Society and Culture* 3, no. 3 (Summer 2004): 1–10.

————. "The New Darwinism in the Humanities. Part I: From Plato to Pinker." *Hudson Review* 56, no. 1 (2003): 89–99.

Garrard, Greg. "Heidegger Nazism Ecocriticism." *Interdisciplinary Studies in Literature and Environment* 17, no. 2 (2010): 251–71.

Glotfelty, Cheryll. "Flooding the Boundaries of Form: Terry Tempest Williams's Ecofeminist *Unnatural History.*" In *Change in the American West: Exploring the Human Dimension,* edited by Stephen Tchudi, 158–67. Reno: University of Nevada Press, 1996.

Glotfelty, Cheryll, and Harold Fromm, eds. *The Ecocriticism Reader: Landmarks in Literary Ecology.* Athens: University of Georgia Press, 1996.

Godine, Amy. Review of *Clear Springs: A Memoir,* by Bobbie Ann Mason and *Ecology of a Cracker Childhood,* by Janisse Ray. *Orion* 18, no. 4 (Autumn 1999): 74–75.

Grosz, Elizabeth. *Volatile Bodies: Toward a Corporeal Feminism.* Bloomington: Indiana University Press, 1994.

Grover, Jan Z. "Real Places." Review of *Bone Deep in Landscape: Writing, Reading, and Place,* by Mary Clearman Blew, and *Ecology of a Cracker Childhood,* by Janisse Ray. *Women's Review of Books* 17, no. 8 (May 2000): 9–10.

Guignon, Charles B. Introduction. In *The Cambridge Companion to Martin Heidegger,* edited by Charles Guignon, 2nd ed., 1–41. New York: Cambridge University Press, 2006.

Gunn, Janet Varner. *Autobiography: Toward a Poetics of Experience.* Philadelphia: University of Pennsylvania Press, 1982.

Gusdorf, Georges. "Conditions and Limits of Autobiography." In *Autobiography: Essays Theoretical and Critical,* edited by James Olney, 28–48. Princeton, N.J.: Princeton University Press, 1980.

Hagberg, Garry L. *Describing Ourselves: Wittgenstein and Autobiographical Consciousness.* Oxford: Clarendon Press, 2008.

Harrison, Robert Pogue. *Forests: The Shadow of Civilization.* Chicago: University of Chicago Press, 1992.

Heidegger, Martin. "Building Dwelling Thinking." In *Poetry, Language, Thought,* translated and with an introduction by Albert Hofstadter, 143–59. New York: Harper Collins, 1971.

————. *The Fundamental Concepts of Metaphysics: World, Finitude, Solitude.* Translated by William McNeill and Nicholas Walker. Bloomington: Indiana University Press, 1995.

————. "Language." In *Poetry, Language, Thought*, translated and with an introduction by Albert Hofstadter, 187–208. New York: Harper Collins, 1971.

————. "The Question Concerning Technology." In *The Question Concerning Technology and Other Essays*, translated and with an introduction by William Lovitt, 3–35. New York: Harper Perennial, 1977.

————. "The Thing." In *Poetry, Language, Thought*, translated and with an introduction by Albert Hofstadter, 163–80. New York: Harper Collins, 1971.

————. "What Are Poets For?" In *Poetry, Language, Thought*, translated and with an introduction by Albert Hofstadter, 89–139. New York: Harper Collins, 1971.

Heise, Ursula K. "The Hitchhiker's Guide to Ecocriticism." *PMLA* 121, no. 2 (2006): 503–16.

Hogan, Linda. *Dwellings: A Spiritual History of the Living World.* New York: Touchstone, 1995.

————. "First People." In *Intimate Nature: The Bond between Women and Animals*, edited by Linda Hogan, Deena Metzger, and Brenda Peterson, 6–19. New York: Fawcett Columbine, 1998.

————. Interview. *Missouri Review* 17, no. 2 (1994): 109–34.

————. An Interview with Laura Coltelli. In *Winged Words: American Indian Writers Speak*, by Laura Coltelli, 71–86. Nebraska: University of Nebraska Press, 1992.

Huntington, Patricia. "Introduction I--General Background: History of the Feminist Reception of Heidegger and a Guide to Heidegger's Thought." In *Feminist Interpretations of Martin Heidegger*, edited by Nancy J. Holland and Patricia Huntington, 1–42. University Park: Pennsylvania State University Press, 2001.

Jordan, William R., III. *The Sunflower Forest: Ecological Restoration and the New Communion with Nature.* Berkeley: University of California Press, 2003.

Kindell, Carolyn, K. C. Smith, and Andi Reynolds. Review of *The Tropic of Cracker*, by Al Burt; *Ecology of a Cracker Childhood*, by Janisse Ray; and *Crackers in the Glade: Life and Times in the Old Everglades*, by Rob Storter. *Southern Cultures* 7, no. 3 (Fall 2001): 97–100.

Kircher, Cassandra. "Rethinking Dichotomies in Terry Tempest Williams's *Refuge*." In *Ecofeminist Literary Criticism: Theory, Interpretation, Pedagogy*, edited by Greta Gaard and Patrick D. Murphy, 158–71. Urbana: University of Illinois Press, 1998.

Leakey, Richard. *The Origin of Humankind.* New York: HarperCollins, 1994.

Lopez, Barry. "Landscape and Narrative." In *Crossing Open Ground*, by Barry Lopez, 61–71. New York: Vintage Books, 1989.

Love, Glen A. *Practical Ecocriticism: Literature, Biology, and the Environment.* Charlottesville: University of Virginia Press, 2003.

Love, Jennifer. "Rhetorics of Truth Telling in Linda Hogan's *Savings*." In *From the Center of Tradition: Critical Perspectives on Linda Hogan*, edited by Barbara J. Cook, 81–96. Boulder: University Press of Colorado, 2003.

Lovitt, William. Introduction. In *The Question Concerning Technology and Other Essays*, by Martin Heidegger, translated and with an introduction by William Lovitt, xiii–xxxix. New York: Harper Perennial, 1977.

Markie, Peter. "The Cogito and Its Importance." In *The Cambridge Companion to*

*Descartes*, edited by John Cottingham, 140–73. Cambridge: Cambridge University Press, 1992.

Maxwell, William. *So Long, See You Tomorrow*. New York: Knopf, 1980.

Mazel, David, ed. *A Century of Early Ecocriticism*. Athens: University of Georgia Press, 2001.

McFarland, Sarah E. "Invisible Birds: Domestic Erasure in Terry Tempest Williams' *Refuge*." *Southwestern American Literature* 29, no. 2 (Spring 2004): 45–52.

Meeker, Joseph W. *The Comedy of Survival: Studies in Literary Ecology*. New York: Charles Scribner's Sons, 1972.

Merchant, Carolyn. *The Death of Nature: Women, Ecology and the Scientific Revolution*. New York: Harper Collins, 1980.

Mitchell, Charles. "Reclaiming the Sacred Landscape: Terry Tempest Williams, Kathleen Norris, and the Other Nature Writing." *Women's Studies* 32 (2003): 165–82.

Momaday, N. Scott. "Native American Attitudes to the Environment." In *Seeing with a Native Eye: Essays on Native American Religion*, edited by Walter Holden Capps, 79–85. New York: Harper and Row, 1976.

———. "The Native Voice in American Literature." In *The Man Made of Words: Essays, Stories, Passages*, by N. Scott Momaday, 13–20. New York: St. Martin's Griffin, 1997.

Nadler, Steven. "Descartes' Dualism?" *Philosophical Books* 38, no. 3 (1997): 157–64.

Oelschlaeger, Max. *The Idea of Wilderness: From Prehistory to the Age of Ecology*. New Haven, Conn.: Yale University Press, 1991.

Olney, James. *Metaphors of Self: The Meaning of Autobiography*. Princeton, N.J.: Princeton University Press, 1972.

Olson, Steve. *Mapping Human History: Genes, Race, and Our Common Origins*. Boston: Houghton Mifflin, 2002.

Ray, Janisse. *Ecology of a Cracker Childhood*. Minneapolis: Milkweed Editions, 1999.

———. *Wild Card Quilt: Taking a Chance on Home*. Minneapolis: Milkweed Editions, 2003.

Richardson, Tina. "Corporeal Testimony: Counting the Bodies in *Refuge: An Unnatural History of Family and Place*." In *Surveying the Literary Landscapes of Terry Tempest Williams: New Critical Essays*, edited by Katherine R. Chandler and Melissa A. Goldthwaite, 229–38. Salt Lake City: University of Utah Press, 2003.

Rigby, Kate. "Earth, World, Text: On the (Im)possibility of Ecopoiesis." *New Literary History* 35, no. 3 (Summer 2004): 427–42.

Riley, Jeannette E. "The Eco-Narrative and the Enthymeme: Form and Engagement in Environmental Writing." *Interdisciplinary Literary Studies* 10, no. 2 (2009): 82–98.

———. "Finding One's Place in the 'Family of Things': Terry Tempest Williams and a Geography of Self." *Women's Studies* 32 (2003): 585–602.

Robertson, Sarah. "Junkyard Tales: Poverty and the Southern Landscape in Janisse Ray's *Ecology of a Cracker Childhood*." In *Poverty and Progress in the U.S. South since 1920*, edited by Suzanne W. Jones and Mark Newman, 167–75. Amsterdam: VU University Press, 2006.

Rockefeller, Steven C. "Crafting Principles for the Earth Charter." In *A Voice for Earth: American Writers Respond to the Earth Charter*, edited by Peter Blaze Corcoran and A. James Wohlpart, 3–23. Athens: University of Georgia Press, 2008.

Rozemond, Marleen. *Descartes's Dualism*. Cambridge, Mass.: Harvard University Press, 1998.

Shepard, Paul. *Coming Home to the Pleistocene*. Washington, D.C.: Island Press, 1998.

———. *Nature and Madness*. Athens: University of Georgia Press, 1982.

Silko, Leslie Marmon. "Interior and Exterior Landscapes: The Pueblo Migration Stories." In *Speaking for the Generations: Native Writers on Writing*, edited by Simon Ortiz, 3–24. Tucson: University of Arizona Press, 1998.

Smith, Andrew. "Hearing Bats and Following Berdache: The Project of Survivance in Linda Hogan's *Mean Spirit*." *Western American Literature* 35, no. 2 (Summer 2000): 175–91.

Smith, Steven B. "An Exemplary Life: The Case of René Descartes." *Review of Metaphysics* 57 (March 2004): 571–97.

Sturrock, John. "The New Model Autobiographer." In *Autobiography: Critical Concepts in Literary and Cultural Studies*, edited by Trev Lynn Broughton, 1:187–98. New York: Routledge, 2007.

Tallmadge, John, and Henry Harrington, eds. *Reading under the Sign of Nature: New Essays in Ecocriticism*. Salt Lake City: University of Utah Press, 2000.

Walsh, Bryan. "Paying for Nature." *Time*, February 21, 2011, Global 1.

Watson, Jay. "Economics of a Cracker Landscape: Poverty as an Environmental Issue in Two Southern Writers." *Mississippi Quarterly* 55, no. 4 (Fall 2002): 497–513.

Wee, Cecilia. "Cartesian Environmental Ethics." *Environmental Ethics* 23 (Fall 2001): 275–86.

Williams, Susan Millar. "Home, Difficult Home." Review of *Wild Card Quilt: Taking a Chance on Home*, by Janisse Ray. *Women's Review of Books* 20, nos. 10–11 (July 2003): 22.

Williams, Terry Tempest. *Refuge: An Unnatural History of Family and Place*. New York: Vintage, 1991.

Wilson, Edward O. *Biophilia: The Human Bond with Other Species*. Cambridge, Mass.: Harvard University Press, 1984.

———. *In Search of Nature*. Washington, D.C.: Island Press, 1996.

Young, Julian. "The Fourfold." In *The Cambridge Companion to Martin Heidegger*, edited by Charles B. Guignon, 2nd ed., 373–92. New York: Cambridge University Press, 2006.

———. *Heidegger's Later Philosophy*. Cambridge: Cambridge University Press, 2002.

Yuki, Masami. "Narrating the Invisible Landscape: Terry Tempest Williams's Erotic Correspondence to Nature." *Studies in American Literature* 34 (1998): 79–97.

———. "Sound Ground to Stand On: Soundscapes in Williams's Work." In *Surveying the Literary Landscapes of Terry Tempest Williams: New Critical Essays*, edited by Katherine R. Chandler and Melissa A. Goldthwaite, 81–93. Salt Lake City: University of Utah Press, 2003.

Zimmerman, Michael. "Heidegger, Buddhism, and Deep Ecology." In *The Cambridge Companion to Martin Heidegger*, edited by Charles Guignon, 2nd ed., 293–325. New York: Cambridge University Press, 2006.

———. *Heidegger's Confrontation with Modernity: Technology, Politics, and Art*. Bloomington: Indiana University Press, 1990.

Zuelke, Karl. "The Ecopolitical Space of *Refuge*." In *Surveying the Literary Landscapes of Terry Tempest Williams: New Critical Essays*, edited by Katherine R. Chandler and Melissa A. Goldthwaite, 239–51. Salt Lake City: University of Utah Press, 2003.

# INDEX